D1329847

Regaining Paradise

Regaining Paradise

Englishness and the Early

Garden City Movement

Standish Meacham

Yale University Press

New Haven and London

Set in Adobe Garamond with Stone Sans display type by
The Composing Room of Michigan, Inc.
Printed in the United States of America.

Library of Congress Cataloging-in-Publication Data

Meacham, Standish.
   Regaining paradise : Englishness and the early garden city
movement / Standish Meacham.
     p. cm.
   Includes bibliographical references and index.
   ISBN 0-300-07572-3 (alk. paper)
   1. Garden cities—England—History. 2. Planned communities—
England—History. 3. National characteristics, English.
I. Title.
HT164.G7M43 1998
307.76'8—dc21
                                            98-44370
                                                  CIP

A catalogue record for this book is available from the British Library.

The paper in this book meets the guidelines for permanence and durability of the
Committee on Production Guidelines for Book Longevity of the Council on
Library Resources.

10 9 8 7 6 5 4 3 2 1

Contents

Photographs follow pages 56 and 152

Preface

Model towns and villages are dependably newsworthy. Recent articles about the Disney Corporation's garden city, Celebration, in Florida, and the Prince of Wales' village of Poundbury in Dorset attest to the interest—and the controversy—such experiments continue to generate and have generated since their inception over a hundred years ago. My own interest in the subject began when I was a child. I built toy villages with blocks, more often than not patterning them on Celesteville, that exuberant prototype of benevolent urban authoritarianism that is the setting of Jean de Brunhoff's Babar books. My father's commitment to the cause of public housing and my mother's to that of city parks encouraged my early enthusiasm. It was no surprise to me that the first research paper that I wrote in graduate school, under the late David Owen's direction, dealt with George Cadbury's Bournville. I am pleased that I have now returned to Cadbury forty years later, and to a subject that has allowed me to combine my lifelong interest in urban design with my more recent investigations of the history of late Victorian social reform.

For editorial assistance I am indebted to Shirley Quinn and Steven

Salzman; for manuscript preparation, Frances Woods. Of particular help to me during the period when I was conducting research were Robert Lancaster, of the First Garden City Heritage Museum, and the late Brigid Grafton Green, of the Hampstead Garden Suburb Archive Trust. At Yale University Press I have profited from the encouragement and professional support of Charles Grench and Otto Bohlmann. Research for this book was underwritten in part by a grant from the University Research Institute of the University of Texas at Austin.

For permission to quote from manuscript sources, I gratefully acknowledge the First Garden City Heritage Museum, Letchworth; the Hampstead Garden Suburb Archive Trust; the Port Sunlight Heritage Centre; Cadbury Ltd.; the British Architectural Library of the Royal Institute of British Architects, and Jane Ridley (Edwin Lutyens papers); the Birmingham City Archives (Cadbury papers); the Hertfordshire Archives and Local Studies (Ebenezer Howard papers); and the Department of Planning and Landscape, University of Manchester (Raymond Unwin papers).

Small portions of the text have appeared in an essay, "Raymond Unwin: Designing for Democracy in Victorian England," in Susan Pedersen and Peter Mandler, eds., *After the Victorians: Private Conscience and Public Duty in Modern Britain* (London, 1994).

ILLUSTRATION ACKNOWLEDGMENTS

The author acknowledges with thanks the kind permission of the following to reproduce illustrations.

Figs. 8, 15–21, 23, 41–46, 50–56, 58: Architecture Library, University of Texas at Austin
Figs. 11, 14, 22, 24–31, 33–38: First Garden City Heritage Museum, Letchworth
Figs. 39, 40, 47–49, 57: London Metropolitan Archives
Figs. 2, 4–6: Birmingham City Archives (Ms 1536/041 0.02, 0010.7, 1017.9, 1601.07)
Figs. 3, 10: Port Sunlight Heritage Centre
Fig. 7: Bournville Village Trust
Fig. 1: Stefan Muthesius (1972) and Yale University Press

Chapter 1 Introduction:
The Matter of Englishness

This is a book about late Victorian attitudes toward social reform and society. It analyzes the way in which the ideas and ideals that shaped the early garden city movement in England were embedded in a vision of Englishness—a vision articulated with increasing assurance by reformers during the decades before World War I. The book thus joins a growing body of literature on the subject of English tradition and heritage.

To regain paradise, it helps to have a vision of paradise lost. The men and women who founded the English garden city movement conjured their vision of the future from a mythic past, constructing a green and pleasant heaven to replace an ugly and unhealthy urban hell. In doing so, they turned away from an alternative vision articulated by the man whose name was most associated with the early movement: Ebenezer Howard. Howard was a utopian who derived his ideas from other utopians, including the Americans Henry George and Edward Bellamy. His scheme for the design and construction of garden cities, first outlined in *To-morrow: A Peaceful Path to Real Reform* (1898), was an amalgam of forward-looking theories and proposals. Despite its utopianism, Howard's plan was practical enough to appeal to a wide group of middle- and upper-middle-class reformers, who were very much afraid of what the future seemed to promise: physical degeneration, class conflict, and democracy. The early history of the garden city movement must be read against the background of those fears. The years before World War I were filled with alarming domestic strife: violent strikes and talk of syndicalist rebellion; insurrection in Ireland and in the House of Lords; women prepared to wage war for the vote, and men equally prepared to battle them back into submission. That was the reality reformers faced.

If their fears were grounded in those realities, they were fed by literature that prophesied a bleak if not desperate future, especially for those born and bred in cities. C. F. G. Masterman, writing in 1901 of "Realities at Home" in a collection of essays about London, *The Heart of the Empire,* conjured up a disturbing image of a force that, for the past quarter-century, had "been operating in the raw material of which the city is composed," those children "reared in the courts and crowded ways of the great metropolis, with hot, fretful life, and long hours of sedentary or unhealthy toil." The problem of the new century, Masterman declared, would be this "New Town Type," on whom the future of the Anglo-Saxon race depended. Masterman's fellow essayist P. W. Wilson described the present situation in even bleaker terms. What hope could one possibly extract from an urban environment in which children "struggle precariously to a pasty-faced puberty," born as they were "with half a brain, which half is saturated in youth with all the filth—pictorial, verbal, and dietary—that a rotten civilisation can devise."[1]

This language, as much that of outright panic as of fear, was common to the early years of the twentieth century. Garden city reformers remained optimists; otherwise they would not have undertaken their task of urban regeneration. But as they celebrated Howard's ideal and made the garden city their icon, their fear for the future encouraged them to transform that ideal in accordance with an agenda that not only promised physical and social health and harmony but also found its justification in a conservative English past.

Those who have written about Englishness or heritage agree that the concepts are grounded in an invented set of perceptions. Robert Colls and Philip Dodd, in the preface to a collection of essays on the subject, declare that "Englishness has had to be made and remade in and through history, within available practices and relationships, and existing symbols and ideas."[2] These makings and remakings are deliberate activities that have to do not only with invention, but also, as Dodd points out, with "transformation and recovery."[3]

Englishness is not history, although it does derive in part from what Raphael Samuel calls "popular memory": "the very antithesis of written history." Such memory, Samuel observes, has no "developmental sense of time, but assigns events to the mythicized 'good old days' (or 'bad old days') of workplace lore, or the 'once upon a time' of the storyteller."[4] The inventors of Englishness employ history as they make and remake the past; but Englishness is myth in that it obscures or ignores whatever does not respond to present need. It serves a therapeutic purpose by using the past in such a way as to mitigate present fears and perceived dangers. It represents, in Linda Colley's words, the "search for an attractive, usable and above all profoundly reinforcing past."[5]

What requires reinforcing is a sense that present difficulties and uncertainties can be resolved and that such resolution can be discovered within a knowable cultural context. End-of-century malaise appears to call forth this need for reinforcement. A nation sensing itself in tension and therefore divided is all the more prone to unite, as one writer has put it, "around certain talismans and images."[6] So it was in 1900. In Britain, Colley observes, the fin de siècle has more than once deepened "fears of uncontrollable change and imminent loss."[7]

Englishness possessed a remarkable power to seduce. Consider the case of Raymond Unwin, the socialist planner and architect for both Letchworth, the first garden city, and Hampstead Garden Suburb. Unwin's socialism would appear to make him an unlikely disciple of an Englishness that saw resolution in a mythic imagining of pre-industrial, rural, hierarchical society. And yet Unwin played an important role in the invention of just such an Englishness. In a chapter he wrote in 1901 for the book he and his partner, Barry Parker, published on "the art of building a home," he began by extolling socialist cooperation as lying at the heart of any acceptable understanding of community. Capitalism had promoted individualism at the expense of community, as it had promoted competition over cooperation. Socialism taught that "independence is no end in itself, and is only good in that it sets free the individuals to form new relationships based on mutual association."[8] Yet when Unwin struggled to give that association shape and substance he turned to the past. Like so many of his contemporaries, he despised the monotony and grimness of industrial cities and saw these cities as breeding grounds for class animosity. Egalitarian though he professed himself to be, he was attracted to a vision of organic unity that he believed had existed in the hierarchically arranged agricultural villages of the past. Along with other reform-minded men and women, he juxtaposed hierarchy with class, extolling the virtues of the former while disparaging the consequences of the latter. Hierarchy was the backbone of a reassuringly settled community in which men and women lived in harmony with those above and below them, all together subscribing to a mutually agreed upon code of responsibilities and obligations. In contrast, class consciousness encouraged social volatility, a collective sense of the opposition of interests that ultimately gave way to social disorder. Fearing class conflict, Unwin mythologized the past while idealizing it, writing admiringly of the village in terms of both its architectural and social unity.

> There are houses and buildings of all sizes: the hut in which the old road mender lives by himself, the inn with its ancient sign, the prosperous yeoman's homestead, the blacksmith's house and forge, the squire's hall, the vicarage, and the doctor's house, are all seemingly jumbled together. . . . Yet there is no sense of confusion: on the contrary the scene gives us that peaceful feeling which comes from the perception of orderly arrangement. . . . The village was the expression of a small corporate life in which all the different units were personally in touch with each other, conscious of and frankly accepting their relations, and on the whole content with them. This relationship reveals itself in the feeling of order which the view induces.[9]

Unwin perceived the village as an "association for mutual help"; it was that quality that distinguished it from modern urban society, at once atomized by isolating individualism and divided by antagonistic class warfare. Not surprisingly, however, he found it all but impossible to reconcile his vision of a community whose members were "conscious of and frankly accepting" of a set of hierarchical relations with his commitment to democratic socialism. He shared the dilemma with other reformers of his class who, when looking for an escape from contemporary urban disorganization and dysfunction, could see an alternative only in an idealized, pre-industrial past. Unwin tried to wiggle free of the difficulty but enmeshed himself further. "The relationships of feudalism have gone," he declared stoutly; but as to what exactly would take their place he was by no means certain. "Democracy has yet to evolve some definite relationships of its own, which when they come will doubtless be as picturesque as the old forms."[10] Why picturesque? The anti-urban Englishness in Unwin's thinking encouraged him to believe that he could pour the new wine of equalitarian socialism into the old bottles of hierarchical community.

Unwin's vision was not historical. It was, in Samuel's words, without any "developmental sense of time." It came from the past yet lacked the baggage that history would have imposed: the disruptive facts of enclosure, poor law, game laws. Nor is it really correct to call this Englishness an invention by Unwin; "invention" suggests a conscious effort that Unwin does not appear to have made. It is probably more accurate to say that Englishness took hold of Unwin the socialist without his fully realizing that he was in its grasp. Its pervasiveness was as subtle as its vision was appealing.

Englishness, both within and beyond the garden city movement, partook of the anti-urban sentiment reflected in Unwin's observation. Virtue was lodged in country ways, country things, and countryside—the south of England's safe and comfortably knowable thatched roofs, enclosed fields, and soft hills. As Alex Potts has pointed out, there is irony in the fact that it was only when the countryside became marginal socially and economically that its benign qualities—"the ostensible peacefulness of its marginality"—came to represent that which was best, because it was most trustworthy, about the nation.[11] The late nineteenth century was the era of the amateur country photographer, who hoped "to capture and preserve a traditional ideal of rural England."[12] It was also the era of the foundation of the National Trust (1894) and the first issue of *Country Life* (1897). Whether conservative, liberal, or socialist, one could be reassured, as Unwin was, by an Englishness that evoked a healthy out-of-doors life lived within an organic society, based on the mutual responsibility and obligation that myth insisted informed social relations before the coming of industrialization and the city.

Reformers conjured up that particular vision as a way of combating their fears of urban degeneration and class conflict. The highly publicized 1904 Report of the Interdepartmental Committee on Physical Deterioration, Parliament's response to a perceived threat to the nation's health and efficiency, placed the blame for the problem squarely on cities. In addition to breeding disease and degeneration, cities spawned social fragmentation and, ultimately, class antagonism. "When part of society is content with a low life, and another part is indifferent to that content, class warfare is not far distant."[13] Thus wrote Samuel Barnett, founder of Toynbee Hall, the East London settlement house, in 1888, when class tension in London was running high. How reassuring, under those circumstances, to believe that modern industrial cities were an anomaly. Walter Creese points out that Barry Parker and Raymond Unwin, whose work lay at the heart of the garden city movement, believed that the city of late nineteenth-century England was a "monstrosity; . . . therefore [they] had no inclination to redevelop, reform or compromise with it."[14] That overstates the case: both architects eventually devoted themselves to elaborate schemes of urban redevelopment and reform. Yet Creese is correct when he senses in Parker and Unwin, as in so many other social critics, a genuine and almost physical revulsion against the city. Surely these sprawling heaps of humanity—deadly at their polluted centers by reason of the ill health their overcrowding bred, equally deadly on their suburban fringes because of the monotonous lives they engendered—were not reality.

What was reality? Alun Howkins declares that what English men and women have for a century or more responded to as "real England" is a rural England, where "men and women still live naturally. The air is clean, personal relationships matter, (especially between employer and employee) there is no crime (except 'quaint' crimes like poaching) and no violence. . . . It is an organic society, a 'real' one, as opposed to the unnatural or 'unreal' society of the town."[15]

Yet the late Victorian social reformers who believed in that myth realized that they could not simply will the nation back to that perceived reality. If change was to come, they would have to battle for it. They did not abandon the strand of Englishness that drew them into the past. Indeed, they used that Englishness as a talisman, combining it, however, with another set of mythic perceptions that celebrated what they insisted was a peculiarly English political pragmatism and the triumph of late-nineteenth-century commonsense liberalism. As Dennis Smith has effectively argued, all major political parties in the twentieth century have fed from this particular version of Englishness. Smith grounds his case in a passage from James Bryce's *Modern Democracies* (1907). A set of principles, Bryce declares, "has come to so inhere in national consciousness as to seem part of national character." His components: a "respect for law as law," the "traditional love of liberty," the "traditional sense of duty to the community," and the "wish to secure reforms by constitutional rather than violent means."[16] These traditions were said to derive from the Revolution Settlement of 1688 and to impart to the state a "peculiarly 'English' capacity for healing rifts and absorbing its constituents."[17] Here again is Englishness as myth, once more without that "developmental sense of time" that would have had to acknowledge political corruption, working-class radicalism, the exclusion of women, and other realities as it turned reassuring vision into unsettling historical reality.

This consensus Englishness permitted reformers, including those responsible for the garden city movement, to support state intervention and the strengthening of bureaucracy as a way to serve Bryce's "traditional sense of duty to the community." Barnett called himself a "practicable socialist," willing to use the powers of government to ensure the well-being of the English, their communities, and the nation as a whole. He and the hundreds of others who lived politically within the broad confines of Bryce's liberalist Englishness agreed to intervene to an increasing degree in such areas as housing, town planning, and a range of social services between 1890 and 1914. If they were practicable socialists, they were what could just as well be called practicable capitalists; some of those most closely associated with the garden city movement were actively engaged in highly successful capitalist enterprises. They defended the tenets of free enterprise and the market economy, yet they were prepared to depart from the bondage of laissez-faire ideology and to welcome intervention when not to do so appeared to threaten the interests of a citizenry vulnerable to social decay and disorder.

While this second strand of Englishness is important to an understanding of the mentality that shaped the garden city movement, it was not at the center of its early history in the way that the Englishness of pre-industrial rural hierarchy was. Yet if it figures in this study as background rather than foreground, it is nonetheless important background. The movement's leaders drew frequently upon the state for assistance in their enterprises, making what use they could, for example, of the Town Planning Act of 1909, and not hesitating to call on Parliament for special legislation to facilitate the layout of Hampstead Garden Suburb. They welcomed as well the creation of old-age pensions and health and unemployment insurance as tools that would assist them in creating the healthy and socially beneficial communities that were their dream.

Practicable socialists, practicable capitalists—what these men and women tended *not* to be were enthusiastic democrats, thanks to their general unwillingness to trust a half-educated urban proletariat. It was no surprise that the most important garden city and garden suburb experiments, Letchworth and Hampstead Garden Suburb, were governed by nonelected company officials and trustees. In accepting the inevitability of an enfranchised working class, garden city reformers employed Englishness to institute an exclusionary hierarchy. They would use the garden city to define what was English and what was not. And with that decision, they would preserve their role as dominant national arbiters. They were not unwilling to share; indeed, many made it their life's work to disseminate Englishness to the nation at large. But their task was the dispensation. This is your heritage, they proclaimed, which we have defined for you; and we expect that you will be profoundly grateful for what you are about to receive.

The ancient universities—and particularly Oxford—played an important role in making and disseminating late-nineteenth-century Englishness. Matthew Arnold and T. H. Green urged young men to fulfill a definition of "best self" reflected in a set of virtues that transcended class interest. In *Culture and*

Anarchy, Arnold argued the ability of a handful of men and women to rise above themselves in order to realize the "idea of the whole community . . . and to find one centre of light and authority there." Within each class, he wrote, "there are a certain number of aliens, . . . persons who are mainly led . . . by a general humane spirit, by the love of human perfection."[18]

The reformers who were committed to the dissemination of Englishness understood themselves as such aliens. Standing apart from class, they could claim a disinterestedness that fitted them for the task of defining and establishing a culture of Englishness to be spread among those who lived alongside them yet remained ignorant of the source of "light and authority." The Report of the Committee on Physical Deterioration endorsed this message when insisting that people be provided with not only the chance to live healthier lives but also the opportunity to understand how best to live. Increased prosperity posed a real threat, the committee insisted, "accompanied as it frequently is by great unwisdom in [a family's] application to raising the standard of comfort." Instead, the "very growth of the family resources . . . is often productive of the most disastrous consequences."[19] The masses, in other words, needed instruction in the art of applying increased wealth and leisure to the realization of best selves, for their own good and that of the community as a whole. They would realize those best selves by practicing the virtues of an Englishness that would be imparted to them. Until then, they would live to at least some degree beyond the cultural pale. Englishness requires an external "other." "Its definition," as John Taylor observes, "is inescapable from the non-English."[20] It is important to acknowledge, however, that the high-minded proponents of garden cities saw that "other" not so much in terms of social category—the working class— as in terms of cultural deprivation. All were welcome to work their way from the wasteland of cultural otherness into the light and authority that was Englishness. Light *and* authority, be it noted: the crossing required a willingness to surrender old cultural baggage at the behest of an elite that felt no compunction in insisting on its own definition of what was best.

Englishness thus implied a cultural paternalism that again connected the present to the past. The pre-industrial social hierarchy that stretched from road mender to squire in Raymond Unwin's mythic village was refracted in assumptions about this related hierarchy of cultural giver and receiver. One of the first residents of Toynbee Hall, P. Lyttelton Gell, wrote explicitly, in a pamphlet entitled *The Municipal Responsibilities of the "Well-to-Do,"* of how community must be reborn if the Hall was to succeed in its mission.

The whole English class system is based upon the assumption of a resident leisured class . . . , but if the well-to-do fly each evening from the cities where their wealth is created, and if the working classes are left behind when the day's work is done, too fatigued and too uninstructed to care for anything but to refresh their wearied bodies against tomorrow's toil, the social system . . . breaks down.

. . . The departure of the well-to-do from out of the heart of our cities robs each community of the citizens whose duty is to maintain the standard of administration and refinement, and leaves them to become more hopeless and more dingy still. . . . There is only one real solution. The wealthy middle-class deserters from the commonwealth must take up again their civic responsibilities. They have the leisure and the ability, which the poor have not. It is their duty to labour personally at the improvement—material, moral, spiritual—of the masses, by whose labours alone their leisured life is rendered possible.[21]

The passage reveals the extent to which urban reformers understood community as cultural paternalism. The "well-to-do" and the poor each had a set of duties to perform: in the case of the "uninstructed" poor, to accept tutelage from a leisured class of committed social educators in the virtues of an Englishness grounded in a hierarchy of values; in the case of the rich, to afford the poor that instruction, which they were best suited to provide. The same understanding was embedded in the assumptions of the majority of men and women who founded the garden city movement. Englishness was their end, cultural paternalism one of their principal means to its achievement. Though they would frequently disown the paternalist label, their actions continued to prove their inability, if not their unwillingness, to separate means from end. Their insistence that the cities and suburbs that they were creating contain "well-to-do" and poor and provide opportunities for both to come together reflected the faith expressed in Gell's essay: that a genuinely English community could be achieved only through cultural giving and receiving.

Did this amount, then, to a sort of self-conscious and explicit social control? Brian Doyle believes that it did. He argues that the respectable working class was deliberately "colonized" by its "cultural superiors" so as to inhibit the spread of socialism with the "radiance of a common culture and heritage."[22] Philip Dodd addresses the question more cautiously. Although, as he suggests, "there is certainly evidence to support the thesis that Englishness and the national culture were reconstituted in order to incorporate or neuter various social groups"—the working class, women, the Irish—he concludes that "it is unhelpful . . . to see the reconstitution as a simple matter of the imposition of an identity by the dominant on the subordinate." He cites two reasons for caution: first, many of those initially deemed "other" in fact welcomed or at least readily accepted the culture that was being offered them and the nation; and second, the remaking of Englishness "was undertaken at such a variety of social locations and by such various groups that it is difficult to talk of a common intention."[23]

This hesitance is justifiable with regard to the garden city movement. Certainly the "English" enthusiasm for home and garden and for the domestic ideal that lay at the heart of the movement was not the sole property of a reform-minded elite. As to Dodd's second point, it is true that garden city enthusiasts came together from many different social locations. Linda Colley's characterization of the present-day directorship of the heritage movement is a strikingly accurate compendium of garden city leadership in its early years: "the very rich, the very cultivated, the deeply idealistic, the highly entrepreneurial and the downright eccentric."[24] Disparate though the group was, it did nonetheless share a fear for the future well-being of the nation, and a determination to improve the physical and moral well-being of those who existed in unhealthy and demoralizing circumstances beyond their control. Most understood their reform effort in terms of a precious Englishness that needed to be shared by as many people as possible.

Traditionalists as they celebrated the Englishness of a beneficent countryside and its hierarchical community; progressives as they celebrated the liberal Englishness that encouraged direct intervention by enlightened individuals and the state: these were the reformers who brought the garden city movement to life at the beginning of the twentieth century.

Chapter 2 Bournville and Port Sunlight: The Exemplars

A garden city, as defined by its proponents at the beginning of the twentieth century, was one built anew, on open land, according to an overall plan that provided its citizens a chance to live and work in social harmony in a healthy, aesthetically pleasing environment, free from overcrowding and pollution. A garden suburb, while built in accordance with those goals, was not a city unto itself but rather a planned, self-contained extension of a larger urban area.

Garden cities and garden suburbs are not English inventions. Planned communities, whether for working- or middle-class families, are part of the general history of nineteenth-century town planning in Europe and the United States. A *cité ouvrière* in Alsace, established in 1853, and the "romantic suburbs," such as Llewellyn Park in South Orange, New Jersey, and Riverside, Illinois, developed between 1850 and 1870: these and other experiments occurred alongside those in England, which consisted primarily of model villages constructed for rural laborers and factory workers.

Indeed, in the minds of most knowledgeable English men and women at the turn of the twentieth century, "garden city" had all but been defined by the successful experiments in industrial village-making under-taken by two highly visible and widely admired businessmen: the Quaker chocolate manufacturer George Cadbury, who built Bournville, outside Bir-mingham, and the flamboyant soapmaker William Lever, whose Port Sunlight rose beside his factory near Liverpool. Those villages, while in many respects innovative and forward-looking in terms of design, were nonetheless part of a tradition that extended back to Robert Owen's early-nineteenth-century New Lanark. A determination to impose both an environmental and a moral order on his workforce had compelled Owen to redefine the experience of factory life. The lasting fame of his experiments encouraged other factory masters to work variations, far less radical than Owen's, on the theme of environmental im-provement. They derived additional inspiration from the endeavors of pater-nalist landlords, many of whom continued to provide model cottages for rural tenants throughout the nineteenth century.[1]

Much employer-built housing, in Europe and America, was that and noth-ing more: uniform rows of modest dwellings constructed with an eye to cost as well as amenities, often part of an attempt to encourage company loyalty through the provision of schools, libraries, and chapels.[2] A few entrepreneurs moved beyond such rudimentary schemes with attempts to create a genuine community. Prices Patent Candle Company built a village of terrace houses, free-standing cottages, and gardens at Bromborough Pool in 1853. Concur-rently, Edward Akroyd, a Halifax worsted manufacturer, financed model towns at Copley and, after 1859, at Akroydon. His purpose was explicitly improve-ment: "a clean, fresh, well-ordered house exercises on its inmates a moral no less than a physical influence, and has the direct tendency to make the members of a family sober, peaceable, and considerate of the feelings and happiness of each other." Akroyd's vision derived from past images and styles; in this he was part of the tradition of backward-looking reform. He insisted that his architect, the distinguished George Gilbert Scott, design Gothic buildings that would reflect the history of Halifax and provide a "taste of our forefathers" pleasing to the fancy and capable of "entwin[ing] the present with memories of the past."[3] At the same time, he proved himself a social innovator, promoting the sale of houses to working men and their families and providing a range of prices that would attract a mixed citizenry of artisans and clerks.

The most famous mid-century factory community was Saltaire, the creation of Titus Salt, a Bradford tycoon who had made a fortune in alpaca. In 1853 he moved his mill to a site outside the city in the Aire Valley. Over the next ten years a town of 850 houses on twenty-two streets was laid out and built up according to Salt's meticulous specifications, as rendered by the local firm of Lockwood and Mawson. Salt was a friend of the Akroyds; his son married into an equally reform-minded Halifax family, the Crossleys. He is said to have been inspired in his endeavor by a determination to leave a mark on his time—the equivalent of that a nobleman might make through his rank and estates—and by a reading of Benjamin Disraeli's *Sybil.* Saltaire was to be the realization of the model village founded by the novel's Mr. Trafford.[4] Most of the houses that Salt provided his workers were well constructed but small, no larger than those built in Bradford for factory hands during the same period. Rents were modest as well: 2/4 per week for the cheapest, rising to 7/6 for four-bedroom houses occupied by managers and office staff. The town was provided with alms-houses, schools, an institute, a wash-house (because Salt disliked the sight of clotheslines), public baths, a church, and a chapel.

Saltaire's explicit paternalism evoked pre-industrial England and the social and economic relations that had characterized rural communities. Like the eighteenth-century squire, Titus Salt understood his task forthrightly as self-interested, driven by the necessity to enhance his investment. As the squire had looked to his land and his tenants and laborers, Salt looked to his factory and those who worked within it. Like a squire, Salt was not afraid to assert his authority over the community he headed as a way of ensuring his continued economic success. If he concluded that authority could most effectively be imposed by means of traditional, benevolent attention to the well-being of the factory "family" in his charge, he understood as well that the community he had founded would cease to exist if he failed to manufacture alpaca at a profit. Capitalism and altruism together made Salt a paternalist. Living and working in the post-Chartist era, he was determined to discover a way to secure harmonious industrial relations. That his new way recalled the past is not surprising, given the continuing power of the social discipline embodied in customary assumptions of rural community life.

Salt did not live at Saltaire, though he had at one time selected a site there for his house. Yet his improving purposes infused the town with his presence. The community was governed by a thick set of rules and regulations. Salt insisted that the town be teetotal. In the park there was little open space for unsupervised play; no political or religious demonstrations were permitted anywhere. Those who lived at Saltaire did so at Salt's pleasure. If they ceased to work at his factory or for the town, they forfeited their housing. Trade unions were outlawed, though two strikes over wages occurred, in 1868 and 1876. An air of working-class respectability lay as heavily on the town as the factory smoke lay on nearby Bradford. "Walking its streets," two recent historians have observed, "one cannot help feeling like a sober, industrious working man of the better sort, tempted to steal furtively into dirty Bradford for a lubricious pint, before hurrying back to the sand-table town where the men were well-clad; the women had a blooming cheek; [and] drunkenness was unknown."[5] Salt believed that environment produced character. Within the environment of Saltaire he labored to create a serious, disciplined community, one that would profit not only his company but the individuals who lived on its ordered, unlittered streets, within its sturdy, sanitary dwellings.

George Cadbury and William Lever drew inspiration from Saltaire, Akroydon, and the other experimental factory towns of Victorian England. Yet they were not merely latter-day Salts or Akroyds. Their achievements derived from their particular personalities. They were alike, however—and like Akroyd and Salt—in that they sprang from an entrepreneurial class whose place in the history of Victorian social reform has been overshadowed by the achievements of professionals and civil servants.[6] Yet there were within the garden city movement men like Cadbury and Lever, unabashed, unapologetic businessmen, "interested," in the sense that they had a vital stake in the success of their capitalist undertakings, and in the sense that they were members of that class whose relationship with workers was direct if not necessarily confrontational. The history of the garden city movement is, among other things, the history of the way men and women from these two distinct spheres joined forces in a cause that they perceived as vital to their country's health.

Common to both sets of reformers was a measure of paternalistic concern in their undertakings. The most widely advertised precursors of the garden city movement, Bournville and Port Sunlight, were paternalist enterprises. To understand the degree to which paternalism infused those communities, one must understand the extent to which, despite the dedication of Cadbury and Lever to the precepts of Victorian entrepreneurship, paternalist impulses motivated their endeavors.

To comprehend George Cadbury, one begins with the fact that he was a Quaker. The garden city movement derived its energies in part from the broadly Christian morality professed by men such as T. H. Green and the not particularly rigorous doctrinal beliefs of Anglican clergymen such as Samuel Barnett. Many of those engaged in bringing garden cities and suburbs to life no doubt believed that they were working God's will, though they seldom declared explicitly that such was the case. (Some, of course, did not: neither Ebenezer

Howard nor Raymond Unwin, for example, were adherents of any organized faith.) In Cadbury's case, however, religion fueled his sense of social responsibility in a direct and uncomplicated way.

Cadbury's Quaker belief in an "inner light," aglow in the souls of all mankind, compelled him to believe as well in the essential oneness of humanity, and hence in the potential for a "best" in those willing to open themselves to God's love. As his biographer wrote, "The central doctrine of Christianity, as George Cadbury understood it, is that men and women, rich or poor, are infinitely valuable, and that their lives should not be squandered."[7] Because Quakers were denied full participation in national politics until well into the nineteenth century, many focused their energies on the businesses that they conducted with an equal share of energy and success. And in the case of most Quaker businessmen, faith compelled them to practice their calling in a manner commensurate with their beliefs. Cadbury was fond of asserting that "priestcraft" was the primary cause of the death of spirituality, because a priestly caste absolved laymen and laywomen of their individual responsibilities to practice good in the world. "It is so much easier to place responsibility upon the priest, clergyman or minister rather than take a share of the work ourselves."[8] Consequently, Cadbury and other Quaker businessmen understood themselves as compelled to put their moral convictions to work throughout their daily lives, both at home and at the factory. All men and women must be priests in company with those around them, teaching and learning a faith together.

Cadbury's philanthropy was more often than not public advocacy of state-directed efforts to end poverty and improve the conditions under which working-class men and women lived. He was a patron of the National Old Age Pensions League. He publicly advocated doubled death duties and a graduated income tax, using as a platform for his views the *Daily News,* which he acquired in 1902. A dedicated Liberal, he opposed the Boer War and condemned the use of Chinese labor in South African gold mines.

Cadbury pressed for a steep tax on land values that he hoped would result in significant property redistribution, believing that land was "almost as needful as light and air" to the country-starved population of England's cities.[9] He was all but fanatical in his insistence that life on the land—or at least within easy reach of a garden plot—was the nation's panacea. He declared to the first Garden City Conference, held at Bournville in 1901, that his "hobby" since boyhood had been "the idea of getting men onto the land where they could enjoy their gardens." "On Saturday afternoon or summer evening, you may see father and mother and children at work in their gardens. Is not that a delightful occasion for the boys and girls, to be bringing them into contact with Nature, and to love the flowers? One of the most touching things to me is to see the interest and pleasure of town families who come out into the country and who have never before seen the seeds sown and the vegetables grown."[10] Equally touching, perhaps, was Cadbury's faith that sowing and harvesting could produce not just a physical revolution but a moral one, in the course of which the light that lodged within the soul of every man, woman, and child would flame up to produce a national revival of the spirit. If Englishness came to be equated with what was rural and therefore what was healthy and wholesome, it was because of people like Cadbury, whose convictions gave birth to a vision of the future that was accepted by reformers as particularly and appropriately English because it celebrated the countryside and not the city.

Born in 1839, in the Birmingham suburb of Edgbaston, Cadbury was raised by parents whose strict adherence to the restraining simplicity of their faith meant for George and his four brothers and sister a childhood that was severe yet apparently happy. George attended a Friends academy, where he studied classics and modern languages. At fifteen he left school and entered the family cocoa and chocolate business. Education for its own sake was deemed a distraction from the important tasks of earning one's living and cultivating one's soul.

The firm to which Cadbury was apprenticed, and that he and his elder brother Richard inherited when their father retired seven years later, was faltering. The brothers had been willed £5,000 apiece by their mother, and with that capital and their willingness to work very hard for very little they struggled to turn a profit. They all but failed. In 1864, however, they determined to manufacture a better grade of cocoa than they and their competitors had been producing. By extracting cocoa butter from the raw powder, rather than adding flour and starch to temper its presence, they established themselves as the country's first producers of quality cocoa for drinking. In the late 1870s success compelled them to enlarge their plant. Convinced of the beneficial effect of country living on body and soul, the Cadburys moved their business to a site four miles from the center of Birmingham—fifteen acres of woods and meadow along the banks of a stream known locally as the Bourn, site of the village they were to establish there.

Cadbury's biographer described his life as possessed of a "singular unity . . . of one pattern and of one piece."[11] Photographs of Cadbury reflect a serenity derived from his simple, direct religious faith. William Lever, though a practicing Congregationalist, was anything but serene. A business colleague recalled him as "short and thickset with a sturdy body set on short legs and a massive head covered with thick, upstanding hair, [radiating] force and energy. He had piercing, blue-grey, humorous eyes, which, however, flashed with challenge when he was angry. A strong, thin-lipped mouth, set above a slightly receding chin, and the short neck and closely set ears of a prize-fighter."[12] Cadbury radiated saintliness; from Lever there emanated the salty odors of the entrepreneurial buccaneer. "Napoleonic," a reporter from the *Liverpool Daily Post* called him; "overwhelming, everything that means power, strength and creativeness."[13] His heroes were Samuel Smiles, the Victorian propagandist for self-help, William Gladstone, and Abraham Lincoln. His gospel was hard work. "The happiest part of our lives will be whilst we are working hard," he declared to his employees in the first issue of his company's monthly magazine, *Progress*. "Let us . . . not be deluded, any one of us, that a life of ease is a life of happiness."[14]

Lever's early life followed a progressive path of which Samuel Smiles would certainly have approved. He was born into the respectable nonconformity of lower-middle-class Bolton, in 1851. His father, James, a successful grocer, had apprenticed himself at fourteen; he later married the daughter of a Manchester cotton-mill manager. In 1842, James joined a former fellow apprentice in partnership as a retail grocer. In 1864, he acquired control of the firm and transformed it into a wholesale business.

William, like George Cadbury, attended local day schools until he was sixteen, when he joined the firm as apprentice. Once he reached majority he became a partner and soon began an adventurous expansion of the company's undertakings. They opened a branch of the business in Wigan and built larger premises in Bolton. In 1884, William commenced a separate wholesale soap business with his brother James. Like the Cadburys, the Lever brothers pinned their initial success to a quality product: soap made from vegetable oils rather than tallow. By 1887 the business had expanded to the point where new premises were required. Lever purchased fifty-two acres—later expanded to five hundred—near Bebington in Cheshire, and there began construction of the factory town that bore the name of the soap that had already made Lever Brothers internationally famous: Port Sunlight.

Lever insisted unabashedly on the self-interested nature of his philanthropy at Port Sunlight. He declared "emotional philanthropy" a mistake yet argued that good business practice required employers to sympathize with their workers. "The time will come when the unsympathetic and inefficient will be wiped out of existence by the employer who perceives that his people require human sympathy and more thought, more attention and more personal acquaintance than his machines."[15] Sympathy encouraged efficiency; efficiency compelled sympathy: a straightforward formula for progress, to which Lever, as an eminent late-Victorian, remained fervently loyal. His gospel was one of planning, building, and regulating in the best interests of those whose lives he was convinced he must improve.

Lever's entrepreneurial aggressiveness translated into an assertive brand of political liberalism. He stood as a candidate several times before being elected to Parliament in the Liberal landslide of 1906. He sat only until 1909, however, when he retired without much apparent regret. He enjoyed the role of political iconoclast. He championed old-age pensions: "That one Act of Parliament has scattered money up and down the land, . . . prospering everybody." He spoke at women's suffrage meetings: "If women exercised the vote there would be a much keener interest taken in matters of reform." And he argued for the payment of MPs, on the grounds that without that reform, class legislation "from a small section of the nation who never feel the effects of their mistakes" would continue to inhibit progress.[16] Lever's one genuinely radical proposal was that municipalities acquire land and offer it free for the erection of workers' cottages. Such a plan, he argued, was in fact anything but revolutionary. The nation already provided free education to its citizens. Why not land? "To give free land to ensure the proper housing of the people is only an extension of the principle we have already accepted."[17]

Lever's penchant for saying that which no businessman would utter may well have been more the consequence of a puckish desire to astonish than of genuine conviction. Many who worked for him resented what they perceived as an authoritarian streak in his management of industrial relations. Yet, in the manner of the enlightened industrialist of the time, he professed to despise the idea of class warfare. He preached, instead, the identity of the interests of employer and employee and claimed that his goal, the "ideal worth living for," was the "elevation of the workers to the front rank." He insisted that he did not fear the time when working men would command a majority in Parliament. "For myself, I know of no justification for such dread, nor any teaching of history upon which fear could be founded. Revolutions have come from a denial of self-government, not from the granting of full and complete self-government."[18]

All of this cut against the grain of cautious, established thinking. Lever appeared to enjoy tweaking the sensibilities of social reformers whose familiarity with anything beyond the world of Oxford, Cambridge, and London was at best dim. He espoused the cause of education; not, however, as the sweetness and light that Matthew Arnold had championed in *Culture and Anarchy* but as a "fairy godmother" who had presented the modern world with the practical gift of investigation and invention. Lever was one of Arnold's unabashed philistines. He had little good to say of learning for its own sake. "The university man who cannot earn his own living is an uneducated man. The skilled mechanic, or bricklayer, or carpenter, or navvy may not be what we should call an educated man or a scholarly man, yet he is a better educated man than the senior wrangler who is unable to earn an adequate living to support himself."[19]

William Lever and George Cadbury prided themselves on the way they earned their livings and on the way that experience had taught them what they knew best. They came to the business of town planning and housing reform from their experience as industrial entrepreneurs, inspired by a particular understanding of the ways of the world—and in Cadbury's case, of the work of God within it. Though very different, the even-tempered chocolate maker and the ebullient soap maker delighted together in the certainty that their practical, tangible accomplishments gave them the opportunity—indeed, the right—to point the way to others who thought and wrote but seldom as they had done. It was their success as practical men that made their work worth heeding. Through the model villages that they built beside their factories, these two industrialists contributed significantly to a public understanding of what genuine English community might be. Their influence was a measure of the degree to which Englishness was not simply the invention of an Oxford and Cambridge professional elite but the conception of a broad collection of reform-minded men and women.

That conception took shape partly as a result of the paternalism that infused the daily work and home life in both Bournville and Port Sunlight. The hallmark of industrial relations at Cadbury Brothers was an intense personal interest on the part of the owners in the physical and moral well-being of their employees. The aim, articulated in a treatise on the Cadbury managerial system by George's son Edward, was a "combination of business efficiency together with the all-round development of the workers as individuals and citizens."[20] Labor, in other words, was not mere commodity, a dogma derived equally from Quaker belief in the inner light and from the notion that sound business practice required that attention be paid to the health and welfare of those who earned the company its profits.

Social harmony was always the goal at the Bournville works. Although George's son Edward, in his account of the firm's policies, wrote that the loyalty of workers was not to be sought "at the expense of individual autonomy and class solidity," the notion that the interests of the workers, as a class, might differ from those of their employers on any major matter appears never to have entered Cadbury's mind.[21] Edward expressed this primary article of the family faith: "The welfare of employer and employed are not antagonistic but complementary and inclusive, [and] each position brings its duties and its rights."[22] If employees wanted to form unions, let them, since unions increased opportunities to discuss issues of mutual concern. Nothing suggests that the workers themselves at this time saw any reason to challenge the policy of social harmony, even though labor unrest was an increasingly uncomfortable fact of life outside Bournville.

Employees enjoyed a range of educational and welfare benefits. Because the company hired teen-age boys and girls, continuing education became a cornerstone of the Cadburys' industrial relations scheme, an expression of George Cadbury's determination to help those in his charge cultivate their inner light. Boys chose from one of two tracks: the commercial or the industrial. Girls were educated to become wives and mothers, since George Cadbury had no doubts about the importance of a married woman's place at home. Edward Cadbury, echoing his father's sentiments, explained the company's policy of hiring only unmarried women by stating that a "woman cannot give proper care to the home and children if she is spending the greater part of her time in a factory."[23] Employees were afforded exercise opportunities as well, including swimming in the company's baths. For adults, education was provided by a local branch of the Workers' Education Association. A variety of organizations enabled workers to make constructive use of their leisure hours: men's and girls' athletic clubs, reading clubs, a camera club, a music society, and the Bournville Women Workers' Social Service League, whose purpose was "to assist in the improvement of conditions in the lives of women working in the factories of Birmingham"—women, that is, whose misfortune it was not to work at Bournville.[24]

George Cadbury remained as concerned about his employees' health as about their educational well-being. Job seekers under the age of sixteen were no doubt surprised to discover that a dental exam was part of the application process, and even more surprised when presented with toothbrush and powder. Male and female doctors and a staff of nurses kept track of employee illnesses. District nurses worked in concert with the company, visiting those sent home sick and, in the process, advising patients on the best way to ensure a healthy, hygienic household by means of fresh air and appropriate diet. A generous pension plan encouraged employees to retire at age sixty, before illness might compel their departure.

Much of the formalized scheme of industrial relations described by Edward Cadbury in his book *Experiments in Industrial Organization* was instituted early in the century, after George had begun to relinquish control of the business to his sons and nephews. (His brother Richard died in 1899.) Yet the innovations bore the mark of George's convictions about how to run a business, if company success was defined in terms of human betterment as well as financial profit. It was that definition that compelled him to take an interest in the well-being of his employees. The interest was personal—at times intensely so—at least before the workforce expanded into the thousands. In those early years, and in the decades that followed, George Cadbury and his family remained acutely conscious of the charge that they were meddling in the affairs of their employees, and worked hard to keep from being labeled paternalists. An 1882 company pamphlet declared forthrightly that "while the partners, with a degree of sensitiveness that a refined mind can at once appreciate, refrain from exercising anything like a paternal control over their employees, they show practically how much they have the welfare of all their workpeople at heart."[25] What makes this disclaimer noteworthy is the fact that the brothers went to such pains to make it—then and throughout their lives. As Patrick Joyce has demonstrated in his study of mid-Victorian factory masters, many employers were self-conscious industrial paternalists, making no bones about the manner in which they provided their workers with the benefits of a kind of benevolent authoritarianism, much as rural squires had done and continued to do.[26] But the Cadburys, subscribing as they did to the doctrine of an inner light, could not allow themselves to believe that they were exercising control over men and women as worthy in God's sight as they were. Their faith in a democracy of souls encouraged an abiding concern for the "welfare of all their workpeople." But that concern must not inhibit the growth of the individual human spirit.

And yet because of their determination to help their employees discover the "best self" within them, George and Richard Cadbury often treated workers in ways that can only be described as paternal. During the firm's early years, every job applicant was interviewed by one or both of the brothers. Writing in 1912, Edward Cadbury showed how little the procedure had changed over more than thirty years of operation. A director of the firm still interviewed each applicant, then decided the class of work to which the employee was to be assigned, "special note being taken of the tone, character, cleanliness and general bearing," Cadbury noted. "When young persons are selected, the condition of their hands is a very important factor."[27]

In the early years, the condition of workers' souls was also of concern to George Cadbury. A woman card box maker from that time remembered that George took a "personal interest in everything concerning the work people, not only for their physical but their spiritual welfare. It was his object in life to lead all with whom he came in contact to the Lord he loved and served so well." A salesman, who recalled that the brothers were referred to "familiarly (but not disrespectfully)" as "Governor Richard" and "Governor George," "knew every-one in their service. . . . The interest they took in one was that of a friend, and they somehow conveyed the idea that their purpose was to do something *for* one, rather than to get the last ounce in the way of work."[28]

In these recollections, as in all the accounts of the life of the firm, one senses a cultivated perception of Cadbury Brothers not just as a family firm but as a family. When George Cadbury assumed direction of the business, he instituted morning readings for the staff and workers, following a precedent set by both his grandfather and Joseph Fry, a fellow Quaker cocoa manufacturer at Bristol. Another early employee wrote in his reminiscence of the "echoes of thronging foot treads along the corridors, the quieter filing into line through a door into the girls' dining room, then the subdued rustling of taking seats followed by the perfect quiet before the ready rendering of an announced hymn in hearty community singing. Then a few homely words or the reading of a scriptural passage by Mr. R. or Mr. G., and the 10 to 15 minute break in working hours came to an end as to time, but probably not as to influence."[29] One is reminded of accounts of the Victorian ritual of morning prayers: father, mother, children, servants gathered in the dining room to celebrate not merely the beginning of another day under God's guidance but also the family as the institution most seemly in God's sight.

Fatherly direction also showed a sterner side at Bournville. Men and women were segregated throughout the plant to prevent conversations between them that might have had a "demoralizing effect upon both sexes."[30] Slackers were quizzed by members of the staff about their inability to work to standard. Sometimes, Cadbury's biographer A. G. Gardiner reported, "it was found that [a] girl went to bed habitually at too late an hour, so losing sleep. In other cases she rose too late in the morning, so missing breakfast." This paternal solicitude could not help but strike some as intrusive. As Gardiner acknowledges, in matters of conduct the brothers "were rigorous, and in spite of their gentleness of method, they were not seldom charged with being autocratic."[31]

Stern or gentle, Cadburys were everywhere about the place. Much as the squire's heir and relations made their presence felt in the communities over which they presided, so George and Richard and then, in turn, their sons played out their lives within the precincts of the factory and its grounds. The *Bournville Works Magazine* reported their doings assiduously: the election of William Cadbury (Richard's son) and George Cadbury, Jr., to the Council of Greater Birmingham; William's presidency of the Bournville Athletic Club; the marriage of Isabel Cadbury (George's daughter) to Mr. Kenneth Wilson ("director of Albright and Wilson, Ltd., chemical manufacturers, and nephew of J. W. Wilson, MP"); the entry of Lawrence Cadbury (George's son) "upon his business life at Bournville Works." ("There has been no doubt about his popularity at College; he is a keen 'open air' man, being interested in many outside pursuits, particularly in rowing.") Over all lay the presence of George Cadbury, who, with his wife, presided and entertained throughout the year— in a period of two months in 1912, for example, feting all sixty-five hundred employees of the company at their nearby "manor house." At one of these gatherings, the *Works Magazine* enthused, "All heartily enjoyed the happiest of garden parties, as was evinced by the chuckling of the patriarchs bowling the best 'woods,' . . . the noisy exuberance of the skittlers, not to forget the laughter of the little people of the house, to whom the big drum and great blazing brass trumpets proved so irresistible."[32] What all this bespoke was surely something very close to the paternalism that had diffused across the pre-industrial countryside, deny it though the Cadburys might. And this sense of their benevolent presence and purposes—not in any way as conscious agents of some kind of social control, but as exemplifying a model of high thinking and right living— was just as powerfully infused into the life of the village they built beside their factory.

George Cadbury gave a characteristically straightforward apologia for the founding of Bournville village in a 1907 appearance before a church commission investigating social problems. "Through my experience among the back streets of Birmingham I have been brought to the conclusion that it is impossible to raise a nation, morally, physically and spiritually in such surroundings, and that the only effective way is to bring men out of the cities into the country and to give to every man his garden where he can come into touch with nature and thus know more of nature's God."[33] Bournville was a lesson that would teach men how to make that journey. Cadbury had never himself lived in Birmingham; his father moved the family to suburban Edgbaston four years before George's birth. A. G. Gardiner insists nonetheless that Cadbury "never ceased to regard himself as a Birmingham man."[34] Yet his passionate antipathy to all that the city seemed to him to embody, his belief that—as he declared in his statement to the commissioners—cities corrupted their citizens, belies Gardiner's contention. Cadbury may have considered himself a Birmingham man in the sense that he was a man of the provinces. But his primary concern with the city after he had removed his factory from it was to try to demonstrate how grossly it had failed to provide its residents with an environment conducive to the growth of the human spirit.

No question that he had cause for complaint. Unplanned suburbs sprang up around Birmingham at the end of the century, its population rising from 634,579 in 1861 to 759,887 in 1901 to 842,337 in 1911. Housing at the center of town was wretchedly cramped; in 1914 Birmingham still possessed 42,000 dwellings built back-to-back without through ventilation. And surrounding this, according to a 1907 report, "miles of streets have been recently cut and built; the houses . . . look already old and ram-shackle, and a large percentage are always empty, waiting till the place is ripe for further development as a slum."[35]

George Cadbury founded Bournville in 1895. A few semi-detached houses for foremen had been built after the move from Birmingham in 1879. By the 1890s, with shoddy suburbs on the march toward the factory, Cadbury feared that jerry-builders would rob the company and its employees of the environment they had escaped Birmingham to find. He had originally purchased 120 acres for the village; by 1909 it covered 525 acres, which were valued, with the buildings on them, at £251,000.[36] In 1901 the property had been deeded by Cadbury to a charitable trust as a way of ensuring that no one individual, himself included, could profit from the sale of houses whose value was rapidly increasing. Originally he had sold houses on a ground lease of 999 years, declaring that he wished the village residents to live independently as homeowners. But when they began to sell at profits of more than 20 percent, his liberal abhorrence of gains accrued from the unearned increment on land made him change his mind. After the sale of the first 143 houses, the remainder were let at weekly rents, and the management of the property was assigned to the trust, on whose board only Cadburys sat during George's lifetime (the appointment of trustees remained in his hands until his death).

All profits from the venture were invested in building more houses. And since the stated object of the trust was the "amelioration of the condition of the working-class and labouring population in and around Birmingham and elsewhere in Great Britain," the houses built at Bournville were not intended for the exclusive use of Cadbury employees.[37] A further goal—convincing investors that decent housing could produce a decent return—proved elusive at Bournville, as it was to prove in other similar experiments. "There is something almost millennial in the suggestion that 3 3/4 percent would satisfy the ordinary builder," the *Architectural Review* noted sourly in 1906, in comments on a book by W. A Harvey, Bournville's principal architect. "It has still to be shown that such a scheme as Bournville can be dealt with on purely commercial (as opposed to partly philanthropic) lines."[38]

Cadbury involved himself directly in the planning of his village. Trees bordered all the roads, which were forty-two feet wide—unnecessarily wide in the view of some critics.[39] Parks occupied 16 of the original 120 acres. Houses were limited to seven per acre, and, whether free-standing, semi-detached, or terraced, stood on a plot of ground large enough to accommodate the garden that Cadbury deemed so necessary. Given his distaste for cityscapes, the rectangular layout of most of the early streets comes as a surprise. Although, thanks to the abundance of trees, grass, and garden, there is none of the monotony of suburbia in Bournville, the sense one gets is of a frankly urban compactness. The sections of the village that were developed immediately before World War I, however, conform to the more irregular, countrified notions of what was appropriate and pleasing. As often as possible, roads ran north to south rather than east to west, so as to provide sun on both the front and back sides of houses for some part of the day.

Cadbury was, of course, concerned with providing more than an aesthetically pleasing and salubrious outdoor environment for working-class families. Houses, too, were designed to promote healthy lives, and at affordable rents. By 1909 they were let on a scale from 4/6 to 8/ per week, plus rates (local taxes), the range encouraging a variety of renters. A typical home renting for 6/6 contained, on the ground floor, a living room–kitchen, 16 feet by 11 feet, and a scullery; on the first floor, three small bedrooms: a very generous layout when compared with the cramped, airless housing that most workers were compelled to accept in adjacent Birmingham suburbs.[40] A house of this sort would have had no separate bathroom; patented devices for bathing were installed in the kitchen. Toilets were placed in closets adjacent to coal storage bins and were entered from outside the house. These were cost-cutting measures, as was the use of sloping roofs (to reduce brickwork) and stock materials.

Cadbury engaged Harvey, who was from Birmingham, to design almost all the buildings at Bournville. Given his patron's desire to make the gardens far more than an afterthought, Harvey abandoned the urban "tunnel-back" plan, used in the very first foremen's houses built near the factory, which stacked kitchen, scullery, larder, coal bin, and WC in a long extension behind the living room. This was the layout in most recently constructed suburban neighborhoods, and the one employed to ill effect at Saltaire. It resulted, Harvey wrote, in a "narrow outlook upon a cramped yard. The better view of the garden obtained from the back rooms by the avoidance of this is an important consideration."[41] Harvey instead used what he called the cottage plan, which brought outbuildings under the main roof, thereby affording a garden prospect at the rear of the house. Houses were built in attached terraces of varying lengths, with increasing attention paid to how each unit related to its neighbors and to the streetscape, with the street itself treated as one architectural entity.

Harvey's "cottagey" idiom reflected Cadbury's determination to turn his back on anything that bespoke the city. "Roofing ridges should have careful attention, and it is wiser to suppress rather than to sharpen, the better to obtain that rustic appearance suitable to a cottage," Harvey wrote. "Many fantastic ridges, with vulgar finials, are employed in the building of small suburban villas, of a more or less sharp-pointed character, and of a depth out of proportion to the roof, which gives an unpleasant harshness to the general appearance."[42] Softened, "natural" lines replaced the harsh vulgarity of the urban landscape, reminding Bournville housedwellers of where they had come and what they had escaped. Exterior details reiterated the purposeful rusticity that was Harvey's intention. He made a virtue of irregularity: "A small cottage with an equal distribution of equal-sized windows is far from desirable," he wrote. Inside, he frequently introduced "cosy" features like the inglenook, though he warned that "like many old-time features which have been revived during the last few years, the inglenook has been a little overdone."[43] A critic writing in the *Architectural Review* wondered if, in fact, Harvey had not overdone things generally. "A walk through the estate suggests that the architect, in his natural and most admirable desire to escape a dull uniformity, has gone just a little far in the other direction. There are, perhaps, too many 'features.' Gables and chimneys vie with rather larky chimneys and oriels to attract our attention, and the effect is sometimes a little short of restful."[44]

In the matter of gardens, variation gave way to regimentation. Gardening at Bournville was compulsory. A clause in the rental contracts stipulated the standards of neatness and beauty. Before tenants moved in, their gardens, usually four hundred square yards, were planted for them, in beds separated by paths three feet wide—toward one side at the immediate back of the house, to allow for more lawn, then down the middle of the vegetable patch to the small orchard beyond. Wherever possible, crops were sown in rows that ran north to south, to ensure maximum sunshine. Each gardener was provided eight apple and pear trees, twelve gooseberry bushes, one Victoria plum, and six creepers for the house: roses, wisteria, honeysuckle, clematis, ivy, and jasmine. The Trust established a gardening department, headed by an expert trained at Kew Gardens. "Thus," an admiring observer proclaimed, "no matter how poor a man may be, or how ignorant of gardening, when he comes to Bournville there is *no chance for him to get discouraged.*" And if he did, the writer continued, and shirked his horticultural obligations, it was with the knowledge "that there are one hundred applicants for homes on the waiting list all the time."[45]

That George Cadbury was prepared to go to these lengths to ensure his village a regiment of gardeners is a measure of his conviction that gardens were the key to a healthy community. He enjoyed flourishing statistics that proved his point. A study he financed in 1901 showed that Bournville boys were on average four inches taller than their Birmingham counterparts, their chests three inches broader, their weight eight pounds greater. He never tired of preaching his gospel: "A man must have fresh air and come in contact with nature if he [is] to have a really fine physique."[46] Sound bodies would not by themselves produce sound minds. Cadbury and his wife, Elizabeth, gave Bournville its schools, at a cost of £30,000, sparing no money, as Harvey noted, "to make the building itself a permanent means of educating the children." Murals depicted historical scenes; English flowers and foliage were carved into the woodwork.[47] There was accommodation for 540 pupils, in classrooms designed to hold no more than fifty-five.

The schools stood on ground donated by the Cadburys near the green and churches, and the shopping precinct known as the Triangle. It was here that the citizens were expected to come to know one another, in a space designed to encourage the sense of being part of a community. And yet as late as 1907 a writer in the *Economic Review,* J. A. Dale, who may well have been a Bournville resident, was complaining that the village still did not possess a "self," that it was not really a village at all but just another suburb—albeit a far more pleasing one than its neighbors. There was, he wrote, no genuine center "about which Bournville could grow to be something different from a casual suburb." Though the village boasted an institute—Ruskin Hall, with library, reading rooms, and crafts workshops—it had no social club or pubs, for Bournville was, of course, a teetotal community. More surprising at that time, adult residents not employed at the Cadbury works could not use the factory's recreational fields. "Visitors find it hard to believe; those who write about [the Village] do not, as a rule, know." Those most inclined to use sports grounds, Dale opined, were also those who would in general "carry on the village life, and the want of those [facilities] will weaken that life."[48] Perhaps Cadbury supposed that since men and women must spend their leisure hours cultivating their gardens they would not need space for other diversions. Certainly the demands of those gardens were considerable. And because gardening is an essentially solitary enterprise, it no doubt inhibited socializing.

Dale noted that the village contained a mix of inhabitants inclined to make much of numerous existing "social cleavages," which were no more than "tiny gulfs" but were "serious enough to those at whose feet [they] yawn."[49] Here, then, was another factor inhibiting the growth of community. Cadbury had from the first insisted that Bournville was not to be a company town, like Saltaire. At no time were more than 40 percent of the adult male residents employed by the Cadburys. He also hoped that families from various classes might inhabit the same streets. "The manager might live next door to the labourer, the object being to create a mixed community of different social groups."[50] Yet, since the Trust's deed stipulated that it build houses for the "labouring and working classes," few managers lived in the village at all. A 1909 survey found that a little over 50 percent of the adult male residents were factory workers; 36 percent were artisans of various sorts; and 13 percent were "clerks and travellers."[51] There is no doubt, however, that many in that latter group assumed a superiority over the artisans, and that the artisans assumed the same over the factory workers. A community, in other words, very like any other in England at the time, with the exception that all who lived at Bournville were bunched around the lower-middle- and upper-working-class rungs of the social and economic ladder. And that bunching may well have impelled an even more than normally obsessive concern about position, about those gulfs that, if tiny to an outsider, might have appeared as chasms to the office clerk living along-side the boilermaker.

From time to time residents complained that high rents were in fact making the village a community with increasingly few working-class families. A Bour-nvillite who signed himself "Disgusted" to the *Birmingham Daily Mail* in 1902, wrote, "It is all very nice for housing of the poor commissioners and labour delegates to come to Bournville and wander round the model village, and swallow all they are told by the good people who conduct them round, as they point out the advantages of living under such pleasant conditions, and then go away with the impression that the housing of the poor problem is solved here. I think they, like myself, would soon come to the conclusion that the working man, such as Mr. Cadbury presumably seeks to benefit, has very little chance here."[52] In 1911 tenants revolted over the Trust's policy of raising rents between tenancies and of separating the charges for rates from weekly rents, the latter practice requiring annual lump-sum payments beyond the means of many. Much of the unhappiness stemmed from confusion over the nature of the Bournville enterprise. "We were at one time under the impression that Bournville was a model village," the *Architect and Contract Reporter* editorialized at the time of the dispute, "owing its existence and excellence in a considerable degree to philanthropy."[53] Cadbury, of course, insisted that Bournville was an experiment proving that workers could be provided decent housing in healthy surroundings at a modest profit. Beyond the issue of rents, however, lay the larger question of Cadbury's role within the community. Who was ultimately in charge? A village council managed playgrounds, garden shows, and children's fetes, but it had no legal standing, and no power to raise funds compulsorily. Its major function was to serve as a means of communication between tenants and the Trust, on which sat only Cadburys.[54] J. A. Dale, in his critique for the *Economic Review,* wrote that this lack of self-government "depressed public activities." There was danger, he observed, in the goodness of Bournville's "unfailing benefactors."[55]

The urban historians Colin and Rose Bell argue that Bournville was "free from the feudal aspects of many other tycoon foundations."[56] Yet it is difficult not to see those "unfailing benefactors" as philanthropic lords of a manor they had built to suit their high-minded purposes. George Cadbury could not resist the temptation to instruct his tenants in matters of health and hygiene. Every newcomer received a handbook, which included such nostrums as:

- Take no solid food of any kind between meals; this rule applies with double force to children.
- Apples are the most wholesome fruit; they should be used freely, both raw and cooked.
- Breathe through the nostrils with the mouth closed, especially at night.
- The best clothing gives the largest amount of heat with the least possible weight.
- In a truly happy home father or mother will conduct family worship at least once a day when the Bible should be read and a hymn sung.[57]

"It was this care for you," A. G. Gardiner acknowledges, "that made George Cadbury a little trying to disorderly people who loved freedom more than good habits."[58] Whenever possible, Cadbury participated in village events that taught the rewards of diligent behavior: prize days at the schools; prize days in spring and summer, when gardeners were handed six shillings for the excellence of their displays.

Elizabeth Cadbury also fought important national battles on behalf of social reform: she was president of the National Union of Women Workers in 1907. She was nonetheless willing to express her determination to improve the lot of her fellow men and women in the language of paternalistic chivalry. In a speech to a convention of Rotarians, she defined social service as "Noblesse Oblige in the widest sense. Those who are in positions of comfort and prosperity are compelled by that very fact . . . to bring about a condition of affairs under which the benefits they themselves enjoy are shared with those who are less fortunate."[59] At Bournville, she called on every new tenant and at houses where there were newborn babies. The schools were her particular concern. She inspected classrooms and substituted for sick teachers. In her presidential address to the NUWW, she declared, in an obvious reference to her husband, that an employer "can establish a feeling of sympathy between himself and his people akin to the old family feeling that existed between the master and his apprentices in the days before machinery and huge industrial centers." "In most cities," she lamented, "there is no personal interest and no one with higher educational advantages to set the tone or a high moral standard."[60] At Bournville she presided over the manor house, staffed by twenty indoor and outdoor servants, from which she and her husband entertained villagers as they entertained their factory workers.

A. G. Gardiner quotes George Cadbury as saying that "men do not want to be patronized; they want justice."[61] Cadbury did not patronize in the sense that he appears to have used the word; he did not condescend. He did, however, refuse to allow others, including the citizens of Bournville, to come between him and his determination to make his village what he wanted it to be: an example to his country of the way human problems might be solved humanely.

William Lever insisted, too, that he was no paternalist. Indeed, if one examines the history of Lever Brothers following its move to Port Sunlight, it is easy to understand Lever in terms of the up-to-date, hard-driving early-twentieth-century capitalism he so enjoyed preaching. For his company, this meant continuing rapid expansion, aided by advertising campaigns that astonished and increasingly vexed his competitors. The move to Port Sunlight was accompanied by what the company's historian, Charles Wilson, calls a "spectacular leap in production." Annual output increased by 3,000 to 5,000 tons per year.

In its first decade Lever Brothers increased production from 2,946 to 38,788 tons.[62] In 1894, Lever Brothers became Lever Brothers Limited, a public company with an authorized capital of £1.5 million. Lever retained what amounted to absolute control by purchasing first the majority and eventually all of the ordinary shares.[63]

Meanwhile, within the factory, Lever proceeded to implement schemes that would serve his declared goal: "to Socialize and Christianize business relations and get back again in the office, factory and workshop to that close family brotherhood that existed in the good old days of hand labour."[64] Men worked forty-eight hours a week, women forty-five. Wages were paid at trade union rates to a mostly unskilled workforce of two thousand men and sixteen hundred women—this in 1909. Work was performed in well-ventilated rooms with mosaic floors and white or soft green walls decorated with a variety of national flags. Men who did not return home for dinner ate meals they had brought with them in the mock Tudor vastness of Gladstone Hall, which seated eight hundred. Women could obtain cooked dinners in Hulme Hall (named for Mrs. Lever's family), where as many as fifteen hundred meals were provided daily. By 1909, workers could enjoy as well a theater, a concert hall, a library, a gymnasium, and a swimming bath.[65]

Each new employee received a free medical exam; personal accident committees, composed of an equal number of elected and appointed members, ensured that workers received prompt and appropriate treatment. The Employees Benefit Fund, established in 1904 and financed entirely by the company, provided pensions to men after age sixty-five and to women after fifty-five, in both cases to workers with at least fifteen years' service; to those forced to retire as a consequence of ill health or injury; and to widows of long-term employees.[66] Lever announced the scheme in characteristically forthright language. In a public letter to his employees he said that the plan was designed to reward those who had done their duty by the company. "There is no unpleasant taint of pauperising philanthropy in this. . . . Those who do not do their duty to the Firm will never retain their position long enough to entitle them to a pension or their Widows and Orphans to maintenance—the Firm can do without such members of the Staff, and their place will be taken by those who will do their duty better. It is fair presumptive evidence if an employee has remained long enough with the Firm to qualify for a pension he or she has done his or her duty and has earned his or her pension."[67]

The authoritarian tone of the letter was characteristic of Lever's dealings with his workers—or staff, as they were referred to at Port Sunlight. And it was no more evident than in the frequent communiqués and pronouncements that he issued to explain and defend a profit-sharing plan that he instituted at Lever Brothers in 1909. A form of "prosperity sharing" was, as we shall see, a feature of the adjacent village of Port Sunlight. But by the time that a "co-partnership" was launched at the factory, a substantial number of workers lived elsewhere. It was a scheme designed to afford everyone employed by the firm a chance to benefit from its increasing profitability.

Lever insisted that he had designed the plan to "take us back in sympathy for each other and in close relationship to each other to those times . . . when we were all working in one building and under one roof"; times, his son later wrote, that Lever remembered fondly, when he knew all his staff, exercising over them a form of "benevolent leadership, tempered by a strictness that was respected."[68] The scheme was complicated in detail but simple in essence. Workers were encouraged to understand themselves as co-partners through obtaining co-partnership certificates—not shares, be it noted—that had no monetary value but which entitled holders to an annual dividend, once the claims of preferred shareholders had been met and a 5 percent payment had been made to ordinary shareholders. There was but one ordinary shareholder: William Lever. Beyond that, profits were divided equally between the co-partners and Lever, as ordinary shareholder. The scheme would have been impossible, as Charles Wilson notes, had not Lever himself held all the ordinary shares. Dividends to co-partners amounted, indeed, "to an annual gift out of his own pocket."[69]

Lever never disguised the moral purpose behind the plan: to teach the virtue of hard work and of cooperation between management and labor. He believed that his scheme would succeed because it supported the fundamental law of progress: that humankind wants to better its condition by working hard. "It is from the operation of this universal law of self-interest of the individual that all progress has sprung and is maintained." Master and worker shared this instinct; co-partnership would do no more than bring them to a realization of their common interests. "There are not two different . . . ladders, one for the master and one for the workman; they both have to climb the same ladder which is— producing more goods with less labour in fewer hours."[70]

Trade unionists saw co-partnership as a clever, relatively inexpensive way to alienate workers from their true interests. Lever paid their misgivings more than occasional attention. In his 1913 address to the co-partners he declared that co-partnership, far from threatening the "solidarity of labour," as so often charged, if anything threatened the "solidarity of capital," by taking £40,000 from the company's reserve fund and placing it in the hands of workers. "Is not this money in your pockets making for the solidarity of labour?" he asked, to which rhetorical demand his listeners replied with a chorus of "hear, hear."[71] Lever appears, in fact, to have considered trade unions an irrelevance, although he frequently declared that were he a worker he would join one. He insisted that he viewed those trade unionists whom he employed with the same paternal eye that he cast on all his staff. "I make no distinction," he told the 1913 co-partners, "no more than a father would between his boys and girls. You are, every one of you, equally as dear to me whether trades unionist or not."[72] But Lever insisted that unions were powerless to raise wages, a worthy end that could be achieved only through cooperation between management and labor. "The sooner we recognize . . . that we are all on one common platform, that we can work together to increase the fund out of which wages are paid," the sooner we understand as well that collective bargaining will make little difference.[73]

Strikes, of course, manifested a point of view at odds with the notion of a "common platform." Lever made it clear, therefore, that strikers were not entitled to the privilege of co-partnership. "Any man can strike as he likes; I do not mind; but if he does this, he is not entitled, surely, to the same consideration as the man who is helping all he can to keep the business running during this time."[74] No wonder that at least some critics saw Lever's scheme as a cheap bribe for good behavior. Workers held co-partnerships in an enterprise over which Lever exercised all but dictatorial power. "It is as much your business as mine," he preached. "But . . . unless you appreciate my point of view, we are doomed to failure."[75] Yet Lever insisted not just on appreciation but on adherence to his view as well, whether or not it suited his workers' own needs and desires.

Beyond the factory, the benevolent circumstances under which men and women went about their lives in the magic kingdom of Port Sunlight did not allow for much criticism of the lively sorcerer who created it. The allusion to the world of Walt Disney is deliberate. In the village of Port Sunlight, which Lever built for the exclusive use of his workers, one breathes the same air of carefully crafted, fastidious unreality that emanates from Walt Disney World. It was Lever's intention when he moved to Port Sunlight to begin a program of house-construction immediately. By 1898 the original village was complete, with 278 houses, schools, a village institute, and shops. By 1909, 720 houses had been built on an expanded site of 130 acres, housing a population of close to 4,000.[76]

The village was an arm of Lever's elaborate scheme of industrial relations and was financed as such. The early houses were built with company money.

Additional housing and an increasingly elaborate complement of public build-ings and parks were paid for either by Lever personally or through his prosper-ity-sharing scheme, forerunner to the co-partnerships. Every year, the company put back into the village a portion of its profits; by 1903, Lever claimed that one-tenth of Lever Brothers' capital was invested in Port Sunlight. Lever believed that his plan was good business. Contented, healthy employees labored more productively for the company if they understood that the pleasant environment in which they lived was in part the result of their own hard work.

There was also a moral dimension to the scheme, as Lever made clear in an interview in 1903.

> If I were to follow the usual mode of profit-sharing I would send my workmen and work girls to the cash office at the end of the year and say to them: "You are going to receive £8 each; you have earned this money; it belongs to you. Take it and make whatever use you like of it. Spend it in the public house; have a good spree at Christmas; do as you like with your money." Instead of that I told them: "£8 is an amount which is soon spent, and it will not do you much good if you send it down your throats in the form of bottles of whisky, bags of sweets, or fat geese for Christmas. On the other hand, if you leave this money with me, I shall use it to provide for you everything which makes life pleasant, viz. nice houses, comfortable homes, and healthy recreation."

"Besides," Lever added with a characteristically unselfconscious flourish, "I am disposed to allow profit-sharing under no other than that form."[77] Critics of course complained that this was nothing more than the institutional philan-thropy that Lever always insisted he never practiced. W. L. George declared that the "scheme, with its sharing of 'prosperity,' suggests that the employees are receiving doles." Nothing ensured that Lever Brothers would continue to share prosperity in this fashion. "The inhabitants are in the hollow of the master's hand. At present his grasp is gentle, but nothing says it will remain so."[78]

The master's grasp, whether gentle or not upon his employees, was firm when it came to the design of the village and its buildings. Like Cadbury, Lever believed that a healthy environment generated moral improvement. Port Sun-light would be erected on ground with "plenty of space . . . for the workpeople employed, which has always been our idea . . . semi-detached houses, with gardens back and front, in which they will be able to know more about the science of life than they can in a back slum."[79] The village was laid out to conform to its very irregular site, crossed by ravines and dotted with tidal marshes that were gradually filled in and drained. Lever insisted on no more than five houses per acre. Semi-detached groupings gave way quickly to rows of terraces arranged for the most part in large open quadrangles, with allotment gardens filling the enclosed areas behind the houses. Roads were twenty-four feet wide, with another eight feet on each side for footpaths. In the first section developed, close by the factory, a compact hamlet clustered around the school buildings, the houses interspersed with pathways. Later the quadrangles stretched along straighter roads. The effect was not precisely villagelike; it did, however, bespeak a reverence for green spaces and, in the provision of allotments, for the ideal of domestic husbandry.

In 1910, Lever sponsored a competition to produce an overall village plan, something that Port Sunlight had lacked. The winner was Ernest Prestwich, a Liverpool planner and devotee of the American "city beautiful" ideal. His selection indicated Lever's enthusiasm for something beyond the villagelike designs that W. A. Harvey had produced for Bournville. Prestwich's plan incorporated two grand "civic" vistas, the first stretching from the railway bordering the western boundary of the village to the substantial neo-Gothic Christ Church built by Lever in 1904; the second intersected the first and culminated in the neoclassical Lady Lever Art Gallery, which Lever erected in his wife's memory to conform with Prestwich's scheme. Thus Port Sunlight is a strange hybrid—part village, part civic center—tribute, if nothing else, to Lever's own restless enthusiasms, certainly to his ability to express those enthusiasms exactly as it pleased him.

In an address to the Architectural Association in 1902, Lever confessed that he had always hoped to be an architect, ever since he had built himself a rabbit hutch as a boy of nine. "There is no career that opens up such immense possibilities for influencing the world in which we live as that of the architect."[80] Working initially with William Owen of Warrington, and later with several other individual architects and local firms, Lever did his best to influence the world at second hand through the houses and public buildings he erected at Port Sunlight. Cottages were of two sizes: the "kitchen type," with one large living room and scullery downstairs, and three bedrooms upstairs; the "parlour type," with an additional sitting room below and three or four bedrooms above. Living rooms in kitchen type houses were usually fourteen to sixteen feet square, in parlor houses a bit smaller. These dimensions suited tenants, Lever told the Architectural Association. "A workman's cottage must fit like a glove if it is to be a successful attempt to provide for the happiness and comfort of himself, his wife and family."[81] All cottages were provided with inside bathtubs—either in the scullery or in a separate room—and with fireplaces in every bedroom. Toilets were placed in closets outside the scullery, a choice dictated by custom, presumably, since they could as easily have been accommodated inside. Unlike the houses at Bournville, those at Port Sunlight were enclosed at the rear by walled yards, which in turn opened out to the allotment grounds behind them, thus preserving a more urban cast to the village overall.

Lever did not concern himself overmuch with building expenses. Kitchen houses cost £200 in 1889, £330 in 1902; parlor types £350 and £550, in all cases well above the amount deemed commercially viable. The company charged rents to cover the expenses of rates, taxes, and repairs but made no attempt to recoup its investment. Lever admitted that "to build a village such as Port Sunlight is not commercially possible at the present time." Rents commensurate with investment—ten shillings at the lowest, instead of the five charged— would have placed the "possibility of living in such a village out of the reach of ordinary village tenants."[82]

Lever's eclectic tastes dictated style as well as cost. Walter Creese, in his survey of garden cities, calls attention to the fact that at the time Lever began to build at Port Sunlight, the Royal Jubilee Exhibition in Manchester included a temporarily constructed village depicting, according to its catalogue, the "many aspects of the town from the time of the Roman occupation to about the middle of the Georgian era"—the town, that is, before it became a terrifying exemplar of industrial devastation. The result, the catalogue proclaimed, was a "wonderfully delightful jumble of incongruities."[83] Creese suggests that it was this model that Lever had in mind when he created his own jumble at Port Sunlight, remarking that this village, "like so many of the architectural events of the 1890s, became tantamount to a permanent exhibition."[84] An undated document in the Port Sunlight archives lists the "types of architectural styles" in which the village was decorated: Cotswold; Queen Anne brickwork; sixteenth-century brick and half-timber; Dutch gable, seventeenth century; brick and stone, Stuart period; plaster, medieval; plastered rubble, French, sixteenth century; Jacobean brickwork; half-timber, late medieval; Flemish brickwork; Baltic brickwork; Dutch brickwork.[85] At a later date, according to one of Lever's architects, his client suggested that the houses erected along the esplanade leading to the art gallery be designed to represent the various countries in which Lever Brothers had built factories. He settled for cottages in the German style, but only after failing to persuade the architect to draw up a block of Swiss chalets.[86] Lever's enthusiasm for the architecture of northern Europe did not preclude an admiration for old English styles, as the list testifies. Public buildings were, in most cases, variations on late medieval or Tudor themes.

Lever was particularly pleased with the row of shops, including a post office constructed with solid oak half-timbering, "as nearly as the Modern Building Act will allow, in exactly the same way it would have been employed three hundred years ago."[87] Facsimiles of Kenyon Old Hall and Shakespeare's birthplace, as well as Christ Church, a re-creation of sixteenth-century Cheshire Gothic, reminded villagers of their national architectural heritage.

Creese makes the interesting suggestion that Port Sunlight's self-conscious eclecticism was driven by a desire to "heighten, brighten, and intensify the visual by emphasis and juxtaposition." And that desire was in turn compelled by a determination to turn away from the "reality" of the northern industrial city, as Manchester had turned away from its real self in the Jubilee Exhibition. "Thus," Creese writes, "the abstract planner of garden cities, like the abstract painter of post-impressionism, was driven to extremes of intensity by the very excesses of realism he encountered in the conventional, everyday urban environment."[88] When reality is at best drab monotony and at most deadly danger, the temptation to create a fantasia from the shapes and surfaces of past times and foreign places becomes remarkably seductive, especially when the creator possesses an imagination as fecund as Lever's.

Critics watching the village take shape found it difficult to decide whether they liked it. "In some cases," W. L. George wrote, "originality has run rather wild."[89] He blamed the architects and not their patron for the excesses. If the cottages were fanciful, so, to a lesser degree, were their surroundings. Lever Brothers planted and maintained the front gardens throughout the village. George wrote that it was impossible to "traverse Port Sunlight without encountering the gardeners perpetually clipping and trimming; so much so that the close-cropped foliage reminds us irresistibly of the wooden trees that once emerged from our Nuremberg play-boxes"[90]—again, a Disney-like touch of the unreal. Lever's rationale for this service was simple. "No other plan is successful in securing a character to the village," he told the Architectural Association, "and avoiding the unsightliness of here and there the obtrusion of neglected plots of garden which would mar the whole effect." The words "character" and "effect" suggest Lever's determination to create a particular setting. The allotment gardens at the rear of the cottages were another matter, however. They were, Lever declared, the "very safety valve of the village."[91] Unlike Cadbury, who spoke of gardens as a means to the end of a healthy citizenry, Lever stressed the way gardening might induce social tranquility. "Nowhere in the world," he remarked at the opening of a village flower show in 1901, "could one get such relief as from a garden. . . . Gardening would tend to make a man philosophic, because after his experience with plants and flowers, he would look upon the world with a more contented view."[92]

Lever differed from Cadbury as well in his ambivalence about the city. He acknowledged that a picture of cottages "crowned with thatched roof and with clinging ivy and climbing roses" was in itself a "quiet, peaceful influence for good." Yet on other occasions, he spoke of the shame of rural as well as urban overcrowding, and of the fact that man, a social being, naturally migrated to cities, "where he finds the greatest scope for his social instincts, and where his genius and abilities have the fullest opportunities."[93] These ambiguities were mirrored in the general design of the village which, as we have seen, was itself, in plan, an amalgam of rural and urban themes.

There was, however, no ambiguity about Lever's determination to bring his village alive as a community under his direction and supervision. He provided a variety of public amenities: schools, hospital, church and Sunday school, library, museum, technical institute, girls' institute, men's social club, gymnasium, swimming baths, playing fields, and a village inn. Within and around these various buildings there met a host of worthy organizations and societies: a literary and scientific society, parliamentary debating society, musical society, British Women's Temperance Society (Port Sunlight branch), dining club, scholars' ramble club, divine services committee, boys' brigade, university extension classes, photography society, horticultural society, cycling club, bowling club, Young People's Temperance League, Silver Prize band, mutual improvement society, chess club, gymnastic club, swimming club, philharmonic society—the lists in *Progress* stretch on and on, as if to prove the manner in which the community's activities matched in spirit the journal's title.

Christ Church opened in June 1904. Lever's architect William Owen designed it; the company building department built it; Lever paid for it. It was to be interdenominational, a community church "where the worship of Almighty God would be conducted free from all dogma and creed," Lever declared at the laying of the foundation-stone. The first minister, the Reverend S. Gamble Walker, a methodist, was nominally appointed by the divine services committee. But Lever, in his speech of welcome, told those assembled that he had first approached Gamble Walker (soon to become the hyphenated Reverend Gamble-Walker) without the committee's knowledge. "Never tell what you have done until you have done it," he advised his listeners. Gamble-Walker was a typical Lever surprise. He was a socialist, and member of the Manchester Independent Labour Party. Warned that he would come to disagree with the man because of his politics, Lever retorted, "That was the very reason I accepted you, Mr. Walker. There are many ministers who are in sympathy with Capitalists. But I never yet knew a Capitalist who needed anyone to help him, and I think we should have been wasting our efforts if we had selected for Port Sunlight a man who had not thoroughly shown that his sympathies were with the people."[94] Capitalist or socialist, Gamble-Walker was clearly Lever's man, and as such like any country clergyman in a squire-dominated parish.

An odor of high-mindedness infused the doings of the community of Port Sunlight. Schools were up-to-date, with a pupil-teacher ratio of one to forty. After 1908, Lever Brothers ceased to hire anyone between the ages of fourteen and eighteen who was not enrolled in evening or continuation classes. The Technical Institute, founded in 1903, offered courses in building and machine construction, technical and chemical engineering. Employees who attended received wage bonuses from the company. The library, donated by Lever, opened in the same year in a remodeled women's dining hall, with an initial complement of thirty-five hundred "judiciously selected" volumes, half of them fiction. W. L. George, in his 1909 survey, lamented the inclusion of so many novels but reported with satisfaction that about half the borrowers read "exclusively serious books" and that books were lent twenty-five thousand times in any given year.[95] Art exhibitions, which often featured paintings from Lever's private collection, were held regularly. Plays and concerts took place in an open-air theater.

Governance of the community rested in the hands of Lever Brothers, which imposed tenant regulations on its citizens. Among them was the stipulation that "an authorized official of the Company may visit any house at Port Sunlight at any time, for the purpose of seeing that due regard is being paid to order and cleanliness." Tenancies ran from week to week, a rule eliciting from George the observation that the policy placed too much "arbitrary power" in the hands of minor officials "whose action may easily become vexations."[96] Lever insisted that the regulations worked no hardship on the tenants. "We expect [them] to show a proper regard for the property, but within that limit they are quite at liberty to do as they like."[97]

Villagers were at liberty to manage their own affairs only in minor ways. A council met monthly to discuss such matters as the issuance of keys to the allotments, the assignment of practice rooms to the band, and the purchase of sewing machines for the Girls' Social Club. An active ratepayers association was chaired by Gamble-Walker. Its business, however, was not with the company but with the Lower Bebington Urban District Council, within whose precincts both the factory and the village lay. In at least one matter of governance Lever proved himself willing to tolerate opposition and eventual defeat. The Bridge Inn began its life teetotal. When the citizenry objected, Lever called for a referendum, stipulating that licensing would require a four to one majority. Out of 1,100 eligible voters, 599 cast a ballot, and the measure passed by a slim margin.[98]

Despite evidence that Lever occasionally was willing to withhold his hand, observers like George could only conclude that if Port Sunlight was in many ways a worthwhile experiment, it was not one that encouraged democracy. Generally sympathetic to Lever's endeavors, he put the best face he could on the matter. "Democratic feeling seems strong," he wrote, "because the people are being trained in self-governance by means in great part of their societies." The Frenchman Georges Benoit-Lévy was considerably harsher. "The citizenship right of Port Sunlight is a precarious right. . . . The government is essentially autocratic, and Mr. Lever is the absolute master of the property. Port Sunlight is nothing more or less than a private estate very well managed."[99]

None of this appeared to matter much to Lever. His interests lay not in the promotion of democracy, but of order and progress. George called the village a "shrine for the worship of cleanliness." Lever Brothers did, after all, manufacture soap. Angus Watson, in his memoir of life as a Lever Brothers employee, wrote that the "whole village was dominated by the spirit of Soap. . . . You could no more escape from its influence than from the odor (not at all an unpleasant one) permeating it from the great factory plant." Clean, sober, industrious—the citizens of Port Sunlight, George observed, "seem ideally fitted by their residence in a model community to become dwellers in an ideal state."[100] There was no hooliganism, no class conflict; no drunkenness, no wife-beating. Instead, the town boasted healthy, apparently contented men and women who lived longer than their counterparts in London and Liverpool, and whose sons and daughters, statisticians were constantly demonstrating, weighed more and learned faster than did children in nearby schools.[101] If there was an air of unreality about the place, as George implies when he writes of "dwellers in an ideal state," that air should be measured against the harsh, unpleasant reality just outside Lever's "estate."

Lever himself must often have seemed to the residents of Port Sunlight as more than a little unreal; certainly, despite his short stature, as a good deal larger than life. He might manifest himself at any time, day or night. In the spring of 1901, fire broke out in a factory shed and destroyed it. Lever, who was in Bolton, received word too late to catch a regularly scheduled train to Port Sunlight. Undaunted, he and his wife requisitioned a special train and arrived at the blaze shortly after midnight. "After a prolonged visit to the scene of the fire," the

Progress account reported, "Mr. Lever expressed his thanks to the Brigades for their splendid work and their successful efforts in preventing the flames from spreading."[102] At least once a month he would preside over the opening of a new building, or over an entertainment for staff members and their children, or over a regular meeting of one of the many village or works organizations of which he was honorary president. In the course of a three-month period in 1906, for example, he spoke at a ladies' gymnastic display, a tea for the general office staff, the annual social for representatives from the Foreign and Colonial Department, a gathering of visiting Japanese sailors, and a Sunday school anniversary. When the first marriage was celebrated in Christ Church, Lever was on hand with a bouquet for the bride, a "choice buttonhole" for the groom, and a silver-plated tea service as a token of his good wishes for them both.[103]

Throughout the year the Levers entertained at Thornton Manor, a large country house they had built in the midst of an entirely fabricated village, Thornton Hough, complete with half-timbered smithy's shop and chestnut tree. At Christmas time the pace was almost feverish: children's costume parties, and receptions for the entire roster of employees, the Christ Church choir, the Port Sunlight Prize Band, the "old scholars" from the village schools. The chroniclers of these occasions for *Progress* enjoyed pulling out the stops. "The beautiful residence of our Chairman opened wide its portals to receive the workers from Port Sunlight. . . . The honours of the house were well upheld by Mr. and Mrs. Lever and Master Willie Lever [shown, full length, in an accompanying photograph]. The guests, numbering 200, were conveyed in covered carriages from Port Sunlight Village and arrived at the manor between 7 and 8 o'clock. On arrival they were graciously received by the host and hostess and the young heir, the welcome extended to all being warm and cordial." The young heir, thirteen years old, had prepared a speech in which he declared that "he was sure he would be pleased when he was able to enter the business." He pledged to try to do his best but "did not think he would ever be able to do anything better than his father had done."[104] Lever clearly relished the opportunity to play lord of the manor. At a ball the previous year, held to honor various Port Sunlight clubs and societies, he opened the proceedings "by asking the lady present, who had been longest in the employ of the firm, to become his partner in the dance; and this was the signal for all to join right merrily in the mazy whirl."[105] Henry Fielding's Squire Allworthy was no more conscious of his duties or more punctilious in his performance of them.

Lever insisted again and again on the straightforward business relationship that he enjoyed with his employees. At the opening of the library he had donated to the village, he said, "There is too much . . . of what one may call patronage of the working man. . . . Any attempt at patronage or philanthropy in connection with them would not only be a piece of absurdity but it would be an insult." The library would encourage workers to improve their minds and thereby increase their value to their employers. That was the rationale. At the opening of the company swimming baths: "Lever Brothers Ltd. were quite certain that by the use of that bath their employees would improve as human machines. . . . That was a selfish basis, but it was the only one on which independence all round could be maintained."[106]

And yet Lever's relationship with his workers was more complicated than he was prepared to acknowledge—to them, and perhaps to himself. He understood his position not merely in relation to a cash nexus but also in terms of the duties that the position imposed on him, and equally on those who worked for him, in the manner that an eighteenth-century landlord understood his position: as a matter of mutual responsibilities and obligations. Lever had a duty to provide the best accommodation and working conditions for his employees. Their duty, in turn, was to labor diligently on behalf of his interests—which, he would have argued, were their interests as well. In a speech soon after the introduction of the company benefits scheme, Lever cited a recent situation in which workers had, in fact, "failed to recognize their duty towards their employer." Staff members who had neglected to shut off the steam at their workplace before leaving for the day had refused to return to the factory to do so, preferring, instead, to continue socializing at the Bridge Inn. Such conduct, *Progress* reported Lever as saying, "required the exercise of all of the philosophy and firmness of which one was capable. . . . Was it worthwhile to bring out a Benefit Fund that would help those people who were unable to work?"[107] In effect, Lever was saying, I am living up to my responsibility toward you, and you are neglecting your obligation toward me.

Discussing Lever's success at Port Sunlight, his friend, the city planner and architect Thomas Mawson, extolled the virtues of "benevolent autocracy." "The individual with the necessary insight can realize the practical 'Utopia' of the people. . . . [T]hus what has been accomplished by past generations of landowners, not by any means in opposition to their own interests, may be repeated today."[108] Mawson understood Lever and his "practical 'Utopia'" well—better, perhaps than Lever himself.

Neither Bournville nor Port Sunlight were garden cities or garden suburbs, as those terms would come to be defined. They were factory villages. Yet because they existed as well-established and highly publicized experiments, they were the communities that men and women first thought of when the terms "garden city" and "garden suburb" began to receive currency after 1900. That the first annual conference of the Garden City Association took place at Bournville, and the second at Liverpool, near Port Sunlight, was no coincidence. No matter that the two villages differed not only from the radical garden city prototype envisioned by the movement's leading proponent, Ebenezer Howard, but from each other as well—Bournville designed as an experiment in affordable working-class housing in a way Port Sunlight was not. In the public mind they were viewed together as successful attempts to address the urban ills that so threatened the nation's physical and spiritual well-being. Say "garden city" to an early supporter of the movement, therefore, and he or she would think of Bournville and Port Sunlight. And in so doing, that person's understanding would be linked to images and perceptions that were traditional and conservative. In their layout, in the design of their houses, Bournville and Port Sunlight summed up a sanitized and romanticized version of life as it had been. In their governance and, probably more important, in the way daily life was dominated by the presence of their beneficent founders, they bespoke paternalistic hierarchical relationships from the past. If they were experiments in the re-creation of English community, they were not experiments in the creation of democracy. Charmed by the attractive images that Bournville and Port Sunlight offered, garden city enthusiasts the more easily persuaded themselves that their task was as much one of restoration as it was of reformation.

Chapter 3 Ebenezer Howard
and the Garden City
Association

If conservative devotion to an English past fueled much of the sentiment generating the garden city movement, its supporters nonetheless saw themselves as modern beneficiaries of an Englishness of political consensus that accepted the need for private and public intervention to remedy social evils. Reformers in Britain were part of a general European and American effort to enhance the quality of life for that ever-increasing majority who lived in cities. Evidence of this determination elsewhere could be seen in Germany's commitment to town planning at all governmental levels, reflected in such projects as Joseph Stübben's scheme for the redevelopment of Cologne in 1880, which experimented with the concept of citywide zoning, and in Frankfurt's pioneering set of differential building regulations, implemented in 1891. By the end of the century, the French, though not as innovative as the Germans, had instituted programs to control suburban infestation and update city center construction in Paris, Lyons, and Nancy. In the United States, support for urban planning came with the growth of municipal reform movements during the Progressive era, and with propaganda efforts by such publicists as Charles M. Robinson, champion of the "city beautiful" ideal.[1]

Throughout the nineteenth century, those worried about the conditions of urban life in Britain had focused on particular goals—adequate housing, improved sanitation, and the like—rather than on the planning of an entire environment. The construction of Birmingham's Corporation Street under Joseph Chamberlain's progressive mayoral administration in the 1870s was the first concrete manifestation of the "civic gospel" that, by the end of the century, had become more widely accepted as an article of faith. Reformers saw Germany's successes in the field of wide-scale renewal and development as worthy of immediate replication in Britain. Thomas Horsfall, a Manchester citizen and pioneer town planner, observed that in Germany "the Imperial, the State and the Municipal Governments see that the housing question cannot be solved, except by measures which ensure that, not only shall there be an adequate supply of cheap, potentially wholesome dwellings, but also that both the immediate and more distant environment of these dwellings shall be pleasant."[2] And Britain, Horsfall argued, must follow Germany's lead. He was among a growing number who championed town-extension planning, advocating parliamentary legislation that would grant local authorities not only the power to acquire land, but also "the power . . . to make and enforce the strict observance of plans" for those areas once acquired.[3]

In this, he was echoing the sentiments of other reformers, who believed that little progress could be made without a substantial increase in state intervention. Overcrowding—associated with high rents and the lack of decent accommodation—the foulness of air and water, the dreary sameness of landscapes without trees and shrubbery, let alone parks and playgrounds: none of these urban blights could be eradicated individually. Public concern must be translated into public initiative. Progressive reformers pressed for more public control and direction even though the most tangible evidence of state intervention had been the depressing "byelaw streets" that stretched for what seemed endless miles across most inner suburban landscapes. So named in consequence of the 1875 Public Health Act, which established regulations concerning sanitation and construction of individual houses, and strict byelaws governing the layout, width, and construction of city streets, byelaw neighborhoods were an easy target for those arguing in favor of more flexible urban planning. John Sutton Nettlefold, chairman of the Birmingham Corporation Housing Committee, was, like Horsfall, particularly concerned with the matter of town extension. He bemoaned the iron-clad regulations that prescribed uniformity without regard to the intentions or reputation of individual developers, let alone the creation of a generally pleasing environment. The law, he wrote, "gives no power to Local Authorities to differentiate between a public-spirited landowner and the most unscrupulous land speculator and jerry builder." Worse, "the present inelastic byelaw system . . . does not attempt the one thing which might be useful—a comprehensive control of town development."[4] Comprehensive control was what these forward-looking planners increasingly demanded; the opportunity to create a complete environment that would warm the spirits of those who lived within it in a manner denied them by the chilly bleakness of the streets and courts they now inhabited.

During this period, those who had remained concerned with the housing of the urban working class joined the growing number of planners demanding comprehensive state initiatives to provide the poor with decent accommodation. Most, indeed, perceived a direct link between housing reform and town planning, the shape and character of housing estates directly affecting the nature of the broader cityscape.[5] Private organizations such as Lord Shaftesbury's Society for Improving the Condition of the Labouring Classes, the Metropolitan Association for Improving the Dwellings of the Industrious Classes, the Peabody Trust, and the Improved Industrial Dwellings Company had experimented in London throughout the second half of the nineteenth century with schemes providing the poor with sanitary, sturdily built, and almost uniformly dreary-looking living quarters, and investors a return of something close to 5 percent.

Yet by 1890, despite the efforts of individual philanthropists and private investors, the housing situation remained grim—indeed, was growing grimmer. Octavia Hill, an early and vigorous campaigner in the housing wars who was fiercely dedicated to the ideal of individual self-help, nonetheless had pointed out as early as 1875 that all the privately financed schemes for the past thirty years had succeeded in housing only twenty-six thousand people, a figure not much in excess of the increase in London's population every six months.[6] Although by 1890 that figure was closer to fifty thousand, it represented a fraction of those in desperate need of better living space. A Royal Commission appointed in 1884 declared that although there had been "great improvement" over the past thirty years, "the evils of overcrowding, especially in London, were still a public scandal, and were becoming in certain localities more serious than they ever were." It also found that existing legislation governing sanitation and building frequently remained unenforced.[7] The commissioners recommended that local authorities be compelled to administer effectively laws already on the books, that further byelaw controls be imposed to ensure less urban density, and that the government make low-interest loans to facilitate the construction of working-class housing. This was as far as the commissioners were willing to intervene. Lord Salisbury, the Conservative prime minister who had instigated the inquiry, stated his view in the conclusion of the report that the housing problem could be left to the laws of supply and demand, with the exception of London, where he agreed with his fellow commissioners that disused prison sites might be sold below market value for housing. In a speech on behalf of a housing bill that was enacted in 1885, however, he declared himself in favor of the "application of the power and resources of society to benefit, not the whole of society, but one particular class, especially the most needy class in society."[8] Salisbury's ambivalence—his willingness to trust supply and demand, yet his determination to make use of the "power and resources of society"—illustrates the hesitant but inexorable path toward consensus intervention that politicians of all parties were treading late in the century.

Parliament was willing to pass an act in 1890 that provided effective machinery for slum clearance, requiring local authorities, whose hands had been strengthened by the reorganization of local government in 1888, to intervene on behalf of its citizenry to improve and increase its housing. Part III of the act, the most important, enabled authorities to acquire land through compulsory purchase, if necessary, to erect lodging houses, block dwellings, tenement houses, or cottages, and to issue stock or borrow money on the security of rates as a means of financing the projects they might undertake.[9] Additional legislation in the 1890s further enabled the newly established London County Council to pursue increasingly ambitious building programs. A housing act in 1900 extended to rural districts the authority granted their urban counterparts in 1890, permitting as well construction by municipalities outside their own boundaries, thereby opening the way for suburban town extension.

City governments applied the legislation in a variety of ways. Birmingham instigated a scheme of widespread repair and rehabilitation. Liverpool, which had experimented with a council building program as early as 1869, pursued a far more ambitious course; by 1912, it had constructed more than 2,000 dwellings, demolished 5,500, and improved 11,000.[10] Not surprisingly, most attention focused on the ambitious projects undertaken by the London County Council. The Boundary Street and Millbank Estates displayed for perhaps the first time a willingness on the part of the builder, whether private or public, to practice what so many were now preaching: provision of trees and open space; overall layouts that avoided the monotony of byelaw streets and "model" tenements; and attention to architectural detail that suggested an effort to provide tenants with something other than a sanitary barracks. The council's first suburban estate, at Totterdown Fields, although a high-density development, was nonetheless designed on what came to be known as the two-story "cottage" principle. With its wide, tree-lined streets, it departed significantly from the usual pattern of jerry-built working-class suburban developments.

Taken as a whole, these schemes were seen as encouraging examples of what could be accomplished by progressive planners and designers willing to make full use of state and local governmental authority to achieve worthy ends. Yet most reformers remained unsatisfied. Some argued that even in estates as advanced as those of the LCC, building heights and density ensured a less than healthy living environment. "The most enthusiastic advocate of the block system," one critic complained, "cannot claim for it an unqualified success; . . . there is too much herding together in an attempt to put as much as possible on a given area of land in order to make it pay. . . . What we now consider well-appointed blocks of tenements will probably cease to be regarded with much favour in years to come."[11]

Concern focused less on the drawbacks of improvements already made, however, than on what remained to be done. Three hundred and thirty thousand Londoners had one-room dwellings; one-fourth of the dwellings in England contained fewer than four rooms. Housing constructed on newly opened suburban land by profit-seeking developers soon deteriorated. A series in the *Sheffield Daily Independent* in 1904 lamented the "strong flavour of the slums in many of these suburban residences. The back garden resembles a dust heap. Here and there we find outhouses which have lost their doors, and these have disappeared altogether, presumably on the kitchen fire."[12] Government programs, though they had accomplished much, were no panacea. Cities remained terrifyingly overcrowded; suburbs segregated their new residents in semi-squalor. While not abandoning their commitment to state intervention, reformers were driven to look for other ways to solve the ever-present problems of housing and planning. Hence the initial appeal of Ebenezer Howard's bold vision for an urban future embodied in his garden city scheme.

Those attending the first national conference of the Garden City Association at Bournville in 1902, when not exclaiming over the achievements of the Cadbury brothers, no doubt sought to lay eyes on the man whose surprisingly influential tract had inspired the founding of the association: Ebenezer Howard—"Ebenezer, the Garden City geyser," as George Bernard Shaw enjoyed calling him.[13] That Shaw generally respected Howard is a measure of the man's ability to attract support for his grand utopian scheme to revolutionize the English landscape. Given Howard's initially unprepossessing demeanor, the support was all the more noteworthy. Those who did encounter him at the Bournville conference discovered a balding gentleman of mild and respectable bearing, the prototype of lower-middle-class London clerkdom.

What he appeared to be is what he was, up to a point. Howard, born in London in 1850, the son of a nonconformist confectionery shopkeeper, went to work for a firm of stockbrokers at the age of fifteen. At the same time he perfected his shorthand technique by taking down the Sunday sermons of Dr. Joseph Parker, one of the leading nonconformist preachers in London. In 1871, Howard stepped out in a manner belying the notion that his destiny was bound to nothing more than a recorder's notebook: he emigrated to the United States, where he lived for five years. At first he tried his hand as a farmer in Nebraska, where he failed. He moved to Chicago and, with apparent relief, resumed his London career with a shorthand firm. He set himself a course of reading, which included Thomas Paine's *Age of Reason* and the subject that engaged many an earnest young man in the 1870s: the conflict of science and religion. He attended lectures by the spiritualist Cora Richmond, an occultist who preached as well the gospel of social and civic reform, and whose influence on his thinking appears to have been considerable.[14] Chicago, at the time Howard lived there, was recovering from the fire of 1871. In the process it was laying out a city for the future. Whether Howard was inspired by what he saw occurring—a sharp rise in urban land values, for example, and the establishing of urban parks along the lakeshore—remains largely a matter of conjecture. It does appear, however, that Howard was relieved to be back once more in a city. Though he would become an apostle for agricultural districts and suburban greenbelts, he remained throughout his life devoted to urban existence, in a way that set him apart from many of those who subscribed to his scheme for garden cities as a means of national revival.

It was in Chicago that his interest in garden cities was kindled, after he read a pamphlet by an Englishman, Dr. Benjamin Ward Richardson: *Hygeia, or the City of Health.* Richardson had presented his ideas in a speech to the Social Science Association in 1875. Reacting to what seemed to him no more than urban chaos, he argued for the establishment of new cities, characterized by low population density, decent housing, modern sanitary facilities, and open spaces. Howard much later recalled that having read Richardson, he began himself to imagine a "defined conception of an intelligently arranged town, a sort of marriage between town and country, whereby the workers would be assured the advantage of fresh air and recreation and nearness to their work."[15]

Returning to England in 1876—largely, it seems, because he was home-sick—he continued to think about his "defined conception," refining it as he read omnivorously, while working as a shorthand reporter in Parliament. Howard joined that band of high-minded, lightly eccentric middle-class men and women who met in groups in London to discuss with passion the condition of England and the possibilities for its betterment. He belonged to an organization named, rather self-consciously, the Zetetical Society ("zetetic" being a synonym for "inquiring"), whose members included Shaw and Sydney Webb, and whose aim was to further discussion of political, religious, and sexual questions with an open mind and in a decorous manner. He was taken by the writings of two Americans, Laurence Gronlund, whose book *The Cooperative Commonwealth* (1884) championed movement from the city to the country, and Albert Kinsey Owen, a utopian who attempted to found a planned community in Mexico.[16]

Far more influential in the formulation of his ideas about social organization was the work of a third American, Henry George, whose much-discussed tract *Progress and Poverty* argued the case for a single tax on land. The idea, derived from David Ricardo's theory of rent, was not new. Yet George's compelling style, and the appearance of his book at the time of severe Irish land troubles, brought it wide circulation and mass popularity. As Avner Offer makes clear in his analysis of the abstruse debates surrounding George's scheme, Liberals were prepared to make use of George to argue the "equitable re-distribution of the incidence of local taxation" and to press for a tax on assessed values that would bring more urban land onto the market for building. Socialists hoped to apply Georgian doctrine as a device to abolish rent altogether.[17]

Howard, though he was attracted to schemes of land nationalization, stopped short of incorporating that panacea in his published plans for garden cities. Yet he subscribed wholeheartedly to the idea that the unearned increment should serve the common good of the community. Indeed, that tenet became the cornerstone of his proposals. Howard's attraction to the cause of land reform placed him among a growing body of serious-minded and determined men and women whom the economist J. A. Hobson described in 1897 as "typical English moralists." "In my lectures upon Political Economy about the country, I have found in almost every centre a certain little knot of men of the lower-middle or upper-working class, men of grit and character, largely self-educated, keen citizens . . . to whom Land Nationalization, taxation of unearned increment, or other radical reforms of land tenure are doctrines resting upon a plain moral sanction. These free-trading Radical dissenters regard common ownership of land and equal access to the land as a 'natural right,' essential to individual freedom."[18]

Howard's interest in the garden city ideal was encouraged directly by close study of a proposal for a model community, put forward in 1849, which had enjoyed a modestly favorable reception at that time and afterward: James Silk Buckingham's "Victoria," whose features Buckingham had outlined in a treatise entitled *National Evils and Practical Remedies*. Victoria was envisioned as a self-financed enterprise, capitalized at £3 million, each resident to own at least one £20 share. Though the entire development would cover 10,000 acres, the town itself would consist of only 1,000 acres, with its population of 10,000 divided between an outer square containing 1,000 small houses, each renting for £5 a year; a second square of larger houses, at £300 a year, along with a number of public buildings. A development company was to manage the entire community and serve as its sole employer. An agricultural belt, surrounding the town and occupying the remaining 9,000 acres, would supply the ultimately self-sufficient community with its food.[19] One of the features of the plan that most influenced Howard was the concept of community ownership of the land and therefore of whatever might accrue to the community as that land increased in value.

When he came to write his book, Howard cited Buckingham's treatise as an important source of direct inspiration, especially appealing to his sense of himself as a social scientist. He also saw himself as an inventor; indeed, he had contributed ideas that led to the modification of early Remington typewriters. He came to believe in garden cities as machines, describing his particular engine for change in an early draft of his book as the "greatest labour-saving invention yet discovered."[20] Other sources of inspiration were the emigration schemes proposed in the 1840s by Edward Gibbon Wakefield and later modified by the Cambridge economist Alfred Marshall. Wakefield had concerned himself with the need to relieve the crowded cities of early industrial England for the betterment of the health and morals of their distressed and discontented populations. Frightened by the political disturbances of the Chartist period, he saw overseas colonies, governed in such a way as to promote a well-ordered citizenry, as a panacea to his country's problems.[21]

Alfred Marshall, writing in 1884, argued for the relief of London's oppressive overcrowding by the establishment of experimental colonies, this time in England itself, in the countryside far enough outside the capital so as to form distinct urban entities, and not simply further suburban wastelands. Here families from London's working-class slums could come to practice artisanal trades. His proposal was based on his conviction that "whatever reforms be introduced into the dwellings of the London poor, it will still remain true that the whole area of London is insufficient to supply the population with fresh air and the free space that is wanted for wholesome recreation."[22] In this, of course, Marshall was simply echoing the many voices that despaired over the fate of those unfortunate enough to find themselves locked inside cities from which there appeared to be no escape.

A third and particularly revealing influence cited by Howard was a treatise by the eighteenth-century utopian Thomas Spence, entitled *The Rights of Man* and published in 1775. Spence argued that men possessed a fundamental right to both liberty and land. Landlords were usurpers and tyrants, having dispossessed the true owners of their property. To right this fundamental wrong, Spence proposed a utopia—"Spensonia"—in which the land in every parish would become the property of a local corporation, of which all inhabitants would be members. Rents, formerly paid to landlords, would now come to the corporations, which would use them to benefit all their citizens by constructing a variety of urban amenities.[23]

Here were the essential ingredients of Howard's own scheme: the certainty that nothing but an organized system of emigration into the countryside would alleviate the nation's present urban ills; the equal certainty that the solution to new community building lay in common ownership of the land on which that community stood; and the inspiration derived from a specific and—to Howard's scientifically inclined sympathies—practical scheme for the realization of his now fervently held convictions. Without one further catalyst, however, Howard might not have written the tract that was to make him and the garden city both famous. In 1888, the American, Edward Bellamy, published *Looking Backwards,* describing yet another utopia—Boston in the year 2000, a city of open squares, tree-shaded thoroughfares, flashing fountains, and public buildings of imposing grandeur. Organized as a giant corporation, the city was its sole employer, "the one capitalist in place of all other capitalists. . . . The final monopoly."[24] Though Howard ultimately rejected the brand of bureaucratic socialism espoused by Bellamy, he remained profoundly moved by the messianic tone of the book. Lecturing to the Fabian Society in 1901, he declared that "it was the reading of 'Looking Backward' which gave my mind the necessary impetus. Differing as I did with the author on many points, one result of that book was to give to my imagination a very vivid sense of the evanescence of the present forms of the instruments of production and distribution and their almost entire unsuitability and inadaptability to a new order. The chief illustration of this evanescence which forced itself upon my attention was our great cities, especially London, in which I was born and of which I had been so proud."[25]

Throughout the 1890s, Howard experimented in various drafts and speeches with the formulations that he refined and published in 1898 in a small book titled *To-morrow: A Peaceful Path to Real Reform*. Because of the success of the tract and of the movement it inspired, it was reissued four years later as *Garden Cities of To-morrow*. The scheme, as outlined by Howard, was an attempt to marry his appreciation of what the city could offer its citizens with his concern for what it was at present failing to provide. With a diagram depicting "Three Magnets"—town, country, and town-country—he attempted to prove that neither town nor country could by themselves afford their residents a full, productive life "so long as [the] unholy, unnatural separation of society and nature endures. Town and country *must be married,* and out of this joyous union will spring a new hope, a new life, a new civilization." Howard declared it his purpose "to show how a first step can be taken in this direction by the construction of a town-country magnet"; and to demonstrate as well that such a step was practical and sound, "whether viewed from the ethical or the economic standpoint."[26]

He emphasized the degree to which the countryside failed equally with the town to provide attractive, health-giving amenities to its residents. Rural communities lacked drainage and proper sanitary facilities. Much of the land was deserted, and the "few who remain are yet frequently huddled together as if in rivalry with the slums of our cities." This insistence on the importance of rural revival, though central to Howard's vision, never captured the interest of reformers to the extent he hoped it might. Garden city enthusiasts tended to understand their task as the prevention of further urban blight, and its eventual elimination. By focusing as they did on conditions in the cities, they ignored the equally sqalid situation prevalent in large areas throughout the countryside. Howard himself helped contribute to the oversight. "The effect for which we are all striving," he wrote, is the "spontaneous movement of the people from our crowded cities to the bosom of our kindly mother earth, at once the source of life, of happiness, of wealth, and of power."[27] Yet what he was equally determined to encourage was movement in the opposite direction—from rural isolation to "town-country" rejuvenation.

Howard's detailed scheme for his city was not unlike Buckingham's. He envisioned a six-thousand-acre estate to be held in trust by a development company as security for both debt-holders and citizens. One thousand acres would constitute the Garden City itself, which Howard depicted schematically in circular form, with a population of thirty thousand. Around it he proposed an agricultural greenbelt with a further population of two thousand, providing the city with food and raw materials. According to his scheme, a main line railway was joined to the city by connecting sidings that, in turn, fed into a branch line encircling the entire town. Municipal buildings surrounded a small park at the city's center core. Behind them, and separated by a further park, was a circular shopping arcade, a "crystal palace." Around this, a series of concentric avenues circled toward the countryside. Midway between center and outer circumference lay Grand Avenue—in fact a third circular park, this one 420 feet wide and 3 miles long, in the midst of which were situated six schools and churches of various denomination. On the outer ring, factories, warehouses, coal and timber yards fronted the railway. Because the trains would be powered by electricity, their effect on the city's environment would be negligible. Traversing the avenues were six "magnificent boulevards," each 120 feet wide, which divided the city into six wards. Howard hoped that these wards would function as neighborhoods, with the schools serving as community centers. Houses of varying styles were to be built on lots averaging 20 by 130 feet. Some would have common gardens and cooperative kitchens.[28]

Although the company would be the city's sole landlord, it would lease to a variety of enterprises, some capitalist, some cooperative. It would, in all likelihood, undertake to supply utilities itself. But because the object was not monopoly but efficiency, "if any private corporation . . . proved capable of supplying on more advantageous terms, either the whole town or a section of it, . . . this would be allowed."[29] Howard assumed that the city could exist on revenues from rents, calculated so as to pay interest to the development company on its investment that would allow a gradual reduction of that debt and to finance municipal maintenance and construction. He argued that rents would be considerably reduced by the fact that the city was to be built on land that was in the countryside and therefore untouched by rising metropolitan or suburban prices. Howard imagined that most of the housing would be constructed by building societies, cooperatives, or even the company itself, though he feared that if it did so, the company might overtax itself, a prophecy that in fact came true when Howard's ideas were translated into reality at Letchworth, the first garden city.[30] City government would be entrusted to an elected Board of Management. Although Howard provided detailed suggestions as to the board's administrative duties, he failed to consider the degree to which the board might find itself squeezed between the desires of its electors and the demands of the company in whose hands the ultimate fate of the enterprise rested.

One further question remained: the matter of growth. With the last of the city's thirty thousand citizens in residence, other similar cities would establish themselves, using funds provided by the initial company to acquire land nearby. Howard envisioned a ring of garden cities surrounding a Center City of 58,000, linked by an interurban rapid transit system. The entire federation would thus contain a population of 250,000; but because each separate community lay within its own greenbelt and enjoyed the spacious layout that Howard had envisioned, congestion would no longer mar a landscape that was now a true marriage of town and country, the "joyous union" of Howard's dream.

Garden Cities of To-morrow proclaimed a radical solution for England's urban problems. The generally measured tone of Howard's rhetoric helped mask the degree to which he proposed not only a drastically altered landscape but a dramatically different way of living. He encouraged his readers to believe in change as progress, asking them "not to take it for granted that the large cities in which [they] may perhaps take a palpable pride are necessarily, in their present form, any more permanent than the stage-coach system which was the subject of so much admiration just at the very moment when it was about to be supplanted by the railways." Nothing genuinely worthwhile was possible except "by starting on a bold plan on comparatively virgin soil." Only when that fact was understood could his "social revolution" occur.[31] Robert Fishman, writing of the utopian schemes of Howard, Le Corbusier, and Frank Lloyd Wright, emphasizes the thoroughness of their conceptions. "The very completeness of their ideal cities expressed their convictions that the moment had come for comprehensive programs, and for a total rethinking of the principles of urban planning. They rejected the possibility of gradual improvement. They did not seek the amelioration of old cities, but a wholly transformed urban environment."[32]

It was not only the scope of Howard's vision that set him apart from most late Victorian social reformers. It was, as well, his apparent lack of attachment to the traditions and assumptions that were coming to be understood as peculiarly English, and, therefore, in the minds of most urban reformers, important to any scheme of social reconstruction. The lanes and greens of Bournville and Port Sunlight, with their villagey layout and cottagey domestic architecture, were evocations of an English past, conceived as a way of re-creating English community. Howard's city, his scientific "invention" of concentric boulevards and neighborhoods, could have risen as comfortably—more comfortably, perhaps—on the prairie beyond Chicago as on the fields of Hertfordshire, where the first garden city was built. Indeed, Howard's inspirations were as much American as they were English. His journey to the United States as a young man, his enjoyment of life in the raw city of Chicago, his admiration for Henry George and Edward Bellamy—all this shaped his thinking. He once remarked that he was drawn to America by the openness of its society; his subsequent years as a parliamentary reporter and, from 1891, as court reporter with the Royal Commission on Labour, soured him on the governmental process at home.[33] When he came to publish his own manifesto, he prefaced it with a verse by the American poet James Russell Lowell:

> New occasions teach new duties;
> Time makes ancient good uncouth.
> They must upward still, and onward
> Who would keep abreast of Truth.[34]

Lowell speaks in his poem of the need for "new pilgrims." Howard obviously saw himself as one, ready to sail with any who would join him, away from the past toward a new world for which he was now prepared to provide a map.

Howard's utopianism and his willingness to transcend England in a search for social regeneration make the enthusiastic reception of his proposals all the more remarkable. That reception was no doubt a result of the fact that there was, within the garden city scheme, a generous portion of down-to-earth practicality. If his scheme was rooted in the ideas of American utopias, his willingness to temper his vision with pragmatic common sense was English, reflecting that strain of liberal consensus that characterized so many late Victorian reform efforts. He recognized that the most advanced position he was advocating—common ownership and management of land for the benefit of an entire community—was one which would have a broad appeal and therefore would not appear all that radical. In "Commonsense Socialism," a speech delivered to various middle-class audiences during the 1890s, he argued simply that the plan would substitute an "honest landlord, namely ourselves," for the "landlordism" that too often imposed unfair burdens on tenants. His nonconformist background supplied him with an appealing analogy: "The landlord is in every-day life what the priest is in religion. He says, in effect, 'If you want to go to God's earth you must go through me.'"[35] If this was socialism, it was of a kind that Howard's audience would have indeed understood as commonsensical.

A bye-law street. Barrow Hill, Derbyshire, c. 1900. The antithesis of the garden city ideal.

2. George Cadbury, benevolent Quaker.

3. William Hesketh Lever, benevolent buccaneer.

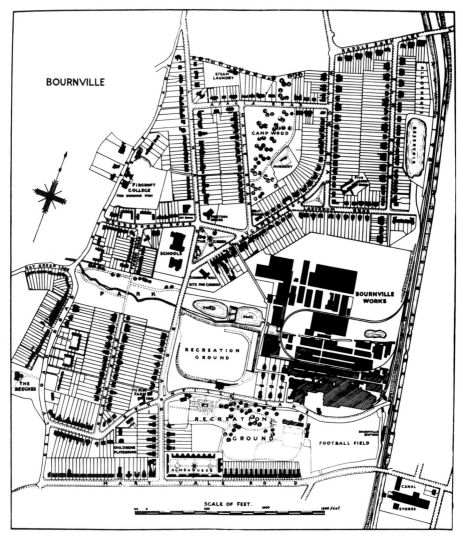

BOURNVILLE

4. Bournville, 1901. Note the prevalence of an urban grid, and the deep lots, designed to accommodate gardens.

5. Bournville. Linden Road, with school tower in the distance.

6. Bournville. Selly Oak Road. "The effect is sometimes a little short of restful."

VARIOUS TYPES OF EARLY COTTAGES

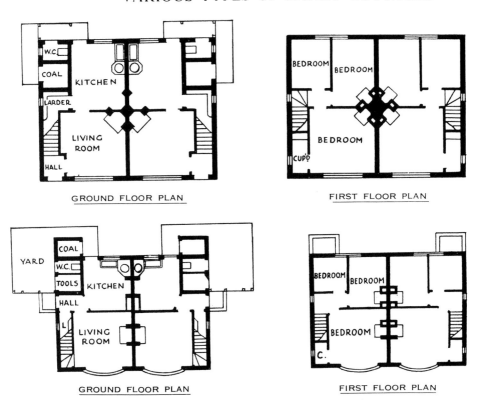

GROUND FLOOR PLAN

FIRST FLOOR PLAN

GROUND FLOOR PLAN

FIRST FLOOR PLAN

7. Bournville. Early cottage plans, illustrating the way in which placement of coal house and WC eliminated back extensions and opened houses to their gardens.

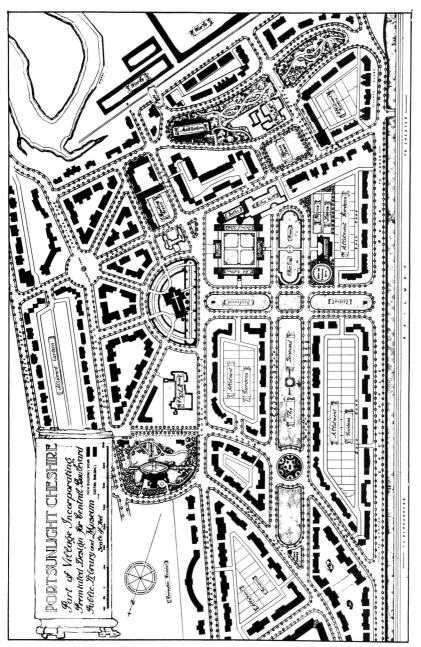

8. Port Sunlight. Ernest Prestwich's 1910 "city beautiful" redesign. The original village lay east of Christ Church.

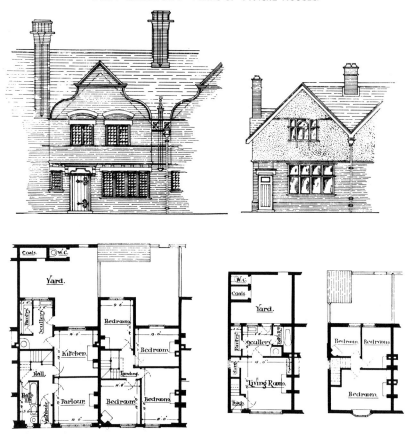

9. Port Sunlight. Plans illustrate "parlour" and "kitchen" houses. Note the use of elaborate and eclectic architectural detail.

10. Port Sunlight. Greendale Road. A reproduction of Kenyon Old Hall, reflecting the influence of the Manchester Royal Jubilee Exhibition.

11. Ebenezer Howard, utopian.

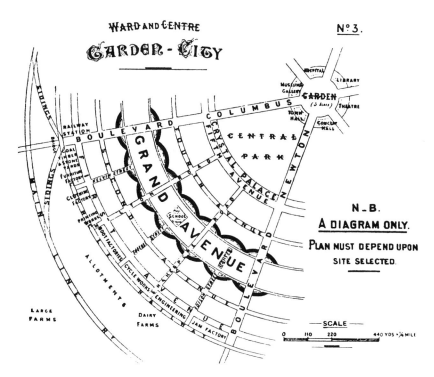

12. A segment of Howard's scheme for Garden City, from *Garden Cities of To-morrow.*

13. Walter Crane's frontispiece for
Garden Cities of To-morrow, evoking
a romanticized medieval past.

14. The Parkers and Unwins at Buxton, 1898. Raymond Unwin is standing at left, Barry Parker at right. Parker's mother and father are seated in chairs. Ethel Parker Unwin is at lower right, next to the Unwins' son Robert.

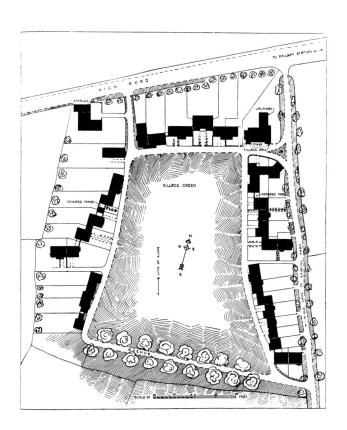

15 and 16. "Design for a hamlet," from Parker and Unwin's *The Art of Building a Home,* demonstrating their affinity for small community clusters.

17 and 18. "An artizan's living room" and design for a village common room. Both from Parker and Unwin's *The Art of Building a Home*. The designs illustrate the manner in which the architects attempted to combine cosiness with high-mindedness in their work.

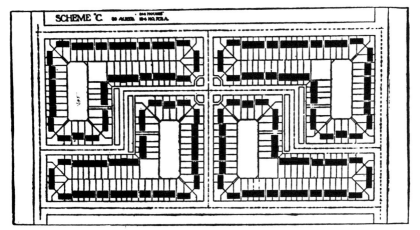

Diagram I.—Scheme showing **20** *acres laid out with* **12·4** *houses per acre, roads included,* **248** *houses in all. The measurement of the 20 acres is taken to the centre of the 50-feet road surrounding the area, and the land is developed by means of 36-feet roads within the area.*

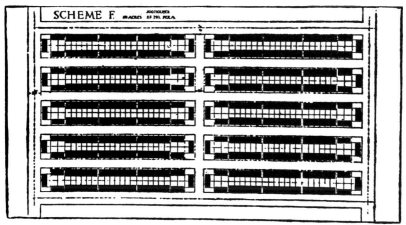

Diagram II.—Scheme F, showing **20** *acres laid out with* **25** *houses per acre, roads included,* **500** *houses in all. Size of roads as in Diagram I.*

19. The advantages of low-density development. A diagram from Unwin's *Nothing Gained by Overcrowding!* Unwin based his argument on the dubious assumption that land could be readily attained at agricultural prices.

20 and 21. Illustrations from Unwin's *Town Planning in Practice.* The aesthetic advantages of irregularity.

22. The "official" plan for Letchworth, 1904. Though modified, it remained the basis for the design of the city. The axial plan is surprising, given Parker and Unwin's preference for the natural, and may be a reference to Ebenezer Howard's original scheme.

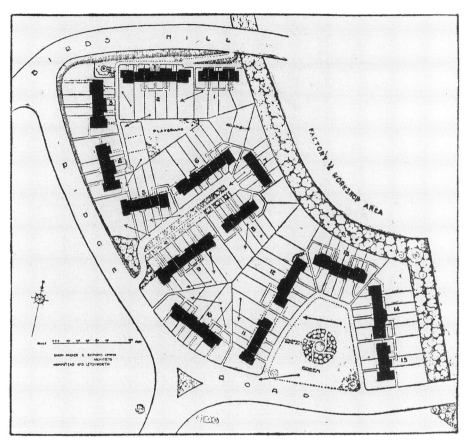

23. Bird's Hill Estate, Letchworth. The realization of Parker and Unwin's "hamlet" scheme.

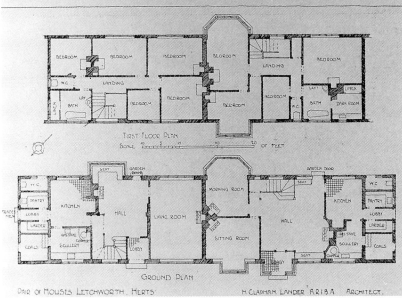

24. Baldock Road houses, Letchworth. Designed by H. Clapham Lander. The "cottage" redesigned for upper-middle-class clients.

25. Laneside and Crabby Corner, Letchworth. Parker and Unwin's own houses. Parker later added a sleeping tower on the right end of the building. Together the houses were called Arunside.

26. St. Brighid's, Letchworth, designed by Parker and Unwin. Built to welcome light and air.

27. Interior, house on Willian Way, Letchworth. Robert Bennett and Wilson Bidwell, architects. Plain living and high thinking.

28. Rushby Mead, Letchworth. The absence of hedges was expected to encourage neighborliness.

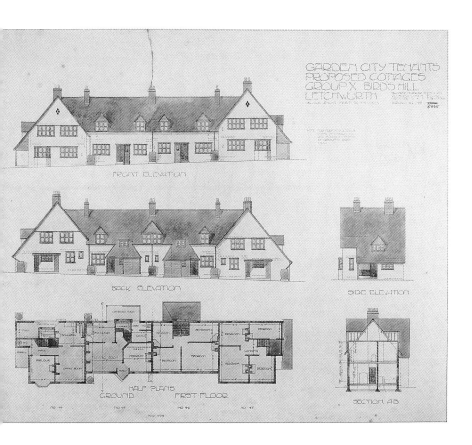

29 and 30. Bird's Hill, Letchworth. The acme of garden city planning.

COMMON VIEW, LETCHWORTH.

31. Workers' cottages. Common View, Letchworth. "If their Ideal City had got to Common View, with its deplorable buildings and settings in six years, what would it get to in twelve or twenty years?" Debate reported in *Letchworth Citizen*. October 29, 1910.

SKETCH PLAN

THREE BEDROOMS & BOXROOM OVER

Cost per foot cube, 3¾d. for the Exhibition ; actual cost, 4½d.

[Robert Bennett, A.R.I.B.A., and Wilson Bidwell, Architects, Letchworth

WILSON BIDWELL, delt

32. The Cheap Cottage Exhibition at Letchworth, 1905. Designed by the reputable Letchworth firm Bennett and Bidwell, the house was constructed of weather board (clapboard) on a wooden frame to save money.

CARTOON No. 8,–A LETCHWORTH DEPUTATION TO THE DIRECTORS.

"The proceedings were quite *en camera*, and we believe that an amicable understanding was quickly arrived at."

33. Cartoon. *Letchworth Citizen.* June 26, 1909. The directors are all W. H. Gaunt, the estate manager. The gentleman with the bag of resolutions is Ebenezer Howard.

34. Howard Hall, Letchworth. Designed by Parker and Unwin. Meeting place of the high-minded. "So many opinions, . . . and so definite."

35. Cartoon. *Letchworth Citizen.* May 15, 1909. "Letchworth Cranks." In the foreground, W. H. Gaunt (left), Raymond Unwin (center), and Ebenezer Howard (right).

36. Food Reform Restaurant and Simple Life Hotel. Leys Avenue, Letchworth.

37. The Cloisters, Letchworth. W. H. Cowlishaw, architect. Where men and women "bathed in energizing currents of the Intellect."

38. "The spirit of the place." Letchworth. May Day, 1912. Ebenezer Howard is second from left.

Howard's radicalism was tempered as well by his reiterated plea for cooperation. He assumed that what he called "pro-municipal" work—work undertaken by citizens on behalf of their community—would engage the cooperative
spirit of most garden city residents. "Those who have the welfare of society at
heart" would work together "in the free air of the city" to "quicken the public
conscience and enlarge public understanding." Howard permitted himself a
brief, sharp thrust at class-based trade union agitation: "If labour leaders spent
half the energy in co-operative organization that they now waste in co-operative
disorganization, the end of our present unjust system would be at hand."[36]
Sentiments of this sort made Howard's "commonsense socialism" sound remarkably like the "practicable socialism" of Toynbee Hall's Samuel Barnett.
Indeed, a speech that Howard delivered in 1900, entitled "Responsibility of the
Masses for the Condition of the Classes," espoused the pure milk of Toynbee-
ism. "A right view of human relationships" was possible only when the attitudes of the masses and the classes harmonized "to form something like a
complete whole." "Extreme poverty and extreme wealth would be gradually
banished from our midst if a vision of life, entirely free from class bias and class
prejudice and class feeling could become ours, for working then for national
ends and not for selfish purposes we should strive with one accord to make the
world a better place."[37] Reading and listening to Howard, one could forget that
his proposal had to do with a major reorganization of society and assume,
rather, that his goals merely coincided with those of others bent on the remaking of community in a less cosmic fashion.

True, not everyone welcomed his scheme. Edward Pease of the Fabian Society dismissed *To-morrow* with contempt. Howard, he wrote, proposed to pull
down existing cities and substitute his own, "each duly built according to pretty
coloured plans, nicely designed with a ruler and compass." Pease would have
none of it. "We have got to make the best of our existing cities, and proposals
for building new ones are about as useful as would be arrangements for protection against visits from Mr. Wells's Martians."[38] A similar attitude, which one
can imagine struck those who professed it as a good deal more "commonsense"
than Howard's, was expressed in the *Builder*. "[The scheme] is so fanciful, and
the projects suggested are so impossible of realization, that it does not appear
desirable to comment upon it at length."[39]

Yet Howard's ideas gradually gained increasingly wide and sympathetic audiences, probably because there appeared to be something in this plan for everyone. C. B. Purdom, who was to become one of the garden city's stoutest
defenders, explained the gathering enthusiasm in terms of political appeal:

"The Socialist liked it because of its semi-municipal character . . . ; the Conservative because it professed a way in which private enterprise could help solve the housing question; the Liberal because it was a project of land reform."[40] In 1912, the newspaper baron Lord Northcliffe, writing to decline an invitation to a dinner in Howard's honor, testified to the fame his book had by that time achieved. With characteristic directness and certainty Northcliffe declared, "I have always said that yours is the most concrete example of the force of an idea that has ever come within my knowledge."[41]

Because public ownership of land was a cornerstone of Howard's vision, he had received support from the outset of his campaign for garden cities from the Land Nationalisation Society, a group of advanced liberals and semi-socialists dedicated to the same cause. When growing enthusiasm for Howard's ideas gave birth in 1899 to the Garden City Association, a number of leading members of the society lent their backing to this closely related enterprise. The association's first secretary, the barrister F. W. Steele, had served in the same capacity at the LNS. The society's president, the eminent scientist Alfred Russel Wallace, had characterized Howard's proposal as "perhaps the only [one] that goes to the root of the matter without being of such an alarming nature as to be for the present outside the sphere of practical politics"—additional evidence of the general appeal of the garden city concept.[42] Yet further confirmation of that fact lay in the acceptance of the association's chairmanship by Ralph Neville, K.C., a Cambridge graduate, former Liberal MP, and later judge of the High Court. Neville had written on land ownership, arguing that the principle of property in land was not, in fact, embodied in the common law but was the outcome of historical circumstance. His reputation in high political circles served the immediate interests of the association well, as did the appointment of a Scotsman, Thomas Adams, as secretary.

Adams, a former Liberal Party agent with a keen appreciation of the importance of favorable public relations, lost no time enlisting the aid of George Cadbury in organizing the national conference held at Bournville in September 1901. Three hundred delegates attended, including representatives invited from local borough councils, along with a small army of pressmen, who reported the proceedings in a generally positive manner. Neville had induced the Liberal Party ornament Earl Grey to take the chair, and announced the objective of the meetings as consideration of the "experiment of [Messrs] Cadbury in moving their works to Bournville, the difficulties and advantages which attend the removal of works from large cities to new districts; how local districts . . . can cooperate with such movements . . . so that new towns may be established on land to be purchased for the community."[43]

In the first paper read to the conference, Neville, the respectable Liberal, nonetheless argued that the "supreme merit" of Howard's proposal was its insistence on the common ownership of land and the implications that such a policy would have for the prosperity of the garden city community. This, even more than provision of the "advantages which it was desirable that [its citizens] should enjoy," made the experiment worth trying. The automatic increase in land values occurring once the city began to rise, that unearned increment that now went to individual landlords, would be used instead to benefit all the city's residents. Neville promised a gain "so enormous that if it could be calculated it would stagger you." He prophesied that once one garden city had shown what could be done, local governments across the country would quickly follow. He announced, finally, that the Garden City Association fully intended to float a company, secure land, and begin erecting a model that would point the way "towards solving great social questions."[44]

This was heady rhetoric. In emphasizing Howard's insistence on common land ownership, Neville was advertising the most radical element in the scheme. And yet he and his fellow enthusiasts were strikingly successful in wooing a large following of the eminently respectable. The next year, nearly a thousand delegates attended a second conference at Liverpool and Port Sunlight. By the end of 1902, following the reissue of Howard's book, the association boasted membership of thirteen hundred. Among the lengthy roster of vice-presidents were various peers, bishops, members of Parliament (twenty-three in all), plus a sprinkling of industrialists, including Cadbury and Lever. Only members of the labor movement were notable for their absence from the list.[45] Garden cities had in no more than three years become a thoroughly respectable cause.

Declaring one of its principal goals the conduct of "experiments in the common ownership of land," the Garden City Association moved quickly toward its goal of establishing a first city.[46] Under Neville's direction, the association's council formed Garden City Pioneer Company, Ltd., with capital of £20,000, to prospect for a site. Members of that board included Neville; Aneurin Williams, a liberal MP and ironmaster; Edward Cadbury, George's son; Thomas Ritzema, editor of Cadbury's *Daily News;* Thomas Idris, a London manufacturer of mineral water; Franklin Thomasson, a cotton master; and Howard Pearsall, a civil engineer. Howard was named managing director, charged with finding a site for the first garden city. Once the board had selected the site that was to become Letchworth, it reconstituted itself, in September

1903, as First Garden City, Ltd., with capitalization of £300,000 and with the addition of William Lever as board member.

Until World War I, the movement continued to enjoy widespread public support and a generally favorable press. Press cuttings books in the First Garden City Heritage Museum at Letchworth—nineteen large scrapbooks covering the years 1902 to 1914—are filled with articles from across the country, many of them apparently based on releases issued by Adams. As the first garden city rose at Letchworth, the press was urged to attend groundbreakings and other events noteworthy to garden city promoters if not to the general public. On the occasion of the opening of a temporary railway station at Letchworth in April 1905, the *Evening Standard* observed that "no doubt a movement like this garden city one is liable to be ridiculed as the dream of enthusiasts." In fact, the *Standard*'s reporter assured his readers that the scheme was far from an ill-devised charity; it was instead "an attempt to solve a problem that has been before the people since the time of Elizabeth, viz., the overcrowding of cities, and [how] to solve it on an economic basis."[47] A year later, following the annual conference of the association, *The Times* pronounced a benediction on the enterprise that echoed sentiments widely expressed before 1914. "The more experiments of the kind tried at Letchworth, the better for society. Every carefully considered attempt to disperse population instead of concentrating it is for the good."[48]

During the decade before World War I, a great many such attempts were made, though only Letchworth conformed in any degree to the garden city concept as proposed by Howard. It was far easier to lay out garden suburbs, the most famous being that at Hampstead, or what came to be called "garden villages," on the model of Bournville and Port Sunlight. The Alkrington Hall Estate in Manchester, Bristol Garden Suburb, Ltd., Cardiff Workers' Garden Suburb at Glyn-Cory, Warrington Garden Suburb, Hull Garden Village, Gidea Park at Romford, Fallings Park Garden Suburb in Woolverhampton, Ruislip Manor near Harrow—these and other developments attested to the general appeal of *The Times*'s injunction to disperse populations, and at the same time to the unwillingness or inability of planners and developers to take the bold steps necessary to create an entire city de novo.[49]

Construction of garden suburbs was encouraged by the Town Planning Act of 1909, which empowered local authorities to impose a plan upon land in line for development adjacent to an existing town. Planners were authorized to supersede existing byelaws in order to provide for a variety of road patterns and to limit the number of houses per acre. Though welcomed as official recognition of the value of the garden suburb ideal, the law distressed garden city advocates. "The essential idea of town-planning as it is practiced in England is the antithesis of the Garden City idea," lamented C. B. Purdom in 1913. "The town-planner says: we want to lay out in advance the land over which our towns are to spread; . . . we want to prepare for the endless growth of the huge monster. The Garden City says: we need to put a limit to the size of the town: we need to preserve these fields so that they shall not be destroyed; we need to remake town life in small towns in the midst of the country."[50] There was, indeed, precious little of Howard left in most of the town planning schemes arising from the act of 1909. When the Garden City Association, in 1907, changed its name to the Garden Cities and Town Planning Association, it was acknowledging the degree to which the bold vision of *To-morrow: A Peaceful Path to Real Reform* had been occluded by reformers' willingness to work for more readily achievable half-measures.

Dilution of Howard's original vision at the hands of town planners did not mean abandonment of the garden city idea by its original advocates, however. The zeal with which promoters remained determined to see Letchworth succeed was a measure of their belief that garden cities were a dream worth realization. How to explain the continued acceptance of Howard's ideas by men and women not easily given to advocating utopian schemes for social reform? The precedents of Bournville and Port Sunlight unquestionably served to win public support for a scheme that was in most respects very different but could be made to seem quite similar. Even Howard—who grew increasingly frustrated by public willingness to identify any development with a bit of green within its midst as a garden city—willingly played up the Bournville–Port Sunlight connection when it seemed to suit his purpose. In the preface to a book on garden cities published by the association in 1906, Howard asked, "Are not Saltaire, Bournville and Port Sunlight witnesses and proofs of what can be done if only we make a fresh start, turn over a new leaf, and dare to do what our friends declare impossible?"[51] Though he employed the example of factory villages to do no more than preach the possibility of general urban change, he must have realized that their mention would reassure readers of the movement's respectable lineage at the risk of conflating Cadbury's and Lever's experiments with his own.

The understandable temptation to make use of Bournville and Port Sunlight in this way could, on occasion, backfire. In a letter in the association's files, Fred Knee, the general secretary of the Workmen's National Housing Council, accused Thomas Adams of misleading the public by insisting that the Bournville experiment proved that working-class housing could be built in such a way as to provide the tenant decent accommodation and the investor a modest profit. "You say that Mr. Cadbury has been successful on purely business lines. This is the first I ever heard of such a thing, and shall be obliged [if you can] let me know the commercial rate of profit he gets on his housing outlay." Knee—whose Council's object, according to its stationery, was "to induce Municipal Authorities to provide Good Houses for the People at Cost Rents"—was suspicious of schemes that smacked of philanthropic do-goodism, which is how he saw not only Bournville but the garden city proposal. "I can only hope you will hurry up and get your scheme through," he concluded, "so that its futility may be the more quickly demonstrated, and the people be induced to set to work at their own housing."[52] Knee's remonstrance is evidence of the degree to which working-class organizations mistrusted and hence steered clear of the association and its efforts. But for every skeptic suspicious of the links between Cadbury, Lever, and the proposal for garden cities, there were no doubt many more who found that connection reassuring.

The general public was heartened as well by the respectability of the directorship of both association and company. Neville and Adams made a determined effort from the start to attract the great and the good. The consequence was an organization that bespoke authority and tradition: aristocratic notables; high-minded reformers like Alfred Marshall and the Samuel Barnetts; and experienced and successful businessmen, such as Cecil Harmsworth, brother of the proprietor of the *Daily Mail,* not to mention the men who sat as directors of First Garden City, Ltd.

Yet at the heart of the enterprise lay the principle of common land ownership. As time passed, however, and as theory became practice, that vital element, so important to Neville as well as to Howard, was threatened for the sake of the immediate and expedient need to see a city arise from the woods and fields of the Hertfordshire countryside. Soon after the Bournville conference of 1901, George Bernard Shaw drafted a letter to Neville, which Howard's biographer Robert Beevers has discovered among Shaw's correspondence in the British Library. Whether or not Shaw sent the letter—and it is Beevers's guess that he did—he lay his finger on the contradiction that he believed to be the scheme's inherent flaw. No matter how carefully Neville designed the deed of trust that would ensure the unearned increment for community use, as soon as he and his fellow directors attempted to lure capitalist business to the city they would encounter resistance to their determination to subordinate individual to common interest.

Shaw pointed out that the garden city needed capital more than capitalists needed the city. Writing as if he were himself such a capitalist, Shaw observed that "when we invest capital in an enterprise, we retain control of that enterprise, and do good works out of our private incomes from it." He anticipated that the businessman contemplating a move to garden city would have nothing to do with a trust deed that limited his profit, though he might be willing to accept a 5 percent maximum in dividends on shares in the city trust, for the improvement of local amenities—which improvement would also, of course, enhance the capitalist's investment. But, in the end, nothing could prevent a majority of shareholders from deciding to sell their shares in the freehold of the city on the open market—a situation that, as Beevers points out, did arise in the 1960s and was only prevented by an act of Parliament.[53]

Had Neville heeded Shaw's advice and eliminated the principle of common ownership of the unearned increment, he would have gutted Howard's scheme and frustrated his own expectations. And so he left it in. But from the start he recognized that investors would need assurance that garden cities, if they were restricted by a covenant protecting unearned increment, were nonetheless a sound financial risk. He struggled to bring his philosophical commitment to land reform into line with his impatience to see the experiment at Letchworth succeed. At the 1901 conference he had gone so far as to declare that his plan embodied the principle of Henry George's single tax on unearned increment. George's plan could be imposed only gradually on the country as a whole, he realized. But that was not the case when founding a city anew. "We are not talking about a town for our grandchildren and great-grandchildren; we want a town for the people of today, and if we do not get a town such as we wish for, or something like it, for the people of today, I do not think that the grandchildren and great-grandchildren will be worth having a town for at all."[54]

Neville was compelled to harness his impatience to the fact that the company had to raise capital of £300,000. If the principle of common land ownership was to be preserved, then some other way must be found to attract investors. The company was floated on stock with a dividend limitation of 5 percent; its directors hoped that the promise of that amount would be enough to ensure sufficient investment. Yet Howard refused to understand how important the promise of 5 percent was to the enterprise. Neville wrote him, objecting to his assumption that "whether [investors] are likely to get any dividend at all for one, two or a dozen years will not affect the amount of their subscription." Following a speech in which Howard declared that investors must expect that they might lose money in an effort that was worth the risk, Neville all but lost his patience. He again wrote to Howard: "For months the Board have striven to put the investment on a business footing and have abandoned cherished projects on the very ground that for mere philanthropy without hope of return the money would not be forthcoming. . . . [Y]ou must bear in mind that there is another side to the ethical question, and that is loyalty to the Board. . . . I feel sure that you have not realised the inevitable effects of such remarks as these quoted [from Howard's speech]. They can be made in one speech; they cannot be explained away in a hundred."[55]

Neville's concern was well founded. Public support for the garden city concept did not initially translate into a general willingness to risk capital in the Letchworth experiment, especially if it embodied a radical land reform scheme. The association's leadership might enthuse. Other potential investors were more difficult to persuade. At the end of the company's first year, only £100,000 had been subscribed. William Lever recommended that the directors sell off some of the property to speculative builders. When outvoted, he resigned. In the end, the reputation of the individuals who directed the company's fortunes, and their increasing ability at Letchworth to realize a city from the ground up, assured enough investors for the project. In 1912, the company turned a modest profit for the first time. Though there was constant fear on the part of the directors that the public would perceive garden cities as no more than a crankish fad, the company's tangible success, and its ability to capitalize on that success in the press, built confidence and trust enough to allow it to proceed. Howard was himself a partial casualty of the process, however. Following the misbehavior that so concerned Neville, he was removed from his position as managing director in 1903 and relegated to the tasks of writing and lecturing, while attending to the design of Letchworth. From that point on he was the increasingly isolated emblem of a movement that was fast becoming a serious—and occasionally precarious—business enterprise.

One further financial circumstance helped ensure increasing faith in the garden city experiment. Most of the houses at Letchworth, and many in other communities eager to call themselves garden cities or garden suburbs, were built with money raised by so-called co-partnership societies. The concept did not originate with Howard or with the Garden City Association. The first society was registered in 1888, and tenants had used the device to build houses in Bournville. The scheme was simple: a society purchased or leased land, laid it out for building in a healthy and aesthetically pleasing fashion, and erected dwellings for stockholders desiring to become tenants. Houses were let at rents that would permit the payment of a modest 4 to 5 percent dividend. Tenant stockholders deducted maintenance expenses and divided surplus profits, which they received as additional stock, until they had accumulated stock in the amount of their houses, at which time they ceased to pay rent altogether. Though the tenant did not own his house, nonetheless—in the words of a brochure written to promote the plan—"There is a sense of ownership arising out of the possession of stock and the participation in profit that is valuable in influencing national thought along sane and sober lines."[56]

Therein, of course, lay the appeal to middle-class investors in First Garden City. A purchase of company shares would indirectly encourage working-class self-help and thus the reformation of working-class character by facilitating the spread of co-partnership housing estates. At Letchworth, Garden City Tenants Ltd., Letchworth Cottages and Buildings, Ltd., and the Howard Cottages Society were among those formed to finance the construction of artisan dwellings. That these were, indeed, houses for artisans and not laborers was a fact dictated by the nature of co-partnership, which required an investment beyond the means of most unskilled workers.

Nothing prevented nonresidents from investing in co-partnership building societies; they were touted to the middle-class investor as a particularly sound venture. In an article extolling co-partnership, Henry Vivian, an MP and housing reformer who had founded Garden City Tenants, listed as "advantages to the capitalist" the facts that it was in the tenants' interest to work for higher profits by maintaining their properties, and that the share capital of tenant members provided a fund from which arrears in rent could be drawn. "Loss by arrears in rent," he concluded, "is therefore practically impossible."[57] This appeal of co-partnership to outside investors worried the labor movement and was another reason why it remained at arm's length from the enterprise. The financial editor of the left-wing *Daily Herald,* in a 1912 article attacking the "Co-Partnership Oligarchy," quoted a speech delivered at the national Liberal Club in which Vivian, according to the *Herald,* encouraged outside investors as a way of checking the power of tenant shareholders, "who may be here to-day and gone to-morrow, against the permanent interests of the Society; . . . the outside shareholder, deriving a fixed interest only on his capital, has absolutely no motive for acting contrary to the permanent welfare of the Society."[58] The *Herald* complained that as a consequence of Vivian's policy, tenants were finding it all but impossible to acquire shares over and above their dividends. If true, their difficulties were further evidence of the degree to which the garden city movement had come to be led by men whose enthusiasm for reform was balanced by their determination to control its course themselves.

That fact, as much as anything, lent the enterprise credibility in the eyes of potential investors. Very little had been written about how these new communities were to be governed. Those who hymned the virtues of garden city life almost never spoke of it as a vehicle for the promotion of broad-based citizen participation in the management of citywide civic affairs. Workers might become shareholders in co-partnership societies; they might manage the business of their various social and cultural clubs and committees, as they did at Bournville and Port Sunlight. As for anything much more than that, the apologists were silent. Howard's scheme for an elected board of management was never realized at Letchworth, Neville and his fellow directors fearing that it might result in a kind of political unpredictability—if not instability—threatening to potential investors.[59]

In the end, therefore, bold proposals for land reform or house building might not appear that radical, since their direction was to remain in the hands of reliably sensible trustees. What, indeed, was the difference, in terms of tangible results, between the scheme for land disposal as eventually settled upon at Letchworth, and that enshrined in the mythology surrounding the much-admired village of old? In both cases an unelected authority—a benevolently inclined, improving landlord—claimed to impose its will for the benefit of the community as a whole. In both cases the authorities defended their rule as beneficial to that of community, insisting that the system of primogeniture, in one case, or of a self-perpetuating body of governors, in the other, would best advance the well-being of those whom it was their obligation to serve.

Throughout the early history of the movement, those who spoke and wrote on its behalf echoed the themes that were to give it a peculiarly "English" and an ultimately conservative cast: the fear of cities as breeding grounds for an unhealthy, inefficient, and socially dangerous population; and the need for the reestablishment of communities that would efface the corroding effects of class conflict by restoring that sense of mutual obligation and responsibility that had characterized the social relations of pre-industrial England.

In his opening remarks to the Bournville conference, Neville sounded the note that he and other garden city enthusiasts were to reiterate as they preached their reformist gospel: that garden cities would eliminate physical deterioration and promote national efficiency.

> The question really is a national question, nay it is more than that, it is an Imperial question—and it is a question of paramount importance to the Empire, because . . . the ultimate destiny of our Empire depends upon the character and capacity of the citizens of this country. . . . Unless we do discover some means of mitigating the evil

[of urban overcrowding] and restoring healthy conditions of life to our population, we are ultimately doomed to failure in the fierce rivalry which we have now to undergo, and which we must undergo in the future. . . . You have in Garden Cities a system which ensures the best physical development of the great majority of the male population.[60]

A redistributed population would inevitably become a healthier population. Writing three years later on the "Basis of British Efficiency," Neville linked the factory system, "with its accompanying aggregation of population," with physical decline. He could see but one remedy: "the redistribution of people upon the land; . . . the carrying on of manufacturing under satisfactorily hygienic conditions," an impossibility in existing great towns.[61]

The association's monthly journal, *The Garden City* (in 1908 renamed *Garden Cities and Town Planning Magazine*) continued to print statistics to support the claim that life in garden cities was far healthier than life elsewhere in England. In 1913, the editors accompanied figures showing Letchworth with an infant mortality far lower than the national average with the observation that at Letchworth the smallest working-class houses were never built more than twelve per acre, whereas "working-class dwellings in most industrial districts number thirty, forty or even fifty to the acre."[62]

Garden city advocates believed that their re-created communities would be conducive to moral as well as physical regeneration. Neville implied as much in a 1904 lecture on the movement and its purposes. "I am convinced that the redistribution of the people upon the land would do more to transform members of the working class than any other conceivable alternation of the conditions under which they live. It is not generally recognized . . . what effect healthy bringing up and healthy conditions of life have upon a man, or the extent of the evils induced by want of fresh air and insufficient outdoor exercise."[63] Though there is a degree of ambiguity about Neville's declaration, his meaning seems clear enough: life within garden cities will make workers more generally responsible as citizens. The point was made explicitly several years later in a speech by Sybella Gurney, honorary secretary of the Co-Partnership Tenants Housing Council, to the Sociological Society. "What we need is to get a more general understanding of the meaning of citizenship. A mere change of external surroundings is not enough. The children in garden city and suburb conditions should develop into better citizens than their parents. A generation should grow up there ready to sacrifice if need be material things to things of the spirit."[64]

Howard himself espoused this belief in the beneficent power of garden cities to compel the sacrifice of special interests to communal ones. In his speech at the Bournville conference he imagined a working class willing to take a reduction in pay—assuming that conditions would prevent a loss of real wages—so as to assist manufacturers in recovering the costs of their move to a garden city. "And thus I can imagine," he added, "this further result: the workmen and the employer, by this common effort to establish better conditions, being brought into more harmonious relations, with the result that the quantity and the quality of work would alike rise with enormous benefit to both as well as to the consumer."[65]

Reluctance to think in terms of a democratic future was tied to nostalgia for the hierarchies of pre-industrial community. James Bryce, addressing the association conference in 1906, spoke of a "community such as London was in the Middle Ages, when rich and poor lived in sight of one another, and where institutions such as Trade Guilds . . . bound up the interests of the employers with those of the humbler workers in the same craft." A garden city, he predicted, would be such a place, where the "relation of the classes is represented in a more natural and wholesome way than in an immense place like London or Manchester."[66] A writer in the *Independent Review* two years before compared the garden city community with that of the pre-industrial, squire-dominated village, "where the lord of the estate has built churches and schools, and is in many places also responsible for the moral and social well-being of his tenants." He extolled the "experiments of Mr. Cadbury and Mr. Lever"—once again conflating factory villages with garden cities—whose generosities "do not find a place in our . . . textbooks of political economy."[67] Barry Parker, the socialist planner and architect at the heart of the movement, was, like his partner Raymond Unwin, seduced by pre-industrial landscape. He predicted that garden cities built on the principle of co-partnership housing would foster an "organized civic life such as distinguished our old-time villages, . . . [to] take the place of the ugliness and lack of organization which characterizes the buildings produced by the extreme individualism of recent times."[68] With language such as this, Howard's garden city was shed of its utopian-American visionary origins, and clothed instead in the conservative images of Englishness.

When, in 1902, Howard reissued *To-morrow: A Peaceful Path to Real Reform* under the milder title *Garden Cities of To-morrow,* the frontispiece of the new edition, by Walter Crane, reflected the degree to which the movement was prepared to look backward in a manner Howard never intended. Rather than evoke the futuristic diagrams that accompany Howard's text, Crane showed readers an enthroned medieval princess, holding aloft the model of a medieval city in her delicately medieval hand. If, as Howard's biographer points out, Crane's drawing illustrates the fact that the movement had attained social respectability, it demonstrates as well the degree to which its respectability was linked to visions from a mythic English past.[69]

Chapter 4 Barry Parker
and Raymond Unwin:
Principles and Practice

The seductive power of an English past helped shape the character of the two most famous prewar experiments in garden city and garden suburb planning in England, at Letchworth and at Hampstead. That character emerged, in large measure, from the work of the architects Barry Parker and Raymond Unwin, whose designs brought the communities to life.

Parker and Unwin were members of the loose confederation calling itself the Arts and Crafts movement. Drawing inspiration from the ideals of John Ruskin and William Morris, the architects, designers, and artists who constituted its membership understood their mission as the creation of a more aesthetically honest and hence morally invigorating environment. Some professed one or another variety of socialism; others did not. But all saw industrial capitalism as the cause of the ghastly landscape of late nineteenth-century England. They believed it responsible as well for the insensitivity of most urban dwellers to the visual squalor they endured and for the spiritual obliviousness that inhibited them from altering it. Arts and Crafts architects assigned themselves a central role in reconstituting the environment, bringing citizens to their senses and encouraging them to lead happier, more worthwhile lives. In the words of W. R. Lethaby, "Architecture was . . . not a superficial veneer, the supercilious trick and grimace of art; . . . it was the construction of buildings done with such fine feeling to fitness, such ordinary traditional skill, selection and insight, that the work [is] transformed into delight, and necessarily delights others."[1] The architect wedded various crafts in pursuit of a pleasing and uplifting whole. Uniting science with art, the higher arts with the lesser, he ensured that each project resulted not merely in a building but in a work of art of lasting benefit to the community in which it stood.

The architect was to turn England's citizens to the task of freeing themselves from the urban existence that held them physical and spiritual prisoner. Arts and Crafts apologists spoke little but ill of modern cities and suburbs. M. H. Baillie Scott, for example, poured scorn on the byelaw street: "If it were conceded that in the planning of the terrace house it is first of all essential that there should be a seldom occupied sitting-room with a bay-window commanding a view of another similar bay-window on the opposite side of the street . . . that the interior of the house should be subdivided as far as possible with as many little apartments as possible . . . that the comfort of the family is really quite a secondary matter in comparison to the proper respect due to furniture, for the proper display of which the house is built . . . one might, perhaps, then admit that the stereotyped plan is the best that can be arrived at."[2] Though more than willing to design city buildings, Arts and Crafts architects continued to despair at what they saw as the sham that urban life had become. Not surprisingly, they looked to the countryside, and to the architectural traditions of the past, for instruction and inspiration. C. R. Ashbee, one of the leading Arts and Crafts apologists, urged the duty of his fellow architects "to maintain wherever we can the type of building [typical of] each county." "Centuries of wisdom," he insisted, were stored in each particular type: "The stone building of the Cotswolds, ashlar, rubble and dry walling; timber work and pargetting in Essex; half timber and brick work in Staffordshire."[3] There was an integrity not only in those distinctive buildings themselves but—Ashbee seemed to imply—in the very words describing them: ashlar, pargetting. In company with most of his Arts and Crafts colleagues, Ashbee preached against the cheap uniformity of modern design and construction, urging instead the preservation of those materials and techniques that had made building in past times what it no longer was, the pursuit of an ideal.

Through individual commissions, speeches and writings, and the work of such organizations as the Art Workers' Guild and the Arts and Crafts Exhibition Society, members of the movement spread their gospel during the last years of the nineteenth century. The emphasis was on the domestic and the natural. Style for its own sake was scorned, as was anything that smacked of conventional pretentiousness. "Simplicity, sincerity, repose, directness and frankness are moral qualities as essential to good architecture as to good men," wrote C. F. A. Voysey in an article titled "The English Home."[4] And Voysey implied that good architecture of the sort he envisioned would help produce good men.

If these architects were in revolt against the high Victorian urban architecture of their immediate predecessors, they were nonetheless themselves high Victorians in the seriousness with which they went about pursuing aesthetic satisfaction. Baillie Scott wrote of an "ideal" evening, as he imagined it occurring in the hall of an "ideal" suburban house of his design in the 1890s. "I should like to picture to you a musical evening in this hall. In the ingle, seated on the broad seats, a company of friends are gathered around a blazing wood fire on the wide brick hearth, which lights up the burnished copper of the fire-dogs and the heaps of logs piled on each side of the hearth. There is no glaring gas, but here and there lamps and candles throw a suffused soft light. Above in the gallery are the musicians, and the strains of a violin are heard to advantage, while the position of the player gives an air of mystery to the music which greatly adds to the effect."[5] Baillie Scott does his best to evoke the medieval, both in the design of the hall and in the prose with which he describes it on this particular evening. One wonders what that violinist might have been playing: almost certainly something English; nothing later than Arne or Purcell. Above all, Baillie Scott wants his readers to appreciate the worthiness of the scene: honest bricks and copper; a log fire rather than coal; candles, not gas.

This was the sincerity of which Voysey wrote, and which Arts and Crafts practitioners strove to infuse into the houses they designed and built for a clientele prepared to reform their own manners and way of life while they were busily reforming others'. Like these clients, the architects who served them believed that they had a duty to instruct. Architecture was a mission, a way of awakening in the consciousness of housedwellers a best self derived from their everyday surroundings and from which they came to know and understand what "best" meant. In the process of that awakening, architects and clients together invented an Englishness, as Baillie Scott invented his "evening," using a mythic past to reinvigorate and reinspire the present. Those clients were largely from the upper middle class. Among them were garden city enthusiasts whose seriousness and vision matched that of the Arts and Crafts aesthetic. Hence their respect for the work of Parker and Unwin.

Raymond Unwin and Barry Parker were born into the north of England middle class. Unwin's father, Edward, lived a maverick life. As a young man he worked in the Yorkshire cloth trade, and despite the eventual collapse of the family business was apparently successful enough to hold on to property in Sheffield, on which he later depended for income. Raymond, born in 1863 in the West Riding village of Whiston, began his schooling at Rotherham. Soon thereafter, the family moved to Oxford. Edward took up a Fellowship at Balliol College, where he had received his degree some years earlier. Family legend has it that he was befriended by Arnold Toynbee, the economic historian, and T. H. Green, the idealist philosopher.[6] He ultimately resigned his fellowship for reasons of religious conscience. He remained in Oxford, however, as an academic coach. Raymond attended Magdalen College Choir School, leaving to begin training as an engineer. In 1885, he accepted a position as draftsman-fitter in a Manchester cotton mill.

Raymond Unwin's daughter maintained that at this time her father spoke with Samuel Barnett, a family friend, about his future. "Raymond," he is supposed to have asked, "are you more interested in making people good or making them happy?"[7] The question implies that Unwin was contemplating a career as a clergyman. The answer, presumably, was given in favor of the latter option. And general happiness, Unwin soon concluded, depended on the realization of a socialist society in Britain. Yet Unwin's particular brand of socialism, reflecting the high-mindedness characteristic of so many late Victorian social reformers, promised to make its beneficiaries both good *and* happy. Certainly that was the implicit—often explicit—purpose of the housing that Parker and Unwin were to design and the communities they were to plan.

During his years at Manchester, Unwin played a prominent role establishing a socialist presence within the city. He met William Morris and Ford Madox Brown, who had come there to supervise the painting of the town hall murals. That acquaintanceship encouraged Unwin to join Morris's Socialist League; in 1886 he was serving as first secretary of the league's Manchester branch. When he was twenty-four, in 1887, Unwin left Manchester for Chesterfield, where he went to work as chief draftsman for the Staveley Coal and Iron Works. There he designed his first houses—employees' cottages—threatening to resign if prevented from including bathrooms in the plans. He joined the Sheffield Socialist

Society and wrote for Morris's *Commonweal*. He spoke regularly at outdoor meetings, most of them staged to increase local union membership. At Clay Cross, in the summer of 1887, Unwin reported in his journal that at the end of his prepared speech, "I . . . just went on speaking about [the] union and trying to make things better and said if they did not live to see it they would still be able to die feeling they had left the world better for their children."[8]

Unwin was conscious at this time of a compelling need to "make things better." He understood evil and misery as an "injunction for us to mend our lives in some way or the general conditions of life."[9] He began to mend his own life by befriending those in Sheffield and Chesterfield whose lives he hoped to improve. The northerners he met impressed him with their seriousness and their integrity as working men. "There is something interesting in these fellows, uneducated simple fellows, . . . living together a life so much more noble than most of us are able to do."[10] Yet he was unable to rid himself entirely of the itch of class consciousness. At a local flower show, which he attended with a working-class friend and his family, he "could not help feeling that I did not like the foreman and so on at the works . . . to see me with, and probably conclude I was connected with, a working man and his family. I tried to shake off the feeling and couldn't. . . . I do despise myself for it and though I don't let it influence my conduct much still I can't help feeling a humbug because I have the feeling at all." Unwin struggled against the temptation to patronize, seeking to respond to the poverty of short-time workers as one human being to another. He was prepared to give the money he had expected to invest in his penny savings account to an underemployed miner: "I don't like saving when I come across something like that." Yet he remained conscious of the distance that separated him from the men and women he believed himself destined to help. After a bank holiday walk through Chesterfield: "Feeling rather sad; that black hole of a town weighed heavily on me. . . . There is something depressing in seeing a lot of English townspeople out for a holiday. Beer, betting, etc."[11]

Unwin's high-minded socialist's sense of the way things might be drove him to disparage the banality of the way things were. A constant striver toward what he believed to be the best, he wanted others striving alongside him. He had heard John Ruskin lecture at least once at Oxford and, as a young man, continued to read and ponder what he wrote. In his inaugural address as president of the Royal Institute of British Architects in 1931, he declared that he did not feel the least need to apologize for urging the importance of harmony and beauty at a time of severe national hardship. "If you feel that I have stressed this aspect too much, I may perhaps recall that my early days were influenced by the musical voice of John Ruskin, vainly trying to stem the flood of materialism which seemed to him to be overwhelming the arts, and much else; and later by the more robust constructive personality of William Morris and his crusade for the restoration of beauty to daily life. Those were times when it was very interesting to be alive."[12]

More than merely interesting: Unwin appears to have leapt at the challenge that Ruskin and Morris flung at the feet of their materialistically minded fellow countrymen and women. In the same address, he quoted Morris: "Beauty, which is what we mean by art . . . is no mere accident of human life which people can take or leave as they like, but a positive necessity of life, if we are to live as nature meant us to—that is, unless we are content to be less than men."[13] Morris's insistence that beauty was to be vigorously cultivated in all aspects of daily life encouraged the young Unwin to look everywhere for what was beautiful, just as it inspired him, as he matured, to design beyond single buildings to entire landscapes. Walking through the Staveley factory in 1887, he noticed a man at work making girders, and saw the beauty—the "higher morality"—in that labor because of the way it was being done. "He took great notice of a bit of praise, and although he is working piece work he tries to do everything the very best way even when it was longer."[14]

The relationship between beauty—whether in art, architecture, or daily work—and morality was one that Unwin tried hard to express through his own life. His effort to do so as a young man was inspired not only by the writings of Ruskin and Morris, but by those of James Hinton, an eccentric surgeon and philosophical writer whose posthumously published collection of meditations, *The Law-Breaker and the Coming of the Law,* was yet another attempt to link beauty to the living of one's life. As his biographer has written, "What Hinton realized as beauty in art he believed to be possible in morals," and possible for all men and women. Jesus was Hinton's lawbreaker. His offense lay in His affirmation "that *all* were ready, able to worship God in spirit, and in truth, and that what was needed was that the laws . . . that implied that they were not must be thrown down."[15]

The inclusiveness that Hinton celebrated linked his thought to that of Edward Carpenter, the man who more than any other helped Unwin discern the socialist vision that best accorded with his intentions for himself and his hopes for his fellow men and women. "From about the year 1881, Edward Carpenter became a great influence in my life," he wrote in 1931. The two had met following a lecture that Carpenter had delivered in Chesterfield. Years later, in an essay in praise of Carpenter's life and spirit, Unwin, recalled the "sense of escape from an intolerable sheath of unreality and social superstition" that he had experienced on his first reading of Carpenter's lengthy prose poem *Towards Democracy*.[16] Carpenter's socialism, like Morris's, celebrated the sturdy individual farmer or artisan: "Who is this, . . . easy with open shirt and brown neck and face . . . through the city garden swinging? . . . There was a time when the sympathy and the ideals of men gathered round other figures; . . . but now before the easy homely garb and appearance of this man as he swings past in the evening, all these others fade and grow dim. . . . And this is one of the slowly unfolding meanings of Democracy."[17]

For Unwin this became the quintessential meaning of democracy, and of his socialism. His creed was in some ways conventional: for example, he joined the chorus of those demanding common land ownership. "The land of a people does and always will belong to the people," he declared in a speech in 1886. "And they have the right to make such arrangements for its management as shall best conduce to the public good."[18] Unwin parted company, however, with those socialists who were demanding increased state intervention. Though willing to acknowledge that state-imposed restrictions had improved conditions in mines and factories, he argued that "the law is a poor and clumsy way of enforcing regulations which should be adopted voluntarily and carried out loyally, without need of enforcing."[19] In his journal he criticized an article in *Commonweal,* Morris's paper, by Belford Bax, complaining that Bax's scientific determinism placed him in that "depressing" camp of socialists who had no "faith in man."[20]

Unwin's socialism was grounded in that faith, as was Carpenter's. And Carpenter's, in turn, derived from the writings of Walt Whitman, from Whitman's insistence on a direct maturing relationship between individual men and women and their natural world. In his tribute to Carpenter, Unwin quoted a passage from *Towards Democracy* that had inspired him, linking the beneficiaries of a socialist democracy with the land that was theirs by right: "I see a great land poised as in a dream. . . . I hear the bells pealing, and the crash of hammers, and see beautiful parks spread—as in a toy show. I see a great land waiting for its own people to come and take possession of it."[21]

They were to possess that great land as individuals. Beyond individuals there must, of course, be community. Yet both Carpenter and Unwin found it difficult to give the term specific definition. "The only society which would ever really satisfy [man]," Carpenter wrote, "would be one in which he was perfectly free, and yet bound by ties of deepest trust to the other members."[22] But what was to provide the binding? Unwin never addressed the issue clearly. He had observed how class bound men and women to each other, and he was disheartened by what he saw. Throughout his early writings he returned to the fact of class and the way it had inhibited freedom of individual expression as it had inflamed animosities between social groups, prevented by the perverted loyalties of the capitalist system from working cooperatively toward common goals. "No people can be happy," he was certain, "who are divided one against another by strong class interests." Class was the pathological enemy of a healthy society. Its symptoms might be as mild as the discomfort Unwin had felt when walking with his working-class friends at the Chesterfield flower show, or as severe as the Trafalgar Square riots of 1886 and 1887, or the Dock Strike of 1889. In all cases, however, class kept people apart and hence brought illness on a society that was not healthy unless united in common and worthy purpose.

Unwin found it difficult to perceive the benefits that class consciousness might bring to workers who, linked as they were by workplace and neighborhood, derived security from the mutuality of their experience. The curse of capitalism was its insistence that the individual remain "bound to the actions of his neighbours."[23] Cooperation there had to be. But it was to be the cooperation of individual men and women above class—the strong with the weak. "Our aim is . . . to develop a society in which the good things in life shall be shared—handed round, as it were, to all—not scrambled for, and in which if there need be any extra burden carried at times, it shall not be thrust upon the weakest as it is today, but the strong shall take it."[24]

Unwin's apparently paradoxical grounding of his socialism in individualism influenced the way in which he carried out his mission as architect and planner. He made it his business to improve the quality of life for English men, women, and children—particularly for working-class men, women, and children. He appreciated the fact that those people needed to understand their lives in terms of some sort of social aggregation beyond their individual selves and their immediate families. Yet he appeared unable to work comfortably with the reality of class consciousness. He saw it as his mission to design houses suitable for a democracy of individual selves. And he welcomed the chance to plan communities that he believed would bring those individuals into harmony with one another. Unwin's plans, however, tended to brush aside the immediate, implacable reality of class. In that respect we should perhaps understand them as utopian. Certainly we should see them as an expression of Unwin's own class consciousness.

Recollecting in 1960 the partnership of Barry Parker and Raymond Unwin, Parker's widow declared that Unwin "had all the zeal of a social reformer with a gift of speaking and writing, and was inspired by Morris, Carpenter and the early days of the Labour Movement." Her husband was, she said, "primarily an artist. Texture, light, shade, vistas, form and beauty were his chief concern."[25] Assuming these observations to be true, they explain, perhaps, why Parker left no written trail, as Unwin did, to help explain his commitment to the architectural mission he clearly shared with Unwin. Though Parker was, like Unwin, a socialist, when he wrote and spoke it was more often to provide his audience an understanding of his methods and their purpose than to enlighten them on the philosophy and politics that lay behind the practice of his craft.

Four years younger than Unwin, Parker was the son of an invalid father who had moved to Buxton spa for his health. He grew up in apparent middle-class comfort, and from the time he expressed interest in an artist's career was encouraged to study at ateliers at Derby and then briefly at the South Kensington School of Art.[26] From 1889 to 1892 he apprenticed with the Lancashire architect G. Faulkner Armitage, learning the crafts involved in the construction, decoration, and furnishing of houses, convinced, as a disciple of Morris, that there was no proper way to subdivide the process of house design.

Unwin and Parker were cousins, and, after 1893, when Unwin married Parker's sister Ethel, brothers-in-law. That same year, Parker came to live with his sister and her husband in Chesterfield, where Unwin was designing a small church presented to the Staveley community by the company's board of directors and the Duke of Devonshire. In the obituary that he wrote for his partner and lifelong friend, Parker recalled how he, Raymond, and Ethel had worked together to decorate the church's interior, gracefully evoking the purposeful life of Arts and Crafts practitioners. "Evening after evening Unwin sat placing little glass cubes" for the mosaic he was installing "in position in the cartoon which I had made, in readiness for their transfer to the cement-rendered east wall, while I drew and his wife, my sister, read to us." In 1895, Parker moved to Buxton to be near his ailing parents. One year later the Unwins followed him, and the two architects joined in a partnership that lasted until Unwin went to work for the state in 1914. "No partnership deed was ever drawn up," Parker remembered. "None was needed. Mutual understanding was so complete."[27]

Parker and Unwin prided themselves on the seamlessness that characterized their personal and professional relationship. They were partners, but also, as Parker once remarked, since boyhood they had been all but brothers, their fraternal bond strengthened, of course, by Unwin's marriage.[28] Beyond that, the two shared a sense that their work as architects flowed from common beliefs, and was the natural extension and expression of those beliefs. Arts and Crafts architects believed that the professionalization of their calling threatened the union of the ideal with the practical. Lethaby expressed the fears: "The system of professionalism is an outcome of the vicious idea that the real business of a builder is not to build well—as mercifully many still do—but to cheat."[29] Professionalism forced lives into compartments. In contrast, Parker and Unwin continued to celebrate the wholeness in their own lives. Writing in 1910 for *The Craftsman,* the American Arts and Crafts journal, Parker described a house he had designed for a doctor. He believed that the house expressed his client's determination to live "unprofessionally" and therefore fully. The work of too many a professional, Parker wrote, "is such that the more he becomes absorbed and successful in it, the smaller, narrower and more ignoble becomes his life." For such a man, the "less his house proclaims his calling, the better." But there are others, Parker continued, "those fortunate beings whose occupation is such that to live for it means their best and truest development, and whose friends are those who help them do this."[30] Clearly Parker saw himself as one of those fortunates, and Unwin as one of those friends.

Parker and Unwin spent the early years of their partnership designing houses for middle-class clients in the north of England. They belonged to the Northern Art Workers' Guild, on whose council Unwin sat. The council's purpose was to "maintain the dignity of the Arts and handicrafts and to forward in every possible way the advancement of true and sterling workmanship upon honest and rational conceptions."[31] For an exhibition of members' work in 1903, Parker and Unwin contributed an illustrated article, "Cottages Near a Town," which emphasized site planning and low density, thereby presaging their work at Letchworth and Hampstead.

By that time the partnership had received national attention with the publication of a book of essays, sketches, and photographs describing in detail their experience as designers, and articulating the principles that had inspired their work. *The Art of Building a Home,* published in 1901, was followed the next year with a Fabian Tract by Unwin, *Cottage Plans and Common Sense,* a more succinct statement of their earlier collaboration. In the years that followed, the two men wrote regularly about their work and the ideals that inspired it. Taken together, their books and articles—alongside the buildings they designed—provided a continuing statement about their principles and practices.

Architectural historians have traced connections, both personal and stylistic, between Parker and Unwin and other Arts and Crafts designers. Parker was a friend of the Manchester architect Edgar Wood, a fellow member of the Northern Art Workers' Guild, whose concern to integrate the houses he built with their natural settings foreshadowed the determination of Parker and Unwin to do likewise. M. H. Baillie Scott and C. F. A. Voysey, already practicing when Parker and Unwin formed their partnership, designed in a style that the younger architects allowed to influence their own early houses: Parker and Unwin's Homestead, for example, completed outside Chesterfield in 1903, resembled Voysey's Broadleys at Windermere, built in 1898, in its siting and use of buttresses to accentuate mass.[32]

Similarities of this sort were not surprising given the extent to which these architects subscribed to a common Arts and Crafts canon. Though they soon developed a style of their own, less severe than Voysey's, less self-conscious than Baillie Scott's, Parker and Unwin adhered to the general principles that declared them members of a brotherhood that looked for its inspiration to Morris, and strove to put his preachings into practice. Most important was the insistence that form follow function. Throughout their collaboration the two men never ceased to proclaim that credo. "The essence and life of design lies in finding that form for anything which will, with the maximum of convenience and beauty, fit for the particular function it has to perform, and adapt it to the special circumstances in which it must be placed." That declaration, a paraphrase from a pamphlet Parker had published in 1895, appeared in the introduction to *The Art of Building a Home*. Parker reiterated it in his first article for *The Craftsman* in April 1910, able by that time to look back on the way in which he and Unwin had continued to abide by its injunction: "We saw there could be only one true way of going to work, and that was to build in the simplest and most direct way possible just that which would best fulfill the functions and meet the requirements in each instance, trusting solely to direct and straightforward construction, frankly acknowledged and shown, instead of to decoration and ornament."[33] The house, the streetscape, the town must express through their architecture and planning the purpose of the individual lives lived within them.

In working toward that end, Parker and Unwin enjoined the architect to turn his back on style for its own sake and on surface ornament that had no relation to the structure beneath it. Again, from *The Art of Building*, the lament that "all constructional features, whenever possible, are smeared over with a coat of plaster to bring them up to the same dead level of flat monotony, leaving a clear field for the erection of the customary abominations in the form of cornices, imitation beams where no beams are wanted, and plaster brackets which could support and do support, nothing."[34] In an earlier article Parker had contrasted the farmhouse kitchen with the modern drawing room, to the latter's decided disadvantage. There was about the kitchen the all-important element of "truth and honesty," so different from the "artificiality, falsity, and pretension and sham" of the room whose form may have followed from its function, but whose function itself—the maintenance of false standards and the proclamation of false values—made it hostile to the purposes for which houses must be built.[35]

Parker and Unwin subscribed wholeheartedly to the Arts and Crafts ideal of architect as teacher, compelling his clients to live "better" lives in an environment that left them little choice when it came to defining what was true and honest. In accord with the movement, they asserted that architects needed to extend their control over the entire process of house design and furnishing, imposing a kind of uplifting unity on both dwelling and inhabitants. "It is essential to any good result that one man should design the home as a whole," Parker declared in an early article, "selecting where he does not design and ensuring that the work of all may be done in the spirit of cooperation towards the complete whole which he planned."[36] Only in this way could the architect know that he was fulfilling his own function, that the form his work took was not itself a sham. If Arts and Crafts architects disparaged the word "professionalism," they insisted nonetheless on their responsibility to profess. As Parker and Unwin wrote in *The Art of Building*, "Architecture is rightly called a profession only when the architect advises his client what is best, and brings the whole weight of his knowledge and experience to persuade him from anything foolish, or in bad taste. . . . We have just such power of influencing our clients by helping them towards a more natural life as the doctor has in such matters as diet."[37]

These young architects diagnosed the ills of society in terms of a pathology of social instability and the poison of class consciousness. "Everyone is seeking to get a step further up the social ladder. The result is a demand for houses which look as though they belonged to the social grade next above that of the people who are to live in them."[38] Their prescription was, in Parker's words, to "create a true setting for true lives, stamped with the personalities, individualities, characters, and influence of those lives," yet stamped as well with the architect's own sense of what was required to make life "true."[39]

Parker and Unwin believed that they understood the needs of their clients—better perhaps, than did their clients themselves—and they saw it as their duty to respond to those needs as creatively as they could. True, the architect's compulsion to tell clients what is good for them is by no means peculiar to Parker and Unwin or to the period during which they flourished as young designers. Yet they were more than members of a timeless band of didactic innovators. They were men of their time and of their class, preaching along with other men and women to settlement house audiences, in Fabian Society lectures, to University Extension and Workers' Education Association students a particular brand of culture that they believed would bring about the enlightenment of individuals and the creation of a right-thinking, socialist yet nonetheless particularly English society. They could not trust their clients, however, to define a worthy moral aesthetic of their own. Capitalism had imposed its gimcrack standards on a commercial, classbound society that lacked the education to withstand them. Parker and Unwin saw their designs as just such education. Once men and women had been taught the difference between what was true and not true, through the experience of living within healthy, liberating environments, they would be able to make choices for themselves. Until then, they would need the tutelage of those with a clearer sense than they possessed of what was best for them. Teachers blessed with a knowledge of what is best; pupils willing to defer to that knowledge: such was the essence of high-minded community.

Parker and Unwin believed that architecture must become the "outcome of the life and conditions of the present time," in the words of the latter's biographer: an outcome, but not a reflection.[40] Because present conditions threatened the well-being of England's citizenry, those conditions would compel a change for the better. The art and architecture amid which Englishmen and women now lived, Parker declared in an article for *The Craftsman* entitled "Democracy's Influence on Architecture," expressed unmistakably the materialism and commercial progress that characterized the past century, "as low an ebb as art has ever fallen." Yet democracy's spread was shifting attention to the needs of the newly enfranchised and thereby fostering architectural change. Old-age pensions allowed men and women who might otherwise have been driven to the poorhouse "to keep their little homes together." And democracy's "demand for a fuller and more balanced life" was encouraging a "village" architecture of clubhouses and institutes. These positive changes reflected both an awakened interest in buildings that expressed the democratic ideal, and a willingness of architects to put their tutelary skills to use "for the fulfillment of genuine individual and social needs."[41]

What style was most expressive of these new architectural impulses? Clearly nothing associated with the excrescences of the recent past. A "living" architecture, Parker declared, must be founded on "vital" principles, as was that of Greece and of the Middle Ages. It must not be imitative of those styles, but it must reflect their directness and sincerity.[42] And it must emerge from the past, from the strengths that lay in traditions of honest workmanship and scorn of the cheap and shoddy. Here, once more, the Arts and Crafts credo: *"Let us, then, do nothing different from what we have done before, until we feel it to be better than what we have done before."*[43] That italic injunction in *The Art of Building* signaled Parker and Unwin's determination not simply to respect the past but to understand it as a neglected source for what might be better done. Indeed, as they remarked, "as regards the common things of daily life, the standard of design is so debased that it would be almost impossible to bring out of the past . . . forms for these which would not surpass in beauty those now current among us."[44]

The past bespoke the countryside. Parker and Unwin, like so many late Victorian reformers, hymned the virtues of rural life. In an 1897 speech to the Sheffield Socialist Education League, Unwin celebrated, as Edward Carpenter might have, the simple pleasures of the ploughman's daily routine. Nowadays he might save two hours by plowing an acre by machine. But looked at in terms of "gladdening the hours of labour," "we see first the picture of the ploughman spending his twelve hours in the open air in the company of his horses, of the birds and the beautiful landscape round. He has a long day, truly, but he has a healthy job. He loves his team. . . . He is proud of his straight furrow and spends a happy day."[45] Despite this effusion, Unwin did not pretend that the life of the agricultural laborer was without violence and oppression. In his journal he once observed that the fourteenth century had been "about the best time for workers"; since then they had suffered "centuries of oppression."[46] Yet he joined the chorus that proclaimed the country a robust antidote to urban sickness.

He and Parker also admired the unifying influence that country villages worked on their inhabitants. We have already observed Unwin trapped in the paradox of his respect for the village, a social and economic institution whose hierarchical nature—squire at the top, road-member at the bottom—belied his socialist and democratic sympathies.[47] Yet because the harsh architectural manifestations of the industrial revolution—factory, mill, office, slum—evoked not only physical misery but also a class-divided society, Parker and Unwin were forced to look backward for inspiration. A village's inclusiveness—social and architectural—drew them into the countryside and the past, and to the cottage, the simple, honest home of laborers who, as myth had it, understood themselves connected to a community that acknowledged the value of their contribution to its well-being. That inclusiveness was expressed in village architecture. "The beautiful grouping of buildings and roofs, a grouping which has come so inevitably that it seems as if it would be somewhat difficult . . . to utterly spoil it. Certainly where many buildings of various characters and size are gathered together, as in a village, a picturesqueness of grouping is rarely absent, even when the individual buildings have in themselves no special beauty."[48]

The softness of that scene, as painted in *The Art of Building,* the blending of "the grouping" into surrounding fields and woods, had enormous appeal to these reforming architects. In contrast, "the new strikes a note of defiance with surrounding nature." Unwin's democracy was grounded in Carpenter's insistence on man's rootedness in nature. The harmony of individual with nature remained central to Parker and Unwin's definition of democracy, and to their understanding of how democracy could be expressed architecturally. "Does not the old building seem almost to grow out of the ground in which it stands?" they asked.[49] And did not the old, in that sense, perforce become metaphor for the new?

In designing houses, Parker and Unwin kept two principles before them: the first, that whether planned for rich or for poor their houses would resemble each other in the quality of their designs; the second, that their houses would honestly reflect the human needs of those who were to live within them. A house did not serve its purpose if it failed to encourage healthy lives. Hence they must flood those lives with sunshine. "Every house should at least get some sunshine into the room in which the family will live during the daytime," Unwin wrote. Sunshine must cease to be regarded as merely desirable; "it must be insisted upon as an absolute essential, second only to air space."[50] Parker, in his series for *The Craftsman,* observed that laboratories used to cultivate germs were designed with a northern exposure. "Germs die in the sunlight. If you wish to cultivate a disease you must first have a room facing north in which to do it."[51] The object was not merely to bring sunshine into the house, it was as well to encourage those who lived inside to walk outside. Parker wrote that the incorporation into house design of loggias, porches, balconies—even the humble stoop—meant that fortunately "there is often really no clear line of demarcation between being in the house or in the garden."[52] Unwin was as enthusiastic about the therapeutic effects of gardening as was George Cadbury. He spoke of its educational value in his 1897 speech to the Sheffield Socialists. Gardeners receive from their hobby, he declared, "more education than from many books. All sorts of information . . . which would be so much disconnected matter . . . has a definite place and relation to them through it."[53]

The architects' house designs for the village of New Earswick, founded in 1902 by Joseph Rowntree, another Quaker chocolate manufacturer, afforded them their first opportunity to give their ideas expression in a major project. The essence of the experiment, as articulated in the deed establishing the village trust, was the "provision of a better house, and with it a garden in which the worker can enjoy a fuller and freer life."[54] Dwellings were arranged so as to catch maximum sunlight, even though this meant eliminating back extensions and placing coal bins and larders toward the street and living rooms at the rear, a feature that was not universally welcomed by householders. Some houses had parlors, others one living room measuring a generous twenty feet by twelve and including a bay window. Over tenants' objections, Parker and Unwin placed bathrooms upstairs rather than in sculleries, rightly surmising that this innovation would eventually find favor. Each house was provided with both a front and back garden, a total of 350 square yards having been deemed "the amount of land a man could easily and profitably work by spade cultivation in his leisure time."[55]

Had it been left to the architects, all houses would have been of the parlorless cottage type. Parker and Unwin did their best to promote domesticity by means of one large living room, in which meals were to be cooked and served, children entertained and instructed, and the common life of the family nurtured. Within the room, inglenooks and alcoves would provide the cosiness—a favorite word—so necessary to the household intimacy they were eager to promote. One experienced this "sense of cosiness" far more intensely within the recess of a larger space than in a separate, rectangular room, "be it no larger than a sentry box."[56]

Their affinity for the single, larger living room led Parker and Unwin into a prolonged and ultimately futile battle against the parlor, a room that other Arts and Crafts architects had also disparaged. Their position reflected their willingness to idealize the past and their determination to impose improving patterns upon the present. Parlors symbolized a foolish craving for bourgeois respectability and thus encouraged antidemocratic sentiments of class consciousness. A tiny front room, used no more than once or twice a week, robbed house-holders of desperately needed living space, often boxing them into airless kitchens facing dreary, sunless back alleys. "When mankind first took to living in houses these consisted of one room; perhaps the most important fact to be remembered in designing cottages is that the cottager still lives during the day-time in one room." Parker and Unwin claimed familiarity with how working-class families lived, and an understanding of their needs. "Except by a very careful study of the life which the space is to shelter," Unwin wrote, "it is not possible to design the house so as to properly fit and accommodate to that life."[57] Unwin had studied that life; but he paid little heed to the ingrained and deeply conservative attitudes that helped give it shape. Parlors, though perhaps irrational, nevertheless embodied in an important, tangible form a family's ability to afford something beyond the minimum. The ten-by-twelve room, with its four or five pieces of all-but-functionless furniture, might supply that family with a measure of psychic sustenance as important to its well-being as fresh air and sunshine.

Others argued, indeed, that a parlor served a positive symbolic purpose. The author of *The Country Life Book of Cottages,* published in 1913, defended it on the ground that it was a "symbol of a higher standard of living, and as such has some moral value. It provides a quiet place where elder children can do their home-lessons, a convenience which will be the more real as school age steadily increases."[58] Parker and Unwin eventually surrendered. By 1919, Unwin had yielded to the extent at any rate of acknowledging that "in order to meet the reasonable requirements of the average working-class family, a cottage should contain three bedrooms, a living room, parlour, scullery, bathroom, W.C. and coal stove."[59]

Insistent on the architect's role as designer of an entire household environ-ment, Parker and Unwin encouraged their clients to build in furniture that reflected and enhanced the interior character of the house. They wrote of the importance of "reposefulness"—next to "cosiness" the quality most impor-tant in encouraging domestic contentedness. "If this test of reposefulness is *the* test," they remarked tartly in *The Art of Building,* "the average farm house kitchen has an artistic value far beyond that of ninety-nine of every hundred drawing rooms in the country."[60] By way of contrast, this excerpt from the *Daily Mirror's* 1913 supplement, *The Perfect Home and How to Fur-nish It:* "In the old days . . . the walls were either covered with tapestry, panelled with oak or left plain with a plaster finish. . . . The decorator of today, however, has far greater opportunities at his disposal. Oak panelling, tapestry or plaster walls can be imitated in wall-paper suitable for the purposes where cost has to be considered. Shades of green, brown, red, etc., on plain grounds, as well as imitations of canvas and leather, are a few of the schemes that can be selected for the purpose."[61] The Arts and Crafts world of Parker and Unwin was one in which "it is better to have no ornament at all unless we can have a really good ornament . . . something which it has given pleasure to the worker to produce"—a world of ideals as unrelated to those of the *Mirror*'s "perfection" as was solid oak to imitation canvas.[62] The repetitive insistence of the architects' aesthetic campaigns must be read against the philistine insensitivity of their adversaries.

If the architect's task was to use planning and design to teach his clients a way to live a finer life, it was the responsibility of the completed house to continue that process. "The influence which our common every-day surroundings have upon our characters, our conceptions, our habits of thought and conduct are often very much under-rated," Parker declared in 1895. "We do not realise the power they have of either aiding or hindering the development in us of the best or worst of which we were capable."[63] The battle of the parlor was really a battle on behalf of the development of what was best. Rid the house of its parlor, Parker wrote, only if it is to be replaced by something that will express a "truer refinement in the lives of the working man and his family, . . . some part of real life exchanged for the attempt to affect supposed symbols of gentility." Indeed, he added, unless that change did occur, better to retain the parlor, which perhaps represented a "groping after something better."[64]

In spite of this concession, the two architects never ceased to believe in the morally therapeutic benefit of that one large room, and they continued to design it, whenever they could, into houses for middle-class as well as working-class clients. With inglenooks for warmth and cosiness, with bay windows to catch winter light and summer breezes, it became for them an almost enchanted place where family members might experience a constant lift of spirits. Describing a "laborer's cottage," in *The Art of Building*, they wrote of a "space for a table for meals, and a few shelves for books," then suggested that the family might find a "corner for a piano or desk." Rather than a parlor, the house should contain a study, or more probably a bedroom large enough so that a "portion of it could be made cosy for such a purpose."[65]

Parker and Unwin were fantasizing for the worker and his family the sort of life that they themselves were living at that time, the simple, harmoniously improving life, patterned on Carpenter's example, that they believed best suited the citizens of a modern democracy. We catch a glimpse of it in a memoir written years later by Katherine Bruce Glasier, a close friend.

> It is difficult . . . to even attempt to estimate the inspiration that came in those early days from watching the Raymond Unwins translate into every detail of their daily life and of their simple five-room home . . . their sincere belief in their fellow-workers' right not only to work and wage but to interest and even joy in the doing of that work and assuredly to beauty in their surroundings. . . . The warm curtains at the window, blankets on the bed, cushion coverings and even the hostess's frock and little son's tunic were all made from Ruskin flannel. . . . The joy of embroidering the strong hand-made fabrics . . . working at it of an evening while one or another played or sang or read aloud from some worth-while writer—these became living experiences that could never be gainsayed.[66]

This was the life Unwin and Parker wanted for everyone, the promise of a socialist democracy. And it was a life they stoutly advocated in houses designed not just to shelter but to promote a particular kind of life. Realizing the power of everyday surroundings, Parker and Unwin determined to do all they could, by means of the houses they built, to teach men, women, and children what "best" and "worst" meant, so that they might better strive for the former and shun the latter.

As the two architects expanded their practice they found themselves increasingly engaged in the business of town planning. Unwin, in particular, devoted considerable time to the subject, not only as an active planner but as a writer and a lecturer. His appointment in 1914 as chief town planning inspector to the Local Government Board was a logical extension of pioneering work he had undertaken and innovative principles he had championed before the outbreak of World War I. Though he and Parker are more often remembered for their work at Letchworth and Hampstead, they were responsible for the layout of New Earswick, and for estates near Ealing, Leicester, and Cardiff, and in Glamorgan. They served, as well, as consultants or advisers for the Ruislip Manor estate outside London and for similar co-partnership developments in Manchester and Liverpool. In addition to numerous articles on various aspects of town and suburban planning, Unwin published in 1909 a widely noticed book on the subject, *Town Planning in Practice*, and a pamphlet, sponsored by the Garden Cities and Town Planning Association in 1912, *Nothing Gained by Overcrowding!*[67]

As Unwin's planning concepts matured, he was increasingly drawn to the example of the medieval city, whose walls gave it the sharp definition that its modern counterpart lacked. He deplored the fringe of "ragged edges and waste areas" that belted so many towns. And he urged the development of "some more comely girdle; . . . belts of park land, meadow, wood or orchard . . . might be used with good effect."[68] Unwin's fondness for the medieval urban silhouette reflected his more general admiration for the traditional. He preferred the "local colour and the local beauty that have been characteristic of our towns" to the introduction of schemes imposing an unnatural order that ignored not only site contours but also the history and associations of particular places.[69] Though he never directly disparaged the "city beautiful" ideal, though he insisted that to plan a community with nothing but curved roads was as foolish as to plan one with nothing but parallels and perpendiculars, and though in his designs for Letchworth and Hampstead he took his own advice in that regard, Unwin preferred to let nature shape his plans rather than to impose his plans on nature. "To try and carry through some symmetrical plan at the expense of upsetting the whole of the properties and destroying all the traditions and sentiments attaching to these properties," he wrote in *Town Planning in Practice*, "would be to give our plan a degree of artificiality which in the result would probably vastly outweigh any advantage which it might gain from a more complete symmetry."[70]

What Unwin urged planners to avoid was the mindless repetition of housing patterns and street grids that resulted in nothing more than vast, monotonous tracts, lifeless because they imparted no sense that they were anything more than the sum of countless disconnected bits and pieces of urban landscape. "Nothing more absurd or more regardless of the essential conditions" of city life could be imagined, he had written in his 1902 Fabian tract *Cottage Plans and Common Sense*, than the present custom "to draw out a cottage plan that will come within a certain space and then repeat it unaltered in street after street, heedless of whether it faces north, south, east or west."[71]

Unwin campaigned for variation that would produce what he liked to call "street pictures." Such a picture should encourage those who walked within it to understand themselves as part of the landscape, to enjoy a soul-satisfying urban adventure in which they, the buildings that surrounded them, and the street itself as it led them forward fused into a pleasing, occasionally uplifting, whole experience. Accomplishing this called for a willingness to consider each streetscape afresh, to compose "pictures" appropriate to particular terrain and location. Such composition in turn required flexible building and planning codes. Unwin of course welcomed regulations that limited the number of houses per acre, as the exhortatory title of his pamphlet, *Nothing Gained by*

Overcrowding! makes clear. Yet he chafed at the unwillingness of legislators and bureaucrats to understand that without thoughtful exceptions to their well-meant rules, urban planners would be unable to provide the "pictures" that would breathe life into an otherwise deadened, if sanitary, environment. While, for example, a minimum general road width was necessary for the health and comfort of residents, he observed in a speech in 1910, "from an architectural point of view it is most desirable that the regulations securing this should be so formed as to allow buildings here and there to be brought nearer together than the general building line, to enable some framing or closing of the street view to be secured, and thus prevent the indefinite prolongation of rows of houses too far apart in proportion to their height to produce good street pictures."[72]

Those pictures would be enhanced as well by an intelligent use of building materials. Cities built in past times, before railways facilitated the cheap transportation of stock from one part of the country to another, benefited visually from the fact that construction was limited to local stone, tile, and the like. "The ease with which building materials can be transmitted today does not of itself justify the indiscriminate use of incongruous and inharmonious materials in juxtaposition with one another."[73] Unwin praised the harmonies unconsciously achieved both by the use of common materials and by the organic placement of buildings and tracing of streets and squares. In comparing the older with the newer part of European cities, he wrote, "one realizes that . . . it is the unity of effect and harmony between the parts [within the medieval quarters] that makes them . . . so pleasing, whereas in the newer part of the town, it is the differences between the buildings which are so noticeable, and which destroy all unity of effect."[74]

Unwin derived these ideas in part from the work of the Viennese planner Camillo Sitte, whose respect for the informal nature of medieval townscapes was already beginning to strike young modernists as old-fashioned. "The demonstrations of Sitte were based on the past," Le Corbusier recalled years later. "Indeed, they *were* the past, the rather insignificant flower by the wayside."[75] Which is perhaps why those demonstrations appealed to Unwin. Sitte's emphasis on the correlation of individual buildings to a coherent, humanely scaled whole struck a response in him that confirmed his own sense of how an urban environment could tangibly affect the way people experienced city life.[76] Parker and Unwin believed that once town dwellers grew conscious of themselves as an organic part of the "picture" they inhabited, they would more clearly understand the need to move beyond themselves into the genuine community that their city must become.

At New Earswick they strove to put their town planning principles into practice. The layout of the village followed the River Foss, which bounded the estate on the east and all but dictated the natural configurations that the architects themselves favored. Short terraces of houses were placed at various angles to roads that were for the most part gently curving; narrow carriage-ways and footpaths led off main thoroughfares into grassy plots behind the houses. Because of their determination to provide ample space for gardening, Parker and Unwin, in consultation with the Rowntrees, set a limit of ten houses per acre. Since fewer than two hundred houses were built at New Earswick before the war, low density inhibited to a degree their ability to create those "pictures" they set such store by. Instead, they relied on com-mon materials—whitewashed stucco, clapboards, and red tile roofs—to cre-ate the harmony that they hoped would help promote community. To that same end, they set aside land for a village green, which was eventually sur-rounded by shops, schools, and a church. "The aim . . . has always been not merely to build houses and schools," the chairman of the Rowntree Village Trust declared in a retrospective volume in 1954, "but far more important, to build a community."[77] Certainly that was the architects' intention as well, as their plans for New Earswick suggest.

When planning towns, as opposed to villages, Parker and Unwin believed that community could be encouraged by the construction of miniature villages within a larger urban context. Unwin wrote in *Town Planning in Practice* of the important role that "place" might play in promoting connections outward from individual homes.[78] "Place" meant an enclosed space, something closely akin in shape and feeling to the Oxford or Cambridge quadrangle. Parker and Unwin first recommended this design in *The Art of Building*. They continued to urge its adoption, and they experimented with variants at New Earswick, Letchworth, and Hampstead. They believed it an economical solution to the problem of housing for the working-class, permitting as many as twenty to thirty dwellings per acre, while at the same time providing sunny courtyards and surrounding fields and gardens for tenants: "undoubtedly the most satis-factory arrangement for numbers of such tenements where space is limited," Unwin proclaimed in *Cottage Plans and Common Sense*.[79] Parker was still enthusing ten years later in his series for *The Craftsman:* "I would have swings and sandpits and similar delights in the center of such quadrangles. There might always be trees and grass and flowers as a substitute for the macadamized expanse of the streets."[80]

Within these quadrangles, families would come to understand the virtues of cooperation through the shared use of common facilities: laundries, bath houses, bakeries, and kitchens. "Instead of thirty or forty housewives preparing thirty or forty little scrap dinners, heating a like number of ovens, boiling thrice the number of pans and cleaning them all up again, two or three of them retained as cooks by the little settlement would do the whole, and could give better and cheaper meals into the bargain."[81] At the center of these settlements, Parker and Unwin hoped to see common rooms, to which families might repair after work to enjoy each other's company and engage in a variety of high-minded pursuits. They imagined a room "in which a fire might always be burning in the evening, where comfort for social intercourse, for reading or writing could always be found. Such a room could be used also for music and general recreation, and might add much colour to the lives of all those who frequented it." These rooms were to express what Unwin once declared a city must strive to become: "A place where men and women live a common life for a noble end."[82]

Common rooms were a clear and important statement, as well, of how Parker and Unwin understood the word "community." These were not town meeting rooms. They were not, that is, places where people were expected to come together to understand or practice their civic duties and responsibilities. Although Parker and Unwin were committed democrats, they devoted little time to considering how their buildings might directly promote democratic participation in community affairs. The "common life" they envisioned was one concerned with the dissemination of a common culture. The common room was to be a place where individuals came together to share and appreciate that culture. (At New Earswick it became a "folk hall.") It would contain "deep recesses or ingles with low ceilings, places which by the contrast of their special cosiness should attract people to sit there. If there could be a little gallery for the musicians, a deep balcony overlooking the street or garden for smokers, these would prove great attractions for which everyone would gladly dispense with the adornments usually thought necessary for public rooms."[83] The assumption that everyone would dispense with typical adornments shows the degree to which Parker and Unwin designed for people not as they were but as they wanted them to be, and as they hoped their buildings would make them: individual best selves come together into a community of the high-minded and plain-living.

It was a worthy enough vision. Yet it betrayed a naive faith in the possibility of human change, and in the willingness of people to change at the behest of others. For it argued that working-class men and women, for whom these quadrangles and common rooms were designed, must shed the habits and assumptions of several generations so as to enter a kingdom of noble ends not of their own devising. They were being asked to forsake the shibboleth that "keeping oneself to oneself" was the surest way of establishing respectability of character. They were to be denied the institutions that over the years they had grown to rely on as a way of establishing a community as *they* understood it: shops, pubs, street life—the warp and woof of the urban working-class neighborhood. Sports were deemed unrewarding, at least when compared with gardening. "Will anyone pretend," Unwin asked in his speech on the way to gladden life's hours, "that this is the end of life: to devote one's interest almost entirely to the chances of a game, to have one's head filled with batting averages and cup ties? Truly if we can do no better than this with our spare time, we had better not seek to increase it vastly."[84]

Without condescending to Parker and Unwin's vision, or their scheme for its implementation, one must ponder the thinking that produced it. Unwin on more than one occasion wrote of the need to include sociologists in discussions about the planning of future towns.[85] To what end? Were they to supply material about life as it was being lived—the kind of information that appeared with increasing frequency in a variety of urban surveys before World War I? Or were they to offer suggestions about the manner in which that life might be changed? Perhaps both. But there is no evidence that Parker and Unwin paid much attention in the period before the war to the implications of studies such as Seebohm Rowntree's examination of poverty in York, at least insofar as that work might have provided them with an understanding of the social and cultural world of those for whom they were designing. Did Unwin remember his conversations with workers and their families at Chesterfield? If he did, what had been the nature of those conversations? How much had he tried to discover about the way they lived while he was speaking about the way that they—and he along with them—might want to live? Had he come to understand the central role of shops and pubs in the life of working-class neighborhoods? If so, had he viewed them as in some way subversive, and had he then determined to substitute for them centers of a more uplifting kind?

Parker and Unwin's communal quadrangles would not, in fact, produce the sort of society they hoped to see established, one of diminished class separation. If anything they would further isolate the classes from each other, since no suggestion is made as to how the groupings of thirty to forty families were to be integrated into the unified community of the whole town, that goal to which the two architects were so committed. What the quadrangles would facilitate, however, was the sort of improvement from above that Parker and Unwin, as both utopians and late Victorian social reformers, believed necessary to their country's safe passage by way of a reassuringly English past to an equally English future.

Chapter 5 Letchworth:
Best Laid Plans

"The truth must be told," the *Daily News* confessed in its account of the opening ceremonies at Letchworth in October 1903. "Even in Garden City yesterday, the rain fell pitilessly. But it fell from a clean sky, and far from smudging everything, polished prettily the green leaves, and wrapped distant trees in fairy mist." George Cadbury's newspaper could be counted on to provide an uplifting gloss on an occasion that, however heartening to the spirit, nonetheless tested the mettle of its organizers and supporters. "How it did rain," one of the latter recalled fifty years later. "And how thick everyone was covered in mud."[1] Lord Grey, who had dignified the first Garden City Association conference at Bournville with his presence, was once more on hand, to bestow his blessings on what he left no doubt was a sound, and soundly conservative, enterprise.

No one who realizes that physique and character are the products of environment as well as heredity, can fail to regard the suburban excrescences of our smoke-enveloped and air-exhausted towns with feelings short of positive consternation. Streets upon streets of sunless slums with nothing to relieve their squalid and depressing monotony—little provision for recreation beyond that which is supplied by low music halls and still lower Public Houses; boys turned out of school at fourteen years of age, and no organized influence to mould them into honest citizenship at an age at which their characters are most impressionable.[2]

Letchworth continued to be perceived by its founders, and promoted by them to the public, in these terms: as an engine for social amelioration and national regeneration, and as a response to those fears about Britain's future that lay heavy upon the consciousness of the nation's social reformers. The company's original prospectus sounded the same note. "In the face of physical degeneration, the existence of which in our great towns is incontrovertible, imperialism abroad and progress at home seem alike an empty mockery." The directors proceeded to declare themselves confident, however, that their undertaking would promote the "sound physical development" without which the country was doomed. Three years later, in the first issue of the Garden City Association's journal, the link between the Letchworth experiment and the promise of social tranquility, implied in Lord Grey's remarks, received explicit confirmation. "The elevation of labour will come only as a result of following out this conception, and not as a result of those things which increase the conflict between capital and labour."[3]

Letchworth was constructed on a patchwork of farms near the town of Hitchin, in Hertfordshire, approximately thirty miles north of London on the Great Northern railway line. Company directors had considered three other sites, in Essex, Staffordshire, and Nottinghamshire, all further from London and therefore deemed less desirable. The choice surprised others, who were concerned that thirty miles was not distance enough to quarantine the infant city from London's infections. George Cadbury's nephew William wrote Ebenezer Howard to say that he had imagined the scheme to be directed toward "reviving industry in the purely agricultural and neglected parts of England," though expressing his understanding of the need to be close to a source of labor. Howard had, in fact, envisioned a community no further than thirty or forty miles from London, during discussions with the Land Nationalisation Society in the 1890s about establishing a garden city. In a letter to Alfred Harmsworth at the time of the Letchworth land purchase, he explained that the site would facilitate the attraction of London businesses and residents, and that—as importantly—"because near this huge metropolis, [the] City would command a very large amount of public attention."[4]

Indeed it did, most of it favorable, some of it not. Once the site was chosen the *Builder* expressed grave doubts. "It may well be that with a good train service an agreeable and not expensive collection of habitations for City clerks and others may be established. . . . It is, however, a different matter to unite a business centre to a rural suburb in one place."[5] Others expressed surprise that the area purchased was no more than about thirty-eight hundred acres, far less than the six thousand that Howard had stipulated in his book. Howard acknowledged the discrepancy in his letter to Harmsworth, arguing that to secure a larger tract near London for a reasonable price had proved impossible. The company paid a sum that Howard declared "by no means high"—approximately £40 per acre. The trick had been to negotiate with the fifteen owners simultaneously and in secret so as not to drive the price higher.

It came as no surprise that the tenants on the purchased farms were unenthusiastic about a scheme that meant immediate disruption and eventual removal for them, despite an agreement with the company that no more than 10 percent of their land would be developed in any year. Nor were the inhabitants of Hitchin pleased with the prospect before them. An adjacent city eventually numbering thirty thousand, whether of the garden variety or not, promised just those unpleasant ills that Letchworth's promoters were hoping to cure. "An Old Inhabitant," writing to the *Daily Graphic,* expressed a view that must have upset those who saw garden cities as invigorating environmental assets. "You do not take into account that to nearly all the inhabitants of Hitchin it comes as a terrible blow—to have some of the 'crush and pressure of modern city life,' with all its diseases and wickedness, put down almost in our midst." "Inhabitant" pronounced a rural curse on the whole enterprise: "May your schemes find many difficulties, and Hitchin remain as of yore—'Sleepy Hollow.'"[6]

Letchworth's early history suggests that more than one disgruntled Hitchinite was sending imprecations over the fields toward the fledgling city. Probably the thorniest issue facing the company's directors at the outset was the matter of leases. Here again, as in his disagreement with Neville about how shares were to be advertised and sold, Howard's unapologetically public-spirited vision clashed with the board's willingness to sacrifice even a modified form of utopianism to the immediate matter of pounds, shillings, and pence. Because the company was undercapitalized, its directors were all but desperate to lease properties as quickly as possible, having wholeheartedly rejected Lever's proposal to turn their backs on Howard and dispose of the land in freehold parcels. The nature of the leases was thus of pressing importance. Could they be made attractive to tenants and still honor the principle of community ownership?

The company's prospectus had declared once again its determination to ensure the "retention by the community of the Garden City of the large anticipated increase in the value of the estate caused by its conversion from country to town."[7] Howard proposed to implement this objective in the form of 999-year leases, with tenants responsible for both rent and what he called an "improvement rate." The former would be used to pay interest on the purchase price of the land and to reduce its capital indebtedness; the latter—to be reassessed every five years—would cover the cost of urban services and would reflect the increased value of the land, thus preserving the "unearned increment" for common use. Eventually, once the company's debts were settled, rent payments would cease, tenants remaining responsible only for their continually reevaluated improvement rate.

The scheme, while attractive in its fidelity to Howard's ideals, was at once deemed impractical by those charged with marketing Letchworth to both businesses and householders. In an attempt to compromise, the board did offer perpetual leases with ten-year revisionary periods, and with the provision that increases, if necessary, would be settled by impartial arbitrators. A few such leases were in fact taken up. But they did not work to the immediate advantage of the company, since tenants, knowing that their rents would eventually rise, insisted on a lower initial rate at a time when the directors needed all the cash they could extract from leaseholders. The major difficulty lay, however, with the mortgage companies to whom the leaseholders turned for money to build their houses, who found the scheme unorthodox and hence unappealing. As one of the company's directors, Aneurin Williams, observed in an article on the matter in 1913, "solicitors and mortgagees, being quite uninterested probably in the Garden City idea, intimated that the form of lease was uncouth, that they could not in the least foresee what might happen to their security under it, and in short that they would not touch it."[8]

As a consequence, all attempts to introduce radical changes in leasehold arrangements were abandoned. Regular 99-year leases were offered to householders. In some cases, factory owners insisted on 999-year agreements at a fixed rent and were granted them. In his essay recounting these negotiations, Williams put the best face he could on the matter. He argued that as leasing continued, the rents for more recently acquired land were higher than those charged the initial settlers. "Their coming, and especially the coming of manufacturers, caused a rise in the value of surrounding plots, and when these were let subsequently, the rise went into the public coffer." As further plots were sold, the value of still others would rise in turn, "and thus more of the unearned increment is reaped for the Letchworth public." Williams pointed out as well that the sole landlord, to whom properties would ultimately revert, was the company, a "trustee for the public, not an individual . . . seeking to make his own income as large as possible."[9] Yet nothing could conceal the fact that Howard's dream had been tailored to fit immediate if understandable needs. The compromise—if it can indeed be called even that—"enabled us to get to work," Williams observed. "The whole possibility of making a Garden City depended upon getting manufacturers, and if a man was willing to come with a 999 years' lease, and not willing with a 99 years' lease, then . . . it would not have been in the interest of Garden City to turn him away."[10] Howard accepted defeat with apparent equanimity. "In my book I set forth an ideal to be attained," he wrote less than a year after the groundbreaking ceremonies. "In our practical scheme we have to advance gradually from the known to the unknown."[11]

Further difficulties arose over the leasing and management of the agricultural lands. Howard had been concerned from the start to revive the quality of life on the land; that had been as important a goal as any in his scheme to invent and market his "town-country magnet." The company hoped to implement the goal by encouraging smallhold farming. To this end it provided manure, seeds, and a variety of agricultural implements, and hired out horses and carts on demand. Yet the land proved unsuitable for intensive market-gardening. Farmers competed at a disadvantage with their counterparts in nearby Bedfordshire, where the soil was richer. When the company, in consequence, ceased to press ahead with plans for further division of agricultural land into small leaseholds, critics accused it of betraying another of its initial goals. In 1907, Thomas Adams found himself in a public argument with Howard, in this instance willing to toe the company line. Adams reminded Howard, however, that the garden city had been perceived as a solution to the problem of rural depopulation. "To some of us, that aspect of the problem was as important as that of moving industries out of large towns." Adams complained that a laissez-faire attitude toward the development of Letchworth's greenbelt was inhibiting the smallholdings experiment, by acquiescing in the continuing division of land into unsuitably large tracts. Employing the language of zealous idealism, Adams urged the company to keep faith with itself. "What England wants to-day is not more experience but more faith and stimulus to act on the impulse of what is right and just. All we ask of 'Garden City' is to help lead the way."[12]

The problem was, of course, that Letchworth's founders were struggling to realize two things at once: a town and a vision. Policy changes designed to facilitate the former thus became betrayals of the latter. In 1906, when ground rents on newly opened land were raised well beyond those of earlier developments, angry letter writers denounced the policy as counter to the ideals that had inspired the city's foundation. An irate resident complained that the "movement is in danger of losing its humanitarian and grave idealistic spirit, and getting in return a hard, grasping commercialism. The project must be made to pay, we recognize, but we are in grave doubt as to whether the best way to make it pay is to strip it of its wholesome sentiment and to make rent so prohibitive that people will not come, and that the place will be impossible for the very persons it was originally designed to benefit. In view of the present policy the Garden City Evangel is beginning for some of us to sound rather hollow."[13] Pioneer residents of Letchworth grew accustomed to addressing each other, and the company, in impassioned language of that sort. They had come to Hertfordshire with the Evangel ringing in their ears. They had not imagined that the company's directors, to whose uncertain and inexperienced hands they had entrusted their dream, would sell them short. Yet those directors that year faced these dauntingly unpleasant facts: the capital they had raised, £148,000, did not match the purchase price of the land (£155,000), or the £200,000 already invested in the city's infrastructure. For the directors, the Evangel's call may often have sounded in those early years far more like a death knell.

Shortcomings and compromises did not in the end inhibit Letchworth's slow but steady growth. By 1914 the town had a population of nine thousand, living and working in almost two thousand buildings—over half of them built by co-partnership societies.[14] C. B. Purdom, Letchworth's dedicated advocate and chronicler, believed that the company's general inexperience and its directors' inattention to detail had prevented faster growth. Writing in 1925, Purdom observed that at a certain point it appeared to be the directors' intention to "sit down, collect the revenue and allow the town to grow by its own impetus." Whatever success the enterprise enjoyed came about, in Purdom's opinion, "by virtue of its own inherent good qualities."[15]

Though there is considerable truth in that analysis—certainly with regard to the directors' lack of time and knowledge, the fact remains that the company did labor hard to breathe continuing life into its scheme, and to encourage others to share the excitement that had fueled its own initial enthusiasm. Company staff excelled at public relations. Until his resignation as secretary of the Garden City Association in 1906, Thomas Adams unceasingly promoted the new city to the press. In a typical standard letter, he would provide an editor with a "few facts respecting the progress being made on the Garden City Estate at Letchworth," along with an already written article and an offer of the loan of a "considerable number of half-tone blocks of various sizes" to be used as accompanying illustrations. A 1906 press tour of industrial sites produced a flood of articles in both London and provincial papers, enough to fill eight large pages of the company's press cuttings book. In addition, various organizations were welcomed on tours, which included lunch or tea and a brief speech. Town councillors, adult education classes, YMCAs, the British Association, a parliamentary delegation: such were the inquisitive pilgrims who traveled from London and elsewhere in a typical month to see for themselves.[16]

Those unable to make the journey could satisfy their curiosity by reading one or more of the guides and picture books that the company published, among them *News and Views of Garden City; One Hundred Photograph Views of Letchworth; Letchworth Garden City in Pictures; Garden City in the Making.* Without question, the work paid off: prospective homeowners returned to build, businessmen to relocate. Doubters became converts. Among the latter was the *Builder,* which had expressed a no-nonsense skepticism from the beginning of the venture, weighing in periodically with short comments designed to debunk the vision and to chronicle its imperfect realization. And yet by 1913 it too had come around. Writing of a recent school opening at Letchworth, its reporter observed that any who had attended as well the initial groundbreaking ceremony in 1903 "must have been impressed by the growth of the town and by the unmistakable signs of its prosperity, Letchworth having grown from a few half-completed residences to a place of considerable importance, . . . so laid out that there is every reason to believe that this, the First Garden City, is likely to become all that its founders desired."[17]

To win the *Builder* to its side was a considerable achievement for the company. It was of little consequence, however, when compared with its success in persuading manufacturers to relocate to Letchworth. In his apologia for long-term leases, Aneurin Williams had written that "the whole possibility of making a Garden City depended on getting manufacturers." Understanding this, the company bombarded businesses with material that detailed the advantages of a move to Letchworth. A brochure, *London and the Manufacturer: Letchworth versus London,* provided "some telling comparisons." In London, a "very large firm of manufacturers" paid £1,740 per year in ground rent and rates. At Letchworth, the firm might lease a five-acre site adjoining the railway to accommodate its £10,000 factory buildings, and pay a mere £175.[18] Advertisements appeared in German, French, and American newspapers, according to a

1908 report in the *Manchester Evening News*, "showing the advantages which prospective migrant firms would derive from erecting and conducting factories [in Letchworth,] that new and thriving town." First Garden City staff devised various incentives to encourage domestic manufacturers to make the move, in one case arranging with a co-partnership building society to undertake construction when a company could not raise sufficient capital, in another—that of the Spirella corset firm—agreeing to allow factory construction outside the originally designated industrial zone, a concession that angered many residents.[19]

In his speech to the first Garden City Association Conference in 1901, Ebenezer Howard had catalogued the reasons why it would pay manufacturers to relocate in garden cities. His list became a litany for the company in the years that followed: mainline rail facilities; cheap land and utilities; low rates; and the pleasure and privilege of living and working in a salubrious garden city environment.[20] There were, of course, disadvantages—or at any rate risks. Capital for new buildings was required; skilled labor was scarce. And throughout the first decade of Letchworth's existence, a shortage of inexpensive housing, only gradually eased after 1910, meant that many families sought accommodation in nearby, overburdened Hitchin, and belied the notion of Letchworth as a workers' paradise on a par with Bournville and Port Sunlight. Yet despite these difficulties, by 1912 twenty-eight factories had established themselves at Letchworth, among them an engineering firm, a geyser manufacturer, a number of printing concerns—W. H. Smith, J. M. Dent, the Arden Press, and the Garden City Press—two motorcar manufacturers, the Country Gentleman's Seed Company, the Idris bottling plant (its chairman a company director), along with a variety of smaller woodworking, weaving, and pottery works. Those who made the move spoke enthusiastically of the change. One of the staff from W. H. Smith declared that "we do not feel that any place in England would have suited us so well, or given us such facilities as this place has given us." He reported his workers content. "They like the place, they do not want to go back to London, as we were told they would."[21]

All music to the ears of First Garden City Company, Ltd., whose directors constantly worried that the notion of garden cities was no more than a fad that would frighten away the businesses that Letchworth must attract. Aneurin Williams gave voice to this persistent fear in his report to the company's annual general meeting in 1913. "Some manufacturers," he warned, "seemed still to have the idea that Letchworth is a place of extreme ideas which it might be more cautious to avoid." Williams continued that there were at Letchworth many people who had formed "ideals . . . as to the future of our country." He acknowledged that without their vision there would have been no Letchworth. But he asked their forbearance, as their vision was tempered by reality: "They are apt to be disappointed and to make criticisms." But they must understand the risk they take when they indulge themselves in that fashion. "I do ask our friends to remember that there is always a danger—and I am not speaking now without warrant—lest prospective manufacturers should be frightened away from Letchworth. . . . We must remember that 'no manufacturers, no Letchworth' is an absolutely true statement of the case."[22] Williams was saying, simply, that he, his fellow directors, and, indeed, the citizens of Letchworth were together prisoners of a noble vision that they could only partially fulfill, and of a grim financial reality from which there was no escape. It is against that set of facts and circumstances that one must understand the work of Barry Parker and Raymond Unwin as they labored to bring Letchworth to life.

Parker and Unwin were awarded the contract to design Letchworth in February 1904. Their plan was judged the best of three, largely because of its respect for the contours and existing architectural features of the landscape. The partners' experience at New Earswick no doubt played a part as well in their success, particularly since the Rowntree family sponsored the Letchworth competition. The architects were familiar with the program that Howard had outlined in *Garden Cities of To-morrow*. "I remember well," Parker later reminisced, "how attracted to Howard I was and how completely sympathetic we were in our aims and views."[23] Perhaps because of their attachment to Howard, Parker and Unwin felt obliged to incorporate into their own plan for Letchworth some of the schematic suggestions that he had made in his book. Their proposal certainly displays a propensity for axes and boulevards that would appear to derive from Howard's diagrams, at first glance seeming to bear little relationship to the modest village layout of New Earswick, or to the principles that Parker and Unwin had articulated in *The Art of Building*. At the time of the competition, Unwin had yet to read Camillo Sitte, whose insistence on the charm of medieval urban randomness influenced Unwin's subsequent townscapes.

Closer attention to Parker and Unwin's plan, however, reveals a sensitivity to the particular nature of the site that was clearly absent from the schemes of the two other competitors. Unwin moved to the existing hamlet of Letchworth, at the edge of the site, in October 1903, soon after he and Parker were asked to submit a proposal. On daily tramps he familiarized himself with the contours and major geographical features of the landscape. He insisted that the Ickneild

Way, an ancient road to the north of the railway line, be incorporated into the plan. Nothing could have justified its obliteration, he wrote. "Its origin is lost in antiquity, but it seems to have been one of the most important highways of the country, before the advent of the Romans, so that its age must be counted in thousands of years."[24] Major axial roads were tied directly to existing historical landmarks—Broadway Boulevard, for example, linking the railway station with the spire of the old church in Letchworth village. Norton Common, part of the countryside north of the railway, remained as natural park land between the more densely settled southwestern quadrant and subsidiary neighborhoods to the north and east. Pix Brook, running north and south through the middle of the site, defined a boundary between the more formal blocks at the city's center and smaller quadrangles, reminiscent of those described in *The Art of Building,* toward the east. The plan called for streets of various widths, designed to conform to a particular function and to the terrain they transected. Parker and Unwin battled the company for variety, more costly than uniformity, which the architects understood as monotony. Unwin lectured Thomas Adams on that point less than a year after construction had begun: "In a new village of a few hundred houses, a definite type of street may be used throughout, without the monotony being felt, perhaps, but in a town of the size of the Garden City there will be a great sense of monotony if even two or three stereotyped street plans are kept to; there is ample occasion for very great variety, and such variety would add much to the charm of the place."[25]

Attempts to transpose Howard's circular scheme onto the landscape ran afoul of the railway line bisecting the estate. Because an industrial zone at the periphery of the city, as proposed by Howard, would have lacked transportation facilities, the planners located it to the east, in a clearly defined area unto itself. Unlike Bournville and Port Sunlight, where factory and village lay in symbiotic relation to each other, Letchworth would keep industry at arm's length, a reflection not only of Howard's original scheme but also, perhaps, of Parker and Unwin's Arts and Crafts mistrust of the factory system.

At the confluence of the city's major avenues, an open space at one of the city's highest points was designated the future town square. Unwin hoped to see a cluster of civic buildings arise there in due course. In a 1906 speech he talked of the "fine effect" that one or more tall buildings could have upon the towns-cape, when they were grouped in such a way as "to enhance each other's beauty." Several years later he wrote almost wistfully of the advantages of an enclosed *place,* as he called it, as opposed to the open square that continued to serve the city as its focal point. With Sitte no doubt in mind, he acknowledged that the present arrangement lacked the "sense of enclosure and cosiness which are attractive features of the medieval *place*."[26] Unwin's willingness to acquiesce in the open plan during the city's early years reflected the company's understandable reluctance to build a grand center before there were citizens to fill it. As a 1906 guidebook observed, "The erection of public buildings . . . must follow the building of the houses and the coming of a population, and cannot be expected to precede it."[27] A central shopping precinct would have to await the arrival of more people as well. Developers were not prepared to risk a first-rate retail district until they could expect a decent return on their investment.

At the start, one critic acknowledged, "no one would . . . have had the pluck to build such premises as will doubtless rise when the town has increased in population to a sufficient extent to justify men in speculating heavily in costly bricks and mortar and attractive shop facades."[28] In 1912, Unwin produced an imposing Georgian style design for the town square, containing both public buildings and churches, with shops at the periphery. Little of this was built until the 1920s. Even today the area fails to involve those who walk through it. There is little sense of that "enclosure and cosiness" that Unwin prized so highly. During the early years of Letchworth's development the town's citizens must have sensed this lack, and the degree to which the hole in the town's center inhibited their coming together into something like a community.

Parker and Unwin's scheme relied on smaller subdivisions within the city to encourage social interaction. In a letter to Howard in July 1903, Unwin was already pressing for "building in quadrangles." He mentions a pamphlet that he had enclosed, presumably his Fabian tract *Cottage Plans and Common Sense,* which set forth the concept.[29] Subsequently he and Parker incorporated schemes for a variety of semi-quadrangles and cul-de-sacs into their master plan. They realized them, in collaboration with other architects, in at least three subdivisions on the eastern edge of the city: Birds Hill, Rushby Mead, and Pixmore. Since the plan decreed no more than twelve houses to the acre, the very low density rate and spaces between the individual settlements, particularly during the early years, imparted what must have been an eerie sense of disconnectedness within what was intended to be a unified cityscape. Unwin saw these satellite hamlets as the *places* that Sitte had taught him to admire. In a discussion before a group of architects in 1909, he extolled the "use of *places* and centres, . . . often formed not only of individual *places* but of groups of medievally-inspired *places* which were, he thought, among the most charming features of many continental towns."[30] He had already acknowledged that at Letchworth, however, the distance between the *places* that he, Parker, and others had designed inhibited the expression of architectural commonality and hence of community. "Spaces in the garden city tend to be too large in proportion to the buildings, and we have much yet to learn as to the best treatment."[31]

In the subsidiary "villages" they designed, Parker and Unwin provided few if any shops, apparently ignoring the extent to which they might serve to draw people together. For the Pixmore estate, a tract of working-class housing, they did include an institute, tennis courts, and a bowling green, testimony to their determination, where possible, to provide workers and their families with amenities hitherto understood as privilege rather than right. But men, women, and children living within these clusters were encouraged by the way in which the closes and quadrangles were designed to focus their activities within them, just as the absence of a lively town center inhibited mingling with those who lived elsewhere in the city, as citizens of a community greater than the sum of its disconnected, individualized parts.

Parker and Unwin hoped that some sense of community might be achieved by means of aesthetic control, most notably by imposing rules governing the use of building materials. In a typed list of suggestions submitted to the company, Unwin insisted on "simple straightforward buildings, suitably designed for their respective purposes and honestly built of simple and harmonious materials." There were to be no "artificial attempts at the picturesque," nor any "useless ornamentation." In order to ensure "unity of effect," roofs were to be of local red tiles rather than of the cheaper blue or purple slate used elsewhere in England, and bricks whitewashed or stuccoed if they were of an inharmonious color.[32] A seventy-one-page booklet, issued by the company in 1906, contained 130 detailed regulations, an attempt to ensure that whatever was built at Letchworth would be of sound construction as well as of aesthetically unified design.

Parker and Unwin were retained as consulting architects by First Garden City, Ltd., following the acceptance of their town plan; their office passed on all architectural proposals submitted to the company for approval. The battle to maintain standards was constant and meticulous. In one instance, Unwin fought with Adams over the construction of cheap sheds on smallholders' farms at the edge of the city. Adams, in an uncharacteristic attempt to win the battle on aesthetic grounds, wrote that in fact the "busy appearance" that outbuildings imparted to the rural landscape—even when roofed with felt—added to its charm. Unwin was not impressed. Unless a strict control was imposed, "we shall soon make our building land look so messy, if we allow all sorts of sheds immediately adjacent to it, that we shall frighten away all our best tenants."[33]

The company's directors, anxious to avert financial disaster, were unwilling to allow aesthetic authoritarianism precedence over fiscal responsibility. C. B. Purdom, in his review of Letchworth's first decade, scorned their attitude and conduct. "The officials have gloried in being practical, commercial, unartistic. They have reckoned it a virtue in themselves that they had no taste."[34] Purdom exaggerated company philistinism. The issue, as the directors saw it, was simple survival. As one reviewer of Purdom's book correctly observed, the attempt to maintain strict control was by no means entirely unsuccessful. To the extent that it failed, it did so "because those who desired to build houses saw that they could force the hands of those in authority and took advantage of it, knowing that the financial resources of Letchworth made it difficult to refuse the letting of a single plot."[35]

Beyond the matter of the company's financial exigency lay the equally important issue of building costs. Parker and Unwin's fierce desire for unity of design often stood opposed to their equally unequivocal determination to provide workers affordable housing. After he had left Letchworth, Thomas Adams took a characteristic shot at Unwin in a speech to its men's club, arguing that "it was possible to provide a well built cottage with slated roof at less cost than the tiled one, although he might be laying himself open to the charge of inartistic taste." He noted as well that the maximum of twelve houses to the acre, because it drove up costs, "was bound to place some burden on the poor," a remark greeted by a round of "hear, hears."[36]

A more thoughtful response to the issue of architectural control came in 1910 from W. H. Gaunt, by that time the company's general manager. Some considered him no better than a hatchet man, raising rents and debasing standards in pursuit of a healthier balance sheet. In response to an open letter in the city's monthly magazine signed by "Certain Members of the Arts Club," Gaunt challenged their insistence on a higher standard of architectural control. People, he argued, had come to live in Letchworth for a variety of reasons: for their health, to earn a decent living. "To suggest that this town can be built up in its fullest sense if we discourage those who do not realise the paramount importance of taste in architecture," Gaunt continued, "indicates a limited grasp of why Garden City ever came into being." Nothing in Howard's book, nor in the company's articles of association, suggested that architecture must assume the precedence that the Arts Club members appeared eager to assign it. "This is a residential and industrial housing scheme, a solution of the land question, a remedy for urban overcrowding and rural depopulation, to be organised on an economic basis rather than as a rich firm's toy or luxury"—an obvious swipe at Cadbury, Lever, and Rowntree. Letchworth was intended as a "better town" in all these respects, and not simply in terms of aesthetic distinction. To the extent to which architectural control contributed to the realization of the city's overall goals, it was helpful. "To the extent to which it is carried so far as to discourage enterprise and merit in other directions it will be a hindrance."[37]

Gaunt's was a reasonable enough position. Yet in its determination to understand architectural integrity as no more than ancillary to the purposes of the city, it ignored the basis of Parker and Unwin's belief in the ability of an environment to make people better, and hence denied the ultimate purpose of the Letchworth experiment as they understood it. A year before Gaunt's response, another Letchworth architect, H. C. Lander, had written in *The City* of the manner in which exposure to nothing less than the best in architecture would ultimately improve the way in which men and women lived their lives. Imposed standards would create an "enlightened public sentiment." People would grow "as much ashamed of living in ugly houses as they are of wearing dirty linen." In time tenants living in shoddy houses "would slink home after dark in order to avoid being associated with an ostentatious gim-crack 'villa.'" And ultimately their understanding of what was best architecturally would translate into knowledge about how to realize a better self. They would leave their nasty villas "and get into something more dignified and worthy of the needs of a human family."[38] A thoughtfully planned city, filled with well-designed houses, would inspire its citizens to understand community in terms of an ennobling ideal. Gaunt was correct when he asserted that neither Howard nor the company had articulated this particular principle. Yet in the minds of Parker and Unwin, of Lander, and of the members of the Letchworth Arts Club, it was an article of faith. As they developed their plan for the new city, Parker and Unwin insisted on architectural controls as a way of achieving an aesthetic harmony that would produce high-minded community.

Parker and Unwin's town plan was drafted to promote community through the imposition of environmental control and architectural unity. It made little attempt, however, to achieve the same end by bringing the various classes together. In 1910, in a speech to the Royal Institute of British Architects' Town Planning Conference, Unwin spoke in favor of "as much intermingling of classes as possible." The following year he reiterated the point in *Town Planning and Practice*. "Both in town planning and site planning it is important to prevent the complete separation of classes of people which is such a feature of the English town." Echoing his general mistrust of the institution of class, he criticized urban planning that kept classes apart and thus encouraged "misunderstanding and want of trust" and an "exaggeration of differences of habit and thought."[39] Yet in their plan for Letchworth, Parker and Unwin appear to have made little, if any, attempt to put that precept into practice. Certainly Howard never addressed the issue explicitly. Nor was the intermingling of classes a part of the company's agenda, as it was to be at Hampstead Garden Suburb. No doubt the company saw the matter in economic terms. Rich people would not build houses next to poor people. For whatever reason, Parker and Unwin designed the city with clearly demarked working-class and middle-class districts.

Unwin declared forthrightly that the portion of the site near the old village of Letchworth and within easy distance of the Hitchin railway station was immediately deemed "one of the best areas for the residences of well-to-do people." He added, however, that large houses were erected in other sections of the city, "there being no intention on the part of the promoters to segregate all of the houses of one size together."[40] Yet Letchworth matured as a divided city, especially after 1910, when working-class developments arose in its northeast quadrant. Architectural segregation was compounded by the fact that there were few public amenities to draw people of different classes together. Neither the architects nor the company appear to have been concerned that their plan would encourage class separation. That it did meant that in this respect Letchworth was a faithful replica of the nineteenth-century cities Parker and Unwin so disparaged.

For the citizens of Letchworth, Parker and Unwin did their best to design— and to persuade other architects to provide—the sort of accommodation they had advocated in *The Art of Building a Home.* And in this they largely succeeded, at least to the extent that cost permitted. The principal Letchworth architects manifested a common determination to put Arts and Crafts ideals to work. C. B. Purdom, in his 1913 progress report on the city, observed that the architects' primary challenge had been to conceive a style that drew from both town and country, "the discovery of [a] new kind of town architecture."[41] The architects' general response to this challenge almost always contained a good deal more of the country than the town, however, an unsurprising result, given the prejudices of Arts and Crafts practitioners.

Some of the finest examples of their work lie in the southern half of the city, that area devoted largely to residences commissioned by middle- and upper-middle-class clients. Here, where expense was not the brake on creativity that it was elsewhere, Parker, Unwin, and others designed in a way that must have pleased both them and their clients. A random sampling of the houses in an area south of the Hitchin and Baldock roads shows how architects incorporated features of siting and planning in a manner testifying to their determination to design democratically—that is, to employ the same principles of honesty and simplicity in houses for middle-class families as they did for workers.

Many of these houses, when described in journals or magazines, were referred to as "cottages," though they might contain four bedrooms or more, servants' quarters and spacious rooms for family living and entertaining. The implication, however, was that life as lived inside these walls would bespeak high-minded unpretentiousness. Exteriors were of the simple materials the Arts and Crafts architects set such store by: roughcast stucco, weatherboarding, and tile roofs. Roof lines were punctuated by gables and dormers, placed irregularly and in such a fashion as to allow a roof to sweep down beyond the first story to cover an entrance porch or loggia on the ground level. The pair of houses that Parker and Unwin designed at numbers 8 and 10 Sollershot West, and a similar pair by H. C. Lander on Baldock Road, are in this sense typical of a number of others, including Arunside, the double house in Letchworth Lane that Parker and Unwin designed for themselves and their families. In the case of the latter, C. B. Purdom commented in his Letchworth survey that "they are good examples of Garden City architecture, being buildings suited to the spaciousness of the place, yet proper to the town , . . cottages in the true sense." Purdom liked the way exteriors and interiors harmonized; "for once in a way it is possible to tell from the outside what the inside will be like."[42] Arunside, like the other large houses in Letchworth, put its face to the sun. The plan of St. Brighids, also on Sollershot West, designed by Parker and Unwin for the weaver Edmund Hunter, capitalized on the interrelationship between house and garden and was angled so that those who looked from its many windows saw not neighbors but trees and flowers—another distinguishing feature of garden city architecture.

Interiors in these houses displayed the architects' fondness for that large room that was to bring a family together and breathe homely refinement into its activities. Even in the plans of houses with conventional morning rooms or sitting rooms, such as those in Lander's Baldock Road pair, the hall, with its bays and ingles, is clearly meant to serve as domestic focus. Occasionally architects placed an isolated study, as a "cosy" retreat, next to a larger hall or living room. In Glaed Home, designed by Parker and Unwin for Howard Pearsall, one of the original directors of First Garden City Ltd., the living room, dining room, and hall could be thrown together by means of sliding doors, or divided into separate, more intimate spaces. Even here, in this very substantial residence, there is no drawing room—and certainly no parlor. The determination to avoid sham extended to the interior decoration of these houses. One searches in vain among contemporary photographs for anything resembling an easy chair. Not all the houses built for affluent clients were redolent of the Arts and Crafts ethos. Some were little more than merely suburban. Yet even in the case of one such, illustrated in the November 1907 *Builder,* there is a timid nod, by way of bay windows in the drawing and dining rooms, in the direction of physical health and aesthetic rectitude.

Studying the houses that Letchworth's architectural first string conceived for affluent residents, one gets the sense that the designers relished their assignments, enjoying the opportunity to express their aesthetic convictions for sympathetic clients with ample budgets. Designing for working-class families, however, was another matter. Unlike Bournville, Port Sunlight, or New Earswick, where benevolent manufacturers could be relied on to subsidize worker housing if necessary to assure minimum structural and aesthetic standards, Letchworth was a town where housing for workers had to pay its way. The result was a squeeze that left no one satisfied.

As we have seen, Parker and Unwin strove to impose aesthetic harmony by means of common materials that raised the cost of construction. They fought, as well, for more than minimal interior space. In a 1906 article, Unwin argued that the minimum at Letchworth was too small, "less in several respects than that which is required by the Local Government Board for houses built by Municipalities to house the poorest of the poor." He suggested that room size be increased by cutting costs elsewhere, by leaving brick walls unplastered, for example. "I have lived in a room the walls of which are whitewashed on the bricks; I have come to like the variety of texture which it gives, and certainly cannot perceive any advantage whatever to myself in those rooms which have been plastered, over the one that has not been so treated." Unwin must have realized that such economy would never suit the working-class clients he was designing for; perhaps he made the suggestion in hopes of startling builders into realizing that the only real hope lay not in cutting costs but in raising wages—a socialist's answer to the problem. He concluded his article with the statement that to spend an extra £30 or £40 per cottage beyond the bare minimum of £150 that was the builders' target would be to "improve every part of the cottage immensely." "For the sake of 8d. or 1s. per week in rent . . . can it be wise not to build the good cottage?" This could be accomplished by a comparable increase in weekly wages. "With that extra shilling for the rent of the labourer's cottage we may secure that every cottage built upon the Garden City Estate shall at least be a decent one; and if Garden City stands for anything, surely it stands for this:—a decent home and garden for every family that comes here. That is the irreducible minimum. Let that go and we fail utterly."[43]

Parker and Unwin, and the architects who worked alongside them, never ceased to struggle against the failure that their high standards and the implacable facts of construction cost made all but inevitable. In cases where they designed for artisans who could afford rents of 7 or 8 shillings a week, they were able to provide houses of considerable style and charm. Those in Rushby Mead, built after 1911 by the Howard Building (co-partnership) Society were of rough-cast brick, with gabled red tile roofs, and occasionally featured hung tiles or weatherboarding. Details such as string courses and drip molding indicate the degree of care that went into their design. Houses of this sort contained a living room, parlor, scullery, three bedrooms, and a bath, and were gaslit. Without question, the Rushby Mead houses, and comparable quadrangles in nearby Birds Hill and Ridge Road, represented the acme of garden city design and a remarkable urban architectural achievement. All opened out to gardens and the sun; together they formed pleasantly soft and varied—yet unified—street-scapes.

At the other end of the scale were houses of no more than 700 to 750 square feet. A dwelling of this sort would contain living room, scullery, three bedrooms, and no bath, cost from £150 to £155, rent for 5/6 a week, and offer its residents little more in the way of space and general amenity than they might find in any conventional suburb composed of byelaw streets.[44] Only the cheapest houses were built without baths. Though there was general agreement as to their necessity, doubts were at the same time expressed as to the frequency of their use. Purdom saw them as a didactic device, if nothing else. "The bath costs hardly anything, and though it is, no doubt, not always much used, the habit of bathing cannot be created if the means do not exist."[45]

Co-partnership building societies struggled to meet the demand for more cheap workers' housing. Letchworth Cottages and Buildings, Ltd., for example, formed in 1907 as a subsidiary of First Garden City, Ltd., built nearly two hundred cottages in four years, some costing no more than £150. The Howard Society completed three hundred cottages between 1911 and 1914; not only those at Rushby Mead, but some as well for considerably less.[46] And yet these and similar efforts by other societies failed to meet the needs of a growing workforce. In 1912, Thomas Adams, now a town planner with the Local Government Board in London, returned to Letchworth to predict that in the coming years the city would require an additional forty-five hundred houses for workers, of which over half must rent for under 6 shillings a week.[47]

The problem received constant airing in the local press. As early as 1906, "Anti-Humbug" was complaining to the *North Hertfordshire Mail:* "The Garden City Tenants, Ltd. [one of Letchworth's co-partnership building societies] goes about in the guise of a semi-religious philanthropy, makes pathetic speeches . . . about high rents . . . and then comes to Letchworth, puts up a lot of inconvenient houses, and charges 8s.6d, a week to men earning from £1 to 24s. a week—with the inevitable result of lodgers, and such an overcrowding scandal that no other town in the country would tolerate it."[48] The Garden City Association's magazine acknowledged the problem in less hyperbolic language the same year, pointing out as well that the housing shortage for industrial workers was exacerbated by the "well-to-do clerk or retired person of small means" who, attracted by the quality of the houses at Letchworth, rented them away from the clientele for whom they were intended. Nor did *Garden City* agree with Unwin that an increase in factory wages would make decent housing more affordable. If wages went up, so would house prices and rents.[49]

Seven years later little had changed. J. J. Kidd, a vocal Letchworth socialist, challenged Howard Pearsall, company director and himself a Fabian, who had argued in the *Letchworth Citizen* that the superior quality of Letchworth houses made them worth the high rents they commanded, contrasting them with inferior London houses at comparable rents. Kidd replied that such comparisons were beside the point. "Letchworth provides the factories and the work yet refuses to construct cottages to suit the hopes of many of the people who are employed here." Nor was he at all convinced that the houses provided were all that fine, no matter what their rent. "All the comparisons in the world will not justify some of the quixotic jumbles called workmen's houses, which we see in some parts of Letchworth, whether the rents be cheap or high." Kidd declared that he would press the local Parish Council to build fifty cheap houses with money borrowed under the Town Planning Act of 1909.[50] Yet Kidd's solution of fifty more houses was no solution at all, given the number needing inexpensive housing.

Purdom, in his survey of the same year, attempted to evade the issue by arguing that Letchworth had never set itself the task of providing housing for the lowest paid workers. Rather, Letchworth had attempted to address the dilemma faced by "the workman who can afford to pay a fair rent, but is unable to get decent accommodation." Yet, Purdom admitted, lower-paid workers had come to town with jobs. When unable to live there, they had found living quarters in the slums of nearby Hitchin and Baldock, where they could rent jerry-built flats for two or three shillings a week.[51] Purdom's conclusion that "Garden City is too close to these old towns" was perhaps true, but it failed to address the dilemma that no one—certainly not Howard, nor Parker and Unwin, nor the company directors—had anticipated when they commenced to plan their city: how to build the decent housing that garden cities, by definition, must have, for workers in industries that, again by definition, a garden city required, yet at rents determined by a steady rise in construction costs and with wages governed by the free-market forces of capitalism.

A partial and not particularly satisfactory answer to that complicated question was provided in 1905 by the first of two Cheap Cottage Exhibitions held at Letchworth. J. St. Loe Strachey, editor of *The Country Gentleman* and therefore concerned about rural depopulation as a result of agricultural depression, asked permission of the company to invite architects and builders to construct cottages for agricultural laborers at a cost of no more than £150, on a site at Letchworth north of the railway. Thomas Adams, conscious of the publicity that such an exhibition would attract, persuaded the directors to provide the land without cost, even though the area chosen was one through which Parker and Unwin had intended to extend the city's north-south axis. The results were no better than mixed. Strachey had stipulated that his intention was to encourage experimentation. Designers and builders took him at his word. Houses were variously constructed of concrete, framed in steel, or prefabricated. Others were merely of extremely simple design and, perhaps for that reason, not without style. If the exhibition proved nothing else, it demonstrated how difficult it was to design cheap decent housing. In most instances, those entries that came in under the £150 limit did so without calculating drainage costs, architects' fees, or even a modest builder's profit into the total. "In some cases," one critic of the enterprise complained, the £150 "covered the bare cost of materials; in more numerous cases not even that."[52] A large number of the sixty thousand visitors to the exhibition came in search of ideas or plans for cheap vacation homes, hence giving to the area where the houses were built, in Purdom's words, "the character of a village of tiny week-end cottages." A representative from the Royal Sanitary Institute observed disdainfully that while impermanent "walls of timber framing or very thin slabs of plaster" might suit the needs of vacationers, they were no substitute for the more solid—and hence more expensive—construction necessary to housedwellers year round.[53]

Nor, despite the crowds, was the exhibition an unmixed blessing for the Garden City Company's own enterprise. In Purdom's view "while it gave the place a tremendous advertisement, [it] did no little harm. It set a rage for cheapness from which Garden City [in 1913] has hardly yet recovered." But worse, the crowds who came saw a city still in its raw, semifinished state, "and gained the place a bad reputation before it deserved it."[54] Unwin believed the entire project misconceived. He and Parker participated by designing Eastholm Green, a grouping of semi-detached cottages at the northeast boundary of the site, reminiscent of the quadrangle scheme that they had proposed in *The Art of Building* and, despite its plainness, not without charm. But in an article written for *Garden City* at the time of the exhibition the two declared that "there is very great danger lest in the present movement in favour of Cheap Cottage building we should make the fatal mistake of regarding the price as the fixed element. It is most necessary to remember that the problem before us is: 'How cheaply can we build a good cottage?' Not 'How good a cottage can we build for £150?'"[55]

Two years later a second exhibition, this time sponsored by the National Housing Reform Council, raised the minimum permissible cost to £175, with the result that the houses designed were of better quality than those of 1905, in terms of both construction and design. Yet the building profession remained largely unimpressed. The *Building News* took the opportunity to disparage not only the exhibition but also the Garden City "do-goodism" that stuck in the craw of those who liked to consider themselves realists. "It is curious to write— that the enthusiasts in the Garden City scheme appear to have discovered an entirely new type of builder, whose mind has been so far etherealized by his sojourn among the charms of Letchworth that he is prepared to erect cottages at a cost which leaves him but a bare margin of profit."[56] No matter that the exhibition was not an undertaking of First Garden City, Ltd.; the fact that it took place in what the *Building News* writer believed to be some sort of suburban never-never land is a mark of the degree to which the company had constantly to guard itself against charges of impracticality and architectural flights of fancy.

Nowhere was it more sensitive to such criticism than in the matter of the design of workers' housing. Whatever their cost, those cottages needed to appeal to the tastes and habits of the families who were to live in them. If they did not, if workers balked at them, companies would be wary of a move to Letchworth. And that would, of course, doom the enterprise. Never could the First Garden City directorship allow itself to forget Aneurin Williams' solemn truth, that the "whole possibility of making a Garden City depended on getting manufacturers."

From the first, workers objected to what they were offered, on grounds of style as well as cost. The parlor debate remained a heated one. The first issue of *Garden City,* published by the Association in 1906, put the matter squarely before its readers: workmen and their wives did not want daily life lived in one room—even if that room was a comparatively large one. "They like the parlor and they mean to have it. They give many reasons for their preference. Such as the necessity of having a place into which to show the casual visitor when the woman of the household is cooking; the need for a place of retirement for the husband when he requires it, and as a sort of storeroom for souvenirs and select pieces of furniture as they possess."[57]

A year later, the issue was window type. Architects preferred casements; residents, sashes. Writing in defense of the former, a correspondent in *Garden City* declared that although the sash window could remain open in most weather in a way casements could not, thereby benefiting householders, the "good-looking [casement] window benefits, too, every passer-by who can appreciate its good points. When I come across a pleasing window, I stand still and gloat over it."[58] That argument would not have cut much ice with housewives, nor with the company tuned to hear their complaints. In 1909, at the time W. H. Smith was contemplating its move to Letchworth, its management sent a deputation of workers to inspect the housing on offer. The results were not encouraging to those determined to teach men and women what they should like.

> The deputation were shown "Art" cottages in different parts of the estate. They were told about the advantage of the "one-big-living-room-with-the-stairs-out-of-it" plan. They said their wives wanted a parlour to see visitors in. They said that in many of the bedrooms there seemed to be no place for the bed, or at any rate for a chest of drawers besides. They said that some of the cottages had doors and latches like chicken houses. They were told that they would get to like the new arrangements. But they declined to try them.
>
> The cottages were good enough as scenery but were not designed to suit the needs or prejudices of the London workman.[59]

Prejudice—and not just that of the London workmen—operated to discredit one of the Letchworth housing projects closest to Howard's heart: Homesgarth, a quadrangle of cooperative dwellings centered around common living rooms and kitchen. Such schemes had been a standard feature of utopian and socialist prescriptions for the future. James Silk Buckingham had included them in his plans for his model community, Victoria; Edward Bellamy had made a point of them in *Looking Backward;* H. G. Wells incorporated them into his *Modern Utopia,* published in 1905, and rhapsodized about them in an article for the *Daily Mail* that same year. "I imagine a number of people living conveniently near one another, and having similar tastes, clubbing for these things: they would all pay a regular subscription for common services and get their meals and so forth at a trifle above bare cost." Wells declared himself partial "to one of the most gracious types of old English architecture, the College," thereby echoing Parker and Unwin in his enthusiasm for this particular form of pre-industrial social organization. Anticipating correctly that communal dwelling places would not appeal to the majority, he doubted "if one could get average working men's wives or clerk's wives into such a place; they would be suspicious of each other, they would quarrel and refuse to speak, and do all sorts of nervous, silly underbred things." (And would, no doubt, bitterly resent the superior demeanor of fellow residents such as Wells.) Yet Wells had faith that because "there are a lot of people in any class above the average," the experiment might succeed; and he suggested Letchworth as a place where such a scheme could be implemented.[60]

Wells was publicizing a concept that had, by the time he was writing in 1905, already received a good deal of favorable notice. As the historian of cooperative living has discovered, proposals for "cooking by co-operation"—clearly not communal living, but a step in that direction—had been aired in middle-class women's magazines in the late 1880s. In the early 1900s, several "distributive kitchens" were operating successfully in the West End of London, at the same time that the Women's Co-operative Guild was experimenting with cooked food shops for the working class in other areas of the metropolis.[61]

Howard had hoped to include communal housing in his Garden City from the outset. In his treatise he made a passing reference to "common gardens and co-operative kitchens."[62] An early draft of the book contained further detail: squares "with dining halls in their centres, with kitchens overhead. Tenants of three or four blocks of houses might share the same dining hall, while others would prefer to do their cooking at home using labour-saving appliances."[63] Parker and Unwin, as we have seen, found the concept a congenial one, combining as it did an idealized notion of social relationships derived from the past with a socialist's vision of a cooperative future. Perhaps the most enthusiastic supporter of communal housing within the garden city movement, however, was the architect H. Clapham Lander, a Quaker, Fabian socialist, and member of the Council of the Garden City Association, who extolled its benefits at the

Bournville conference in 1901. Lander delighted in proclaiming the concept both novel and radical. He associated those Victorian shibboleths, independence and self-sufficiency, with barbarism: "The pre-historic savage was probably the most independent being who ever lived." Civilization brought cooperation. "As man becomes more highly developed the more does the individual unit give way to the social unit." Lander insisted that communal living would prove far more efficient than conventionally organized domestic life at present. The wastefulness of individual fires for cooking and laundering; the squandering of valuable urban space on countless tiny parlors; the money that might be saved on servants, and by purchasing food in bulk: these were matters that could best be addressed by means of cooperative domesticity, a way of living that would inevitably "allow scope for the growth of a broader spirit of brotherhood." "What is economically best," Lander declared, "is invariably morally right. Any system involving material waste stands self-condemned from the ethical standpoint. There are not two laws, one for the spiritual and another for the natural world."[64]

The Garden City Association appended a note to Lander's reprinted speech in its report of the conference proceedings, declaring that while the paper was indeed delivered under association auspices, "the Association as a body is not responsible for the opinions expressed."[65] Even at that early stage in its life the association was conscious of a need to distance itself from attitudes and proposals that might allow critics to characterize the movement and its goals as faddish or extremist. Proponents of cooperative living frightened the fainthearted by insisting that it represented a distinct and imperative break with the past. The otherwise moderately inclined Purdom wrote with reference to the Homesgarth experiment at Letchworth in his 1913 survey that the "ideals of Victorian society about home, the family and women are as dead as all the other ideals of that time. But the houses remain, and the methods of running them, and the relations between mistress and maid. Everything has changed except the houses we live in, the food we eat, the manner of its preparation, and the attitude of the ordinary woman to her servants. . . . We cannot fit the new life into old houses. We want new homes and new towns, and a new kind of domestic policy."[66]

Words such as those no doubt made the directors of First Garden City uneasy. And their uneasiness translated into what was at best an ambivalence toward Homesgarth, while it was being planned and built. Responding to association skittishness, Homesgarth's promoters took pains to present their plans in as unassuming a way as possible. A preliminary prospectus by Howard appearing in the October 1907 issue of *Garden City* presented the scheme as nothing more than a sensible solution to the servant problem. "The project here described will be of special value to those whose incomes are comparatively small, but who wish for comfort, beauty, and order in their surroundings, and who though requiring domestic service, wish to economize in that direction." The result would benefit both mistress and servant, the former by freeing her from the worry of meal planning and the task of supervising a servant, and by providing her with increased privacy; the latter by affording her greater freedom. "The nature of her work and her hours will be clearly defined, and she will be associated in it with other girls her own age."[67]

Two years later, Letchworth Co-operative Houses, Ltd., unveiled a detailed set of plans drawn by Lander and advertised for £10,000 worth of capital in order to begin construction. Once again, the directors—one of whom was Howard—declared at the outset that "by means of co-operative housekeeping in the form here proposed, an important step will be taken towards the solution of the Domestic Servant Problem."[68] Lander's plan included a central building, with common dining hall, kitchen, and accommodation for the domestic staff, along with sixteen houses, some with single bed-sitting rooms, others with one, two, or three bedrooms. The quadrangle, though it was designed to recall medieval Oxford and Cambridge, was nonetheless up-to-date: central heating throughout and a telephone service that connected each house with the manager's office. Rents ranged from £22 to £46 per year; additional charges for meals, cleaning, and gardening rose from £10 to £16. Homesgarth was clearly intended for a middle-class clientele. And though nowhere stipulated, the plans appear to assume a majority of single tenants, the lack of playground space suggesting as well an exclusively adult population.

Homesgarth was opened in November 1910, with eight of its sixteen houses completed. Lady Aberdeen was prevailed upon to lend the occasion dignity by cutting the ribbon in a driving rainstorm. The thoroughly respectable *Westminster Gazette* joined other newspapers in wishing the project well, its report reflecting the degree to which Homesgarth's promoters were successful in putting their moderated message across to the public. "It is an experiment which aims at nothing less than a solution of the domestic servant problem!" the *Gazette* enthused. "An experiment which seeks, on the one hand, to raise the status and to lighten the burden of the servant, and on the other to give to householders the economic advantages of a modified communal basis of living."[69]

Other reports were equally enthusiastic. Yet First Garden City, Ltd., remained wary and unimpressed. That same month, its directors turned down a request from Letchworth Co-operative Houses for further abatement of ground rent, having previously agreed to waive one year's payment, "as in their opinion sufficient concessions have already been made to this Company." When Howard had, two years before, requested that he be allowed to circulate his Homesgarth prospectus to First Garden City shareholders, the directors had bridled, noting only that "permission be given Mr. Howard to examine the Shareholders' list in order to inform the Board how many names he would wish to send to, but that in any event the Letchworth Co-operative Houses Ltd. would have to make it perfectly clear that it was a Company quite independent of First Garden City Ltd."[70] Three months later the directors did authorize Howard to solicit about 250 names. But their determination to distance themselves from what they appear to have perceived as an untrustworthy stepchild helped to ensure that Homesgarth would begin life burdened by debt. In a second prospectus, issued in June 1911, Howard reported that of the £6,000 already expended on the building, only £3,600 had been raised in share capital. He urged potential investors to assist in the completion of a project that was as well a "promising social undertaking."[71]

Homesgarth was never completed as planned. After World War I its name was changed to Sollershot Hall, the cooperative experiment was ended, and additional flats were carved from the original common rooms. A less ambitious attempt at communal housing, for women only, was begun in 1914 when two of Howard's friends, Ruth Pym and S. E. Dewe, put up their own money to finance the scheme in part, the remainder to come from the Howard Cottage Co-partnership Society. Meadow Way Green, close to the town center, was not completed until after the war. It enjoyed a success denied to Homesgarth, largely because of the generosity of its founders and their determination to ensure that their friend's dream might become a reality, at least in a modest way.

Howard never ceased to frighten the directors of First Garden City. He continued to speak out on behalf of communal housing; and, when not muzzled by the need to raise money for the cause from conservative inventors, he made it clear that he was promoting the concept within the larger framework of radical social change. In an article titled "A New Outlet for Woman's Energy," which appeared in a 1913 issue of *Garden Cities and Town Planning Magazine,* he compared the "invention" of Homesgarth to James Watt's invention of the steam engine, both designed to make use of "long-neglected power" and to "open up a new era."[72]

Language of that sort brought trouble down on Howard's head, and not just from directors of First Garden City. In the fall of 1913 he was attacked by Letchworth trade unionists who accused him of suggesting that communal housing would make it easier for women to leave home for factory jobs. Challenged at a public meeting, Howard temporized. "A factory, rightly understood, should be, as it were, an extension of the home. . . . A woman certainly ought not to work all day, either in a factory or in her home." A month later, the issue remained heated. George Bates, an outspoken local politician identified by the *Letchworth Citizen* as a "trades unionist," continued to press Howard. "In reply to stern criticism . . . Mr. Howard admitted that he had thought of the Spirella [corset] factory as a suitable place for . . . mothers to work a few hours each day." He then remarked that he saw nothing inherently wrong in placing small children in daytime creches while their mothers worked outside the home. "A working-class kitchen . . . is certainly not an ideal place for young children, while working, cooking and dusting are going on; a creche might be an ideal place." To which an irate listener responded that he was "against any outside interference with the home."[73]

Howard continued to champion cooperative living schemes for working-class families as well as for single, middle-class professionals.[74] But the appeal fell on deaf ears. As the skeptical *Architects and Builders Journal* observed of a similar working-class experiment at Finchley, "Unless, . . . unobserved by us, an unprecedented change is obliterating the prejudices of the most conservative section of the most conservative people in the world, we cannot conceive that the kitchenless house and the *cuisine* in common are likely to become at all general, or even widely popular."[75]

It is tempting to think of the city's early years in terms of three visions. The first was Howard's, a vision that looked steadily toward the future, whose goal was to make England a more equitable community by ensuring that land was held for the common good and used creatively for the healthy benefit of all. The second vision was Unwin's, inspired as well by hope for the future but drawing sustenance from an English heritage that reached back into the pre-industrial past. Its goal was to make individual Englishmen and women better people by providing them with an improving environment, all the better for having been derived from those "best" things the past could teach the present. The third vision was that of the company's directors—not so much a vision as a determination: to make Letchworth a successful enterprise. In the beginning they had spoken enthusiastically of land reform and of physical and moral regeneration. But once faced with the difficulties of turning vision into reality, they found themselves transforming the means—the garden city at Letchworth—into an end in itself, with the result that Howard's vision, and Unwin's, were sacrificed whenever necessary in order to make Letchworth a self-sustaining city.

By the end of Letchworth's first decade, Howard's vision had been all but swallowed up in the need to reassure investors. Unwin could claim greater success for his. In a 1912 speech, he challenged his listeners "to go down a street of workman's cottages in almost any other town in this country and assume the same critical attitude [as that of Letchworth's detractors]. Do we know any other town where there is not and never can be another slum? Do we know any other where every house has had some thought and care bestowed on it, to adapt it to the needs of its occupants and its position? I know of none such; . . . going as I do constantly to other places, I feel that Letchworth has given a very good lead."[76] To the extent that Letchworth was providing its citizens the opportunity to enjoy healthy lives in an environment in sympathy with aesthetic refinement and in touch with natural beauty, it corresponded to Unwin's aspirations for a new and better kind of English community, in which men, women, and children shared access to what was "best." If Letchworth had not achieved that lofty goal, it had, in the minds of its supporters, come closer than any other city in the nation.

Chapter 6 Letchworth:
"The Spirit of the Place"

The company's unwillingness to allow visionary schemes to impede its determination that Letchworth pay its way helped to produce a feisty spirit of opposition among many of the garden city's early citizens. In designing his utopia, Howard devoted comparatively little attention to how it should be governed. When it came time to build Letchworth, circumstance dictated that initially, for reasons of expediency, decisions would remain in the hands of First Garden City, Ltd. Nor was this deemed a less than satisfactory state of affairs by those responsible for the city's immediate well-being. Viscount Peel, one of the dignitaries called on to speak at the ground-breaking ceremonies in 1903, echoed company sentiment when he declared that he "rejoiced to think that you are going to have something like a paternal government for those with whom you are going to deal, and whom you may include in your city."[1] His lordship no doubt had in mind the pattern of governance in Bournville and Port Sunlight, as well as that still prevailing in many rural communities. "Paternal" management would seem entirely appropriate for a venture of this sort, whose rural setting was to conform to tradition and whose configuration was to echo an idealized past. Yet those in Lord Peel's audience intending to move to Letchworth might well have disagreed with his pronouncement. Indeed, once families began to take up residence and to consider themselves Letchworth citizens, they expected to have a voice in the management of their affairs. And that expectation did not sit well with company managers and directors.

The first fur flew in 1905, with the sacking of Thomas Adams as manager and his replacement by W. H. Gaunt, who came from Lancashire and had played a large part in laying out the Trafford Park industrial estate near Manchester. The fact that Gaunt's experience was largely with factories and hence with company directors, and not with the enthusiastic visionary types who populated Letchworth in its early years, led to an all but inevitable collision. Gaunt had been hired to make the experiment pay its way. One of his first acts was to raise ground rents, a move that not surprisingly angered leaseholders. Residents wrote to North Hertfordshire newspapers, lambasting Gaunt and the directors not merely for raising rents but—an increasingly common extension of the argument—for betraying the ideals of the movement. "Vox Populi," writing in August 1906, insisted that "vital questions such as the housing of the working classes, small holdings, etc., all of which go to the very root of the Garden City principle, are being endangered by the enormous rise in ground rents." The writer attacked the directors for their "aggressive officialism," which "boasts, brags and bullies."[2] What made Vox Populi and those allied with him particularly angry was the fact that they had no democratic recourse from the company's policies, since the company was the de facto government of the city.

A resident's union, elected by full adult suffrage, had come into being soon after the city's inception. Judging by its minute book, however, its chief occupation was discussion of the ill behavior of school children, the preservation of bird sanctuaries, and the organization of social gatherings for newcomers to the city. In July 1905 the union became a council, a change that appears to have emboldened some of its members, along with more vocal Letchworth citizens, to speak out against company policy. The council's president, Dr. Norman Macfadyen, labored to keep tempers even. Addressing the annual meeting in January 1906, he acknowledged that some had expected that he and his colleagues would "carry on a sort of guerilla warfare with the Company's officials." Not so, Macfadyen insisted. Certainly the council was prepared to oppose company policies that might "militate seriously against the interests of the residents and leaseholders," but nothing of the sort had arisen.[3] Rhetoric such as that struck garden city militants as nothing short of collaborationist. A year later a resident complained to the

North Hertfordshire Mail of the "oligarchic spirit" already at work on the council. "The public will trust the Council," the writer declared, "but only if the Council realize that they can trust the public."[4]

Meanwhile, the company proceeded to do what it deemed best, paying as little heed as possible to criticism and importuning from residents and ratepayers. That same year, Harved Craske, the company's secretary, wrote Aneurin Williams, the chairman, disparaging a proposal that the council meet regularly with the directors. Craske reported that during the past year the council had not submitted "any proposal of real value" for the company's consideration. Besides, he continued, "the Directors have first to consider their obligation to their Shareholders, and I venture to think it would be a little difficult for them to accomplish this successfully if the residents were allowed to take part, even indirectly, in the management of the Estate."[5]

If the directors shared Craske's sentiments, they understood nonetheless that as the city grew some form of limited yet legitimate authority would have to be granted to its citizens. In 1907, therefore, the company blessed the establishment of a parish council for Letchworth, amalgamating three preexisting parish councils into one for the entire estate. At the company's annual meeting in January 1906, Williams spoke positively—and patronizingly—of this new initiative. "Your directors feel that their work is to prepare the new town for self-government, and to enlist its aid as rapidly as may be in the carrying out of Garden City ideals. They look forward with pleasure and confidence to the co-operation of the citizens in their new collective capacity." So might a benevolent colonial administrator have addressed an assemblage of "deserving natives" at the same period in some part of the British empire. This paternalistic benediction did not sit well with all the shareholders present. A Miss Young rose to declare that the Parish Council would not go far enough to meet the demands of Letchworth residents who looked on the directors as "an alien autocratic body, whose regulations may be quite opposite to the wishes of the people affected by them."[6]

Few imagined that the change would do much to alter the way Letchworth was governed. The new council was subsumed under a Rural District Council, whose greater powers limited what the Parish Council could accomplish. Nor did the company in any way pull back from the management of the city's affairs. As one disgruntled citizen complained after the first Parish Council election in 1908, its powers were "so very limited that even if the wrong men were elected they could not do much harm." The "real controllers of our destiny" remained the company directors.[7] The writer suggested that the purchase of company shares, which entitled their owners to a vote at the annual general meeting, was the best way to ensure residents a voice in their own affairs.

In 1912 the company demonstrated its willingness to intervene directly and drastically in the politics of the city. In December, Joseph van Hooydonk, the Dutch owner of the Phoenix Motor Company, which had recently moved to Letchworth from Finchley, addressed the Letchworth Citizens' Association on the topic "Letchworth from the Manufacturer's Point of View." In the course of his remarks he attacked the town newspaper, the *Letchworth Citizen,* and its editor, A. W. Brunt, who had been fired from the Garden City Press six years before for leading a strike. Van Hooydonk accused Brunt of publishing only negative "socialist" reports about the city. He declared that "he and Mr. Gaunt" were of the opinion that the paper was of no assistance in encouraging industry to move to Letchworth. When Brunt and a reporter, who were both present, objected to this assertion, Van Hooydonk exploded: "It was no good him saying they came here to build a factory for the benefit of the working man; they came here to make money, and when 'the Citizen' told the world that the place was a hotbed of Socialism he could not send it away to a manufacturer and persuade him to come here, as at once he formed the opinion that he would not be able to control his own men."[8]

Shortly thereafter Brunt was removed as editor by the directors of the *Citizen,* presumably with the approval of the company. Whether Gaunt had persuaded Van Hooydonk to act as stalking horse or whether the company used Van Hooydonk's attack to achieve an end it had for some time desired but had been unwilling to pursue, the episode reinforced a lesson the citizenry already knew: that the company could have its way on any matter, large or small. Angry protests appeared in the *Citizen;* resolutions of regret were passed at public meetings. But as one letter writer observed, the company understood the issue as an economic one: "Whatever may have been the ideals of the founder of the city . . . no such city can ever arise except on one foundation—the solid foundation of commercialism."[9] In fact, the *Citizen* appears to have presented news in a balanced and genteel fashion. If its columns contained criticisms and complaints, they reflected the lively iconoclasm characteristic of men and women attracted by the experimentation that was the company's original raison d'etre. Brunt's dismissal is evidence of the directors' determination to court those commercial interests on whose conservative good will they believed they must rely in order for their experiment to succeed.

The inability of the council to stand in the company's way did not make election contests any less lively. Candidates in the first race ran as self-proclaimed socialists or antisocialists, the latter group affiliated with the Letchworth Social and Industrial League, which announced its intention of combating Letchworth's reputation as a city "run by those extremists who have made the name of Garden City a byword that excites derision and scorn in the country."[10] The Leaguers did not, of course, have in mind the company directors, who actually did run the city. They were instead referring to the numerous committed socialists who had been attracted to Letchworth as a semi-utopian experiment in its early years, and whose political convictions compelled them to speak out, often with noisy certitude, about matters local and national. In 1907 the London *Standard* reported the "migration of a large number of Socialists to the Garden City." Many of the newcomers, the report continued, "possess the most extreme views, and spare no efforts to convert those around them to the same way of thinking."[11]

Years before, in an article for William Morris's *Commonweal*, Raymond Unwin had written of the manner in which socialists could upset a community with their convictions. "To be a socialist nowadays a man must first have enough discontent with his surroundings to look for something better, hence we are a discontented lot." And discontented people, Unwin further observed, "are not likely to live very happily together."[12] That was especially the case in Letchworth, where the socialists' hopes for the city were repeatedly thwarted by a directorship of capitalist landlords. J. J. Kidd, one of the city's most outspoken radicals—and eventually a member of the Parish Council—wrote in 1906, at the time that Gaunt was raising rents, of the "disappointment tinged with bitterness" that had been the consequence of the changes. Why the surprise? Kidd asked. "Will anyone show me how it could be otherwise, in view of the fact that the majority of the people of the British Isles hold capitalist and not collectivist ideals? If the public conscience is still satisfied with the products of capitalism—competition and cheating, shoddiness and sordidness, wealth and want—how can we of Garden City hope to escape its influence?" If those who came to Letchworth in search of an ideal have suffered disappointment, Kidd declared, "I must plainly and even bluntly tell them the fault is their own."[13] Here, as so often at Letchworth, the issue was heightened by casting it against the background of those ideals embodied in the vision of the city's founders. Failure to keep rents low or to provide adequate street lighting—the tedious stuff of municipal politics—quickly was perceived as nothing less than the betrayal of a dream.

Although socialists of various stripes probably comprised a majority in Letchworth, the Liberal and Unionist parties enjoyed considerable support as well. Indeed, the political situation was accurately enough summed up by a Conservative signing himself "Primrose" in a letter to the *Letchworth Citizen* in 1908: "It is surely perfectly clear that at the moment there are in Garden City two bodies, Socialists and Anti-Socialists, who have been striving to get to grips for some time past."[14] Though representation on the council appears to have been fairly evenly divided between the two camps, the socialists were better able to attract outside speakers for their cause. During the early years of the city's history, the *Citizen* was filled with accounts of speeches by the likes of Sidney Webb, George Bernard Shaw, H. G. Wells, R. H. Tawney, Ramsay Mac-Donald, Annie Besant, Will Crooks, Victor Grayson, H. M. Hyndman—all sorts and conditions of socialists, and all prepared to travel down to Hertford-shire from London to see for themselves the extent to which Letchworth met the measure of their own particular vision of a socialist future.

If that vision included the expectation of a classless society, Letchworth was bound to disappoint. The city's inhabitants had not shed the skin of class consciousness as they emerged into their healthy garden city sunshine. One can arrive at a rough estimate of the town's social structure in 1911 from a report on the ratable value of houses published in the *Citizen*. Of the 1,380 houses listed, a little over half—757—were valued at £12 and under, 389 at £25 and under, 154 at £40 and under, and 80 at over £40. Despite the much discussed shortage of working-class housing, the city nonetheless had a population comprised primarily of working-class men and women, a solid lower-middle and middle class, and a small upper-middle class. The large number of owner-occupiers— Purdom estimated them at about 50 percent of the total number of houses— may have meant a larger lower-middle class than the *Citizen's* figures at first suggest.[15]

Middle- and upper-middle class residents moved to Letchworth because they chose to. Working-class men and women followed their jobs. As they arrived, they were encouraged to believe that Letchworth was free from the constraints and tensions of class-conscious cities elsewhere. "We have no feudal survivals, no slums, no snobbery," one resident proclaimed in Letchworth's monthly magazine, *The City*. H. D. Pearsall, welcoming newcomers at the quarterly social of the still-active Residents' Union in 1911, encouraged his audience "to break away from the ordinary mould of English town life with its 'class' distinctions."[16]

Putting "class" in quotation marks could not diminish the reality of its presence, however. The history of industrial relations during Letchworth's early years provides evidence of the extent to which the city was prey to the labor unrest that plagued the country in the years before World War I. The company's determination to project an image of a community sympathetic to the needs of manufacturers meant that the directors and their staff worked constant variations on a general theme that emphasized harmony. "Garden City is not the outcome of impracticable Socialism, or of extravagant co-operative theories," Gaunt wrote in an article promoting Letchworth as an industrial center. "And it is not a region where commercial rules are ignored and interference between employers and employed encouraged."[17] Despite Gaunt's brave words, Letchworth experienced two major strikes in 1912 and 1913. Both originated from a demand for higher wages; both soon produced the issue of strikebreaking by nonunion workers; and both involved disagreements between Letchworth residents, many of whom expressed sympathy with the strikers, and the company, which insisted on remaining neutral but was clearly unhappy with the attention the strikes attracted. Labor disputes were everyday events during those contentious years. But when they occurred within the supposedly tranquil social environment of the first garden city, they became particularly newsworthy.

The 1912 strike occurred at the Lacre Engineering firm, where workers complained of low wages. The men argued that although they had understood their pay might be lower than in other similar factories, they "nonetheless expected to find that wages offered would, in Garden City, with 'ideal conditions and model housing arrangements' be adequate." Instead, they were being paid four shillings per week less than workers at the same jobs in nearby Luton. Here, as so often happened, the expectations generated by the professed vision—"ideal conditions and model housing arrangements"—worked to encourage disappointment and, in this case, industrial action when promise conflicted with reality. At the same time, Lacre's management was prepared to lay much of the blame for the dispute at the feet of the "people of Letchworth." When asked by the *Citizen* what had caused the strike, the works manager was quick to respond: "more than all . . . the work and propaganda of the Socialists of the place. . . . If Letchworth is going to get into the hands of trade unionists it will soon become a place unfit to live in."[18]

Both sides spoke of the existence of this "Letchworth factor" while the dispute continued. As the socialist councillor J. J. Kidd remarked, at one of several open-air demonstrations, "A struggle like [this] would be a mere bagatelle in some places. In Letchworth it meant much." Kidd added that the company had an "important duty in the matter," by which he meant that it should act as mediator. But the company remained determinedly silent.[19] Trade unionists, though disappointed by the company's unwillingness to intervene in any way, expressed their surprise and pleasure at the way the citizenry supported the strikers, not only over the wages issue but in opposition to strikebreaking (the firm had imported nonunion workers after the dispute began). The trade unionist *Daily Herald* acknowledged the "splendid support accorded by the residents of Letchworth, who have contributed £90 to the men's cause." And a spokesman from the Gas Workers' and General Labourers' Union, at another outdoor meeting, expressed his pleasure "that the trade union movement had got down to Letchworth," for he had thought Letchworth "too brilliant a place, and much too dominated by the better classes, for trade unionism to stand a chance of asserting itself."[20] For both sides, the fact that the strike was occurring at Letchworth gave it special meaning and importance. At issue were not only wages or blacklegs but also what the city itself was about.

It was the same the following year, when builders struck for higher wages against the Master Builders' Association, a consortium of local contractors. The workers charged that they had been shabbily treated not only by the association but by First Garden City, Ltd., as well. They argued that the company's unwillingness to provide sufficient cheap housing meant that a disproportionate share of their current, inadequate wages was gobbled up by high rents, thereby reducing their standard of living to a level below what many of them had enjoyed in London. The association's habit of hiring the cheapest possible labor kept highly paid skilled workers from jobs they considered rightly theirs, while betraying garden city principles in the bargain.

"One of the chief objects of the Garden City," an apologist for the strikers declared when addressing the Residents' Union, "is to arrest rural depopulation. But with regard to Arlesley and Stotfold [two nearby villages] the Garden City has had precisely the opposite effect, for the best men of Arlesley now come to Letchworth to work and take away their earnings. The result is the organized workers [at Letchworth] have to compete against a great quantity of cheap labour from the villages and towns round about. Men who came here from London are competed with by youngsters from those villages, who are quite skillful and able to do good work, and who constitute what economists call 'cheap and docile labour.'"[21] One of the strikers, interviewed by the *Citizen*, pointed out the depressing irony that was the consequence of Letchworth's high rents: "The curse of Garden City is the fact that so many labourers live [not in Letchworth but] in villages at a distance, in practically slum conditions."[22]

Although the company recognized the pressing need for more worker housing, it was not about to be drawn into the controversy. To charges that First
Garden City was, because of its association as landlord with building projects
throughout the city, "in the position of employers who are refusing the just and
fair claims of the workmen," the company's secretary, Harved Craske, replied
that "First Garden City, Ltd., takes no part in this, or any other wages dispute
on the estate." Sounding the company's predictable warning about the dangers
of scaring manufacturers from the city, Craske observed, "It is evident that no
employers would bring their workers to Letchworth, if it came to be understood that Letchworth was a place where, in any dispute with labour, the
employer would have, not only the trade organisations, but the owners of the
estate against him."[23]

As with the Lacre strike the previous year, the city was caught up in the
theater of strike activity. The most dramatic confrontation occurred on the
occasion of the opening of the newly completed railway station. In the presence
of a distinguished assemblage headed by the chairman of the Hertfordshire
County Council and the Earl of Clarendon, Lord Lieutenant of the County,
strikers and their supporters appeared carrying placards and banners with
slogans that made pointed reference to the disparity between promise and
performance: "Where Are the Ideals?"; "Fresh Air Increases Our Appetites";
"We Cannot Live on Fresh Air."[24]

Certainly this was not the stuff of Howard's dreams. In a speech to a group of
builders at Letchworth in 1907 he had preached cooperation on behalf of a
noble common purpose, urging them to take particular pains as they built the
houses that were to be occupied by working men and their families. "I want you
to see to it that your labour is as efficient as you can." Sounding the Arts and
Crafts call to good workmanship, he implored that they build well, that their
work be "honest work." If it was, repairs—and therefore rents—could be kept
to a minimum. "Besides, we will enjoy the privilege of living in well-built and
not in jerry-built cottages."[25] That gentle injunction had been drowned out by
1913, when Letchworth's industrial relations were little different from those
elsewhere in England. There were exceptions, certainly: the St. Edmundsbury
Weaving Works, for example, established by Edmund Hunter in a building
designed by Parker and Unwin. As recalled by one of his friends, his was an
enterprise in every way worthy of the vision Howard professed. "Mr. Hunter
was a good, kind, and very considerate manager of this small but unique and
well-known factory, and he treated his work people in such a manner that he
was appreciated and loved by them all. . . . Mrs. Hunter was a sweet and gentle

person. She dressed very artistically and with a good sense of colour, and was very fond of poetry and mysticism."[26]

For a moment we are back in that world evoked by Katherine Bruce Glasier, who celebrated the simple, honest life that the Raymond Unwins led, and "their sincere belief in their fellow-workers' right not only to work and wage but to interest and even joy in the doing of that work."[27] One wonders whether Unwin imagined that all the factories at Letchworth would resemble the St. Edmundsbury Weaving Works, that all employers would be as benevolent as Edmund Hunter. Certainly his distaste for contemporary industrial civilization might have led him—and others at Letchworth who thought as he did—to believe that once the likes of the Lacre Engineering Works were admitted into the precincts of the garden city, its chances for survival as a place expressive of ideals he professed were doomed. A community of equals could not flourish in a city dependent on a class-based industrial system.

At the time of the builders' strike, a Leeds clergyman of the militant Church Socialist League paid a visit to Letchworth. Having walked about the town and talked to its residents, he declared in a speech that "after all, Letchworth is no more than Leeds white-washed. In Letchworth the same system obtains, but it happens to be painted in more beautiful colours. There is the same division of classes, the same separation of members of the human race into workers and men." The speaker praised the "aspect and general laying out of the place" but concluded that "at the back of it all you have not got away from the same system under which we are groaning in Leeds."[28] Had he been there, Unwin undoubtedly would have nodded a sad amen.

As we have seen, Unwin had himself helped to ensure the city's class divisions in the layout of distinct middle- and working-class districts. A reporter for the *North Hertfordshire Mail* who resided in Letchworth asked in 1907 whether Ralph Neville had not been "talking through his hat" when in a recent speech he declared that at Letchworth class distinctions had been abolished. "The audience was a select one," the writer observed, "and vociferously cheered the remark." Yet he queried the genuineness of the response. "How easy it is for us to trip out those platitudes about our dislike of class distinctions." Yet the writer was certain that Neville was wrong, though he had to believe that at Letchworth class did not "exhibit the same petty features as in other places."[29] Another resident writing in his journal the following year on the same subject wondered whether the pettinesses were indeed not just as pronounced at Letchworth as they were elsewhere. "The Common View workman's wife will not associate on equal terms with the Birds Hill workman's wife [a case, presumably, of the working-class distinction between the rough and the respectable]. The carpenters and plumbers on a building will not eat their dinner sitting on the same plank with the hod carriers." The "upstairs," white-collar worker at Dent's publishing works refused to dance with the "downstairs folk."[30] By 1912 even Neville was prepared to acknowledge the facts of social life. He bemoaned the tendency to associate membership in Letchworth clubs with social standing, the fear that "if you joined a tennis club, say, or went to a subscription ball, there was no telling that you might meet Mr. Jones or Mr. Smith whom you did not consider on the same social level as yourself." Neville hoped that those "Victorian" concerns might be soon forgotten, and, ever the optimist when it came to the power of garden city, declared that "Letchworth was just the one place in England" calculated to effect such a change."[31]

Those who, like Neville, had conceived of Letchworth as an instrument for social change, had from the outset insisted that social relations there would not be characterized by the paternalism of which Bournville and Port Sunlight were frequently accused. With those two towns in mind, Howard had declared soon after the city's founding that "the worker in the Garden City is at least as free as he is in the great towns. . . . Whatever advantages the worker gains through living and working under the more wholesome conditions of Garden City are not at the cost of his independence. . . . There is not the slightest suggestion of paternalism, benevolence, or philanthropy in the atmosphere of the place, such as might exist or might be feared in a smaller scheme, or in a town dominated by a single employer."[32] And yet, despite intention, resolve could give way to the patterns of past thinking and behavior. One of the co-partnership building societies sponsored a contest among its tenants for the best-kept cottage. "Lady judges" visited workers' houses, following notice to the tenants, awarding prizes on the basis of tidy interiors and pretty gardens. The scheme flopped. For, as C. B. Purdom observed, "many good tenants did not care to have their houses inspected, and most of the bad ones naturally were reluctant."[33] Even Howard could, on occasion, sound remarkably like George Cadbury. Commenting on his visit to a flower show in 1909: "It did me 'real good' to see how these late Cockneys were already beginning to show skill in their gardens; how they, for the most part, and their children especially, were far better in health than in the great city they have left behind, and how there is among them a great sense of comradeship."[34]

When Howard had boasted that there was not the "slightest suggestion of philanthropy" at Letchworth, he had not imagined that unemployment might become the problem there that it was in other cities. By January 1907, however, conditions had necessitated the founding of a Charitable Relief Society, which the following year became the Letchworth Guild of Help. In soliciting funds the secretary catalogued a "considerable amount of distress, consequent on decreased earnings in the short days and broken weather, and that arising from seasonal slackness in the building trade." He reported that many had insufficient clothing and that children were attending school "underclad, underfed, with boots which afford no protection against mud and wet." The guild broke ground by coopting workers from some of the larger Letchworth firms onto its executive committee. Determined to become an instrument of community rather than class, it expressed its "larger purpose" in terms not of relief but of the prevention of destitution, a "service in which, if it is to be effective, every citizen must share." That was the language and spirit of garden city as Howard and Unwin understood it.[35]

The company also showed itself willing to experiment with innovative schemes for unemployment relief. Twice the directors solicited funds to enable unemployed London workers to move temporarily to Letchworth and work as road and bridge builders and pipe layers. On the first such occasion, in 1905, Thomas Adams, still at that time the company's manager, reported proudly that the men destined for Letchworth had been specially selected in hopes that they might become permanent residents there; that since their arrival their health had improved considerably; and that a football team composed of the recent immigrants had thus far defeated all comers.[36]

These attempts to address unemployment in creative ways did not diminish social divisions at Letchworth. Nor was class consciousness a consequence of economics and industrial relations alone. Cultural attitudes played their part as well in separating working class from middle class. Throughout the early years Letchworth's critics—friendly and otherwise—wrote of the absence of opportunities for working men and women to enjoy the kind of social life they had been accustomed to before moving into rural Hertfordshire. Little more than a month after ground was broken, a letter writer to the socialist newspaper *Clarion* castigated the city's promoters for failing to respect the desires and tastes of the working class. She quoted a friend—"a mere man"—who had attended the opening ceremonies and had waited in the rain "to hear something useful." Instead he had listened to platitudes about slums, pubs, and music halls, which "appeared to run a dead heat as the three misery mills." The *Clarion's* correspondent predicted that if the company did not "provide a place where the working man can get a glass of beer, or a music-hall where he can get away (and his wife too) from the kiddies and washing occasionally, he'll see them somewhere before casting his lot with them."[37]

Four years later a Letchworth resident and writer for the *Bedfordshire Express*, Robert Gernon, aired the same complaint, suggesting that the company had paid no heed to what remained a sore point with an increasing number. Gernon began by attacking the notion that Letchworth should reflect nothing other than the culture of a high-minded minority of its middle class. "We are not all middle-class in Garden City—let us thank the Gods! Neither have we all a pretence to intellectual culture or any social veneer of that kind." Gernon pointed to the absence of much in the way of entertainment that might appeal to a man or woman accustomed to urban ways. Sensitive to the pleasures of city existence in a manner foreign to the mind of someone like Unwin, he wrote of how the "mere fact of being in a town, the movement, the human interest, the atmosphere created by the proximity of people" exerted an influence greatly missed when one is away in the country. "The ordinary man does not like country life. It is too slow, too dead, too solitary for his social instincts. And the life we offer in Garden City, to the men who come from London, is little more than this." Gernon urged the company to build a music hall forthwith, arguing for one on grounds that he hoped would appeal to the company's economic sensibilities. "Manufacturers will not bring their men here unless they can get them to stay." The company must therefore provide not only economic inducements to employers but social inducements to their workers. "And there could hardly be found after cheap cottages a greater social inducement than a good Music Hall."[38]

Gernon's argument fell on deaf ears. In this instance, apparently, high-mindedness—the determination to give workers what was in their own best interest—took precedence over the pressing need to attract industry and its workforce. The company was prepared to cede a point when it came to parlors, but not to music halls. One year before Gernon's article appeared, Thomas Adams, who understood the need that Gernon and others were trying to address, called a meeting to discuss the matter. He was speaking to the Howard Hall Association, the governing body of an institution built as Letchworth's principal cultural center, designed by Parker and Unwin and named for Howard's recently deceased wife. Adams asked the association "to recognise the need to provide for the working men of the estate" and recommended the appointment of a committee of six workmen and artisans to advise the association on how the building might be better used to suit their interests. The committee was duly appointed. But opposing the idea was Ethel Unwin, Raymond's wife, who "did not see that such an advisory committee was necessary, as workmen and their associates would be quite free to make use of the hall." Indeed; but on terms dictated by the middle-class members of the association, whose ideas as to what might be appropriate and inappropriate would not, in all likelihood, tally with those of the men and women whom Adams hoped to attract.[39]

More conspicuous by its absence at Letchworth than a music hall was a pub selling alcoholic beverages. In *Garden Cities of To-morrow,* Howard had written in favor of a municipally licensed public house, arguing that in his garden city a pub would "have many competitors for the favor of the people; while, in large cities, with few opportunities of cheap and rational enjoyment, it has its own way."[40] Ralph Neville appears to have agreed with Howard. In his remarks at the first garden city conference, in 1901, he promised that "in our Garden City . . . the public house . . . will not be the only place where a man can go and enjoy his hours of leisure and find recreation."[41]

As matters transpired, the only place a man could go for such enjoyment was the Skittles Inn, a teetotal establishment whose nominal proprietors were Edward Cadbury and Aneurin Williams, and whose amenities included a skittles alley, bowling green, billiard room, reading room, and bar serving nonalcoholic beverages. It was patronized to a degree by workers; trade unionists used its rooms for meetings, and during the Lacre strike as a dispensary for relief funds. But to many it was a joke. G. K. Chesterton made it the subject of a satire, declaring that while he was prepared to concede that life was not all beer and skittles, "I think it would be yet more . . . monochrome if it were all skittles." Chesterton saw the innkeeper of Garden City as an "emblem of a somewhat larger truth," and one with particular relevance to the attitudes of those determined to shape the culture of the first garden city in their own image. "Just as the Garden City innkeeper wishes to keep 'The Skittles' while abandoning the beer, so our life to-day is marked by perpetual attempts to revive old-fashioned things while omitting that human soul in them that made them something more than fashions."[42] Workers, inconvenienced but not ultimately deterred from drink by the lack of a pub in Letchworth, betook themselves on weekends to nearby villages and towns, thereby bringing down on the city the gentle ridicule not only of Chesterton, but of the local press. The *North Hertfordshire Mail* commented, in August 1907, that

> regularly every Saturday night a large number of men come into [Hitchin] from Garden City, whose chief mission is a tour of the public houses. We have nothing to say against this visit to Hitchin by people in the surrounding townships, which affords, we hope, a pleasant break in their daily routine, and we only give prominence to this matter with the object of saving the town from a reputation for drinking excessively which it does not deserve. . . . The question inevitably arises, what is the

correct policy for Temperance people to take—to discourage a public house at Garden City and add to the drinking at Hitchin, which must over-tax the police staff, or provide reasonable facilities for refreshment in each community.[43]

Three times the licensing issue came before the voters of Letchworth in the years before 1914, the company directors having agreed to a neutral stand on the matter. And all three times—in 1907, 1908, and 1912—the forces of teetotalism carried the day. The debate did little to smooth relations between working and middle classes. Though there were working-class "drys" and middle-class "wets," many perceived the continuing prohibition as an attempt to give workers what was best for them. One such, signing himself "worker," wrote that he was tired of hearing about what the working class needed or wanted.

It would be interesting to peep into the minds of some people who are concerning themselves so much about the welfare of the working man, whether they are considered such a feeble-minded race as to be led like little children by the grandmotherly cant which is so often heard. The object may be well-intentioned, but the only success it achieves is ridicule and contempt. . . . If the appetite for alcohol is thought to be vulgar, conceits and delusions are little better. I think it is reasonable to suggest that as the population of Letchworth grows, so will the hostility and discontent between the two sections.[44]

In one important area, that of education, Letchworth succeeded in designing a system meant to ensure that children would grow up free from class-bred hostility and discontent. At the time the Letchworth tract was purchased, the company had already established a committee to consider the matter of garden city education; by 1905 a reconstituted Letchworth Education Council, which included both Raymond and Ethel Unwin, was preparing a detailed plan for the city's schools. The scheme adopted called for the establishment of a "non-provided" public elementary school. By designating the school in that manner the council would remain its trustees and thus retain a degree of local control that it would otherwise have had to surrender to the county. Under the council's plan, the county would equip and maintain the school. But provision of the building and of money to ensure highly qualified teachers and smaller classes was the responsibility of the council, funds for their work to be provided from a voluntary rate and private subscription.

Unwin wrote of the council's vision for the Letchworth schools in an article for the *Journal of Education*. He declared its goal "the development of the individual, to fit him or her for the common life." Working- and middle-class boys and girls would be taught together and would "share the same training and experience, so that they might be prepared to meet and co-operate in civic and business spheres." The hope was that "from the common discipline of different classes of children a more thorough and complete understanding of, and respect for, the different spheres of life would be likely to grow." Only in a system of this sort, which turned its back on the tradition of segregated education by class that was the hallmark of English schooling, "could anything like equality of opportunity be given." Though eventually some streaming would be necessary in order to accommodate students going on to university, the whole system—elementary, technical, and secondary—was to remain homogeneous, as regarded management, quality of teaching, and social status, so as to ensure that all children shared "in the same school life." Nor was it to be supposed that children of the working class would automatically leave school at fourteen; assistance would be provided to the "specially gifted children of less well-to-do parents."

The plan was a democratic departure from the elitist Education Act of 1902, which had authorized state support for secondary education but kept elementary and secondary streams segregated so as to minimize the mixing of working-class with middle-class children. The council intended to encourage the nurture of individual "best selves" from whatever class, fitting all children for their role in the common life of a more genuinely democratic society. That said, there remained in Unwin's exposition of the council's intentions a whiff of the unconscious condescension that so often infused the well-intentioned thoughts and plans of late-nineteenth-century social reformers. While "the children of the well-to-do" would gain "widened experience and sympathy" from the scheme, he wrote, those of the "less well-to-do" would profit "by mixing with children who may have had a more refined upbringing, and may be expected to have more refined habits and manners."[45] Tell that to respectable working-class parents, and then wonder why they might turn away in anger and resentment. Unwin nonetheless understood the need to convince working-class parents that the system would work to their children's advantage. "On one essential point," Unwin wrote elsewhere, the council would have to solicit understanding. It would have to ask parents "to allow their children to remain longer than was usual in an industrial town"—that is, beyond the statutory age of fourteen.[46]

Until a school was built, children met in quarters leased from the company, which had subscribed funds for general expenses. C. A. Pease, brother of E. R. Pease, the pioneer Fabian, was hired as first headmaster. The classrooms in the first permanent building were designed on an open-air plan, with screened and curtained windows, india rubber and linoleum floors, and cane chairs constructed to withstand moisture. Although the council could not finance its expanded scheme as completely as it had hoped through voluntary taxation, it prevailed upon the county to give it the kind of schools it wanted, with reduced classroom size and central courtyards, planned so that light always fell on the left side of the pupil's writing desks.[47]

Despite initial hopes that most middle-class children would attend state schools, private fee-paying establishments soon began attracting students: a coeducational secondary school; a traditional school for girls; and a boarding school, St. Christopher's, where the meals featured fresh fruit and vegetables, and where morning assemblies were "deliberative rather than devotional."[48]

Letchworth afforded adults two educational institutions. In this case, however, the published curricula suggest an unwillingness to repeat the attempt to bring working class and middle class together in classrooms. The 1909 fare at the Garden City Adult School, which met on Sunday mornings at Howard Hall and was clearly designed as an alternative to church services, included readings from Plato, Montaigne, Swedenborg, the Old and New Testament, Olive Schreiner, "Indian Writings," and Herbert Spencer. Speakers discussed topics as varied as the readings: "The God-Thought in Life," "The Ancient Mysteries," "Wanted: A Good News Paper," "Children and the Poor Law," "Human Nature." The school was clearly a discussion club whose topics and venue, as we have seen, appear to have intimidated most workers from attending. The Evening Education Committee, on the other hand, offered Machine Construction and Drawing; Building Construction and Drawing; lectures on gardening, poultry keeping, and bee keeping; as well as a sociology course that incorporated material used in a similar survey at Ruskin College, the "Workingman's College" at Oxford. Yet despite a set of offerings clearly designed to cater to the working class, the committee had difficulty attracting its intended clientele. "Education classes for the working men had had to be dropped," one disappointed correspondent wrote to the *Citizen,* "because the working men felt uncertain and insecure, and could not settle down, and so lacked the interest necessary to attend."[49] The correspondent did not venture an opinion as to where the fault lay. His observation merely underscores the touchy nature of class relations and class attitudes at Letchworth, and the way they lay close to the surface of life.

During the years immediately before the World War I, Letchworth was in many respects a city of three classes, not two: a working class that had come into being with the advent of local industry; a middle class of manufacturers and businessmen and their families, whose increasing presence so delighted and relieved the company; and a second middle class—or, rather, a first—those who had been among the city's original settlers and whose commitment to Letchworth had stemmed from commitment as well to the ideals of Howard, Parker, Unwin, and their ilk. These men and women led the community in its early years, devising for it a culture that reflected their own high-minded values, and imparting to it a spirit that became its hallmark. As they battled to preserve ideals they began to celebrate what they enjoyed calling the "spirit of the place." In so doing, they celebrated as well an alternative Englishness, one that, while paying homage to past virtues and past pleasures, had about it an air of independence at odds with the paternalism that had shaped life at Bournville and Port Sunlight, and that the company's directorate was not hesitant to impose at Letchworth as well. This Englishness derived from the original hopes for the garden city experiment. While it remained accepting of the English class system and professed cultural hierarchy, it reflected as well Unwin's concern for the individual and Howard's admiration for America and its pioneer spirit. It welcomed the idiosyncratic and rejoiced in the eccentric. In its heyday it imparted a particular quality to life at Letchworth that delighted its free-spirited true believers as much as it annoyed and occasionally horrified its establishmentarian opponents.

This was the Englishness that emanated from Howard Hall, which people used much as Unwin had imagined his common rooms might be used. Stroll inside on a wintry day, one early resident recalled, and you might

> find an artist and some helpers busy decorating . . . with copper plaques, and draperies and festoons of ivy, and you will learn that there is to be a conversazione at night, or an Association meeting, or a Debating Society's Social, or a gathering of new residents. And when you look in again . . . you will probably listen to some quite excellent music, orchestral or otherwise, directed, it may be, by a lady well known in the musical profession; there will be a scene from one of Tolstoy's plays. . . . On other evenings you will find the graver side of life taking its place. There will be discussions upon the Liquor Question, The Unemployed, Methods of Education, Political Organisations, Arts and Crafts, Science and Civilisation, and so forth.[50]

"So many opinions, . . . and so particularly definite," recalled another early resident on the occasion of Letchworth's fiftieth anniversary. "We grew into societies overnight. Everybody knew everybody else, and we all joined something so as to be in the swim."[51] By the summer of 1906 a published guide listed twenty-eight societies. A year later the list had grown to fifty-eight; by 1910 there were ninety, in a city whose population was no more than nine thousand.

Many were unexceptional—the Letchworth Football Club, the Provident Dispensary, the Residents' Union, a variety of religious and political clubs. But many bespoke the particular character of the city and its defining culture: the Anti-Vivisectionist League, the Literary and Debating Society, the Dramatic Society, the Art Workers' Guild, the Theosophical Society, the Women's Freedom League.[52] "For a time," C. B. Purdom reported in his 1913 survey, "every man was a committee man," and "the committee-man became a joke."[53]

One of the most active groups, and one particularly expressive of the cultural uplift characteristic of Letchworth's early years, was the Dramatic Society. In its first annual report, members declared their determination to "prepare the way for a theatre which will express the best thought and feeling of those who are attracted to the new town, and worthily represent the new social movement of which Garden City is an embodiment." A list of the plays performed during the first six years of the society's life shows how seriously it took its own charge: Tolstoy, Shakespeare, Shaw, Yeats, Goldsmith, Synge, Lady Gregory, along with the annual pantomime, written by Purdom and Charles Lee, a local writer and composer, which poked fun at the high-mindedness that the community took so seriously the rest of the year.[54]

An easy target for Purdom and Lee's gentle satire were the oft-lampooned faddists and eccentrics who had come to live in Letchworth in search of their own brand of utopianism. Some of what was considered "crankishness" was nothing more than latter-day common sense. A woman who had campaigned in London for the elimination of lead poisoning in pottery founded a workshop at Letchworth that sold leadless glazed ware. F. J. Osborn, executive secretary of the Howard Cottage Society in the early years and later a highly regarded city planner, recalled on the city's fiftieth anniversary that "the eccentricities of the Letchworth Circle . . . were mostly fashions in advance of their stiff and hidebound time." Sandals were a vogue among this minority, Edward Carpenter's sandal maker having moved from Carpenter's commune at Millthorpe to Letchworth. Hats and gloves were deemed extraneous and affected. Osborn remembered himself as a "youthful no-hatter" whose radical style brought him disapproving stares when he went to work in London.[55] Vegetarians opened the Food Reform Restaurant and Simple Life Hotel. An account of a visit of the secretary of the national Vegetarian Society to Letchworth in 1907 in the *Vegetarian Messenger* suggests why he may have imagined himself closer to his kind of heaven on earth than he had thought possible: "Arriving here on Saturday afternoon . . . he proceeded straight to Howard Hall, where he lectured on 'Health and Food,' with the usual bombardment of questions; from there he went to the Food Reform Restaurant, where he met several friends to tea and afterwards in the Common Room. Then in the evening to the Women's Guild . . . he spoke on vegetarian cookery; cooking and dispensing nut fritters and soup. Then at nine on Sunday morning, at the Adult School, leaving at 12."[56]

Charles Lee, the pantomimist, delighted in recording the idiosyncrasies of his fellow citizens in a journal, excerpts from which were published on the occasion of the city's half-century celebration. He had written of a man he called a "typical Garden Citizen," a bachelor, between forty and fifty, living with his sister, a sandal-wearer, vegetarian and member of the Theosophical Society. "Keeps two tortoises, which he polishes periodically with the best Lucca oil." Over his mantel hung a photograph of Madame Blavatsky, high priestess of Theosophy, beneath which he burned joss sticks, "not for reasons of ritual but to impart a piny flavour to the air he breathes." Lee relished what he referred to as Letchworth's "perpetual feast of the Grotesque." "The leading vegetarian [Howard himself] in heroic attitude on his doorstep, repelling a concerted attack of pie men and butcher-boys: 'I will not have my house desecrated with sausage rolls.'" He enjoyed an occasion when the company sent a representative to a Howard Hall convocation to denounce no-hatters as "unpatriotic citizens, who had not the interests of Letchworth at heart," whose bare heads had driven off many a potential settler. "As soon as he gets out of the station, he meets half a dozen folk of both sexes, all without the conventional headgear. 'Cranks,' says he at once, 'Suffragists, Freelovers, Socialists! This is no place for me,' and off he goes, and the Company is left to mourn its unsigned lease."[57] If on occasion Lee allowed his imagination to embroider plain truth, as some commentators suggested, the richness of his detail and wryness of his observations contribute nonetheless to a re-creation of that "spirit" early residents never tired of celebrating.

Religion of one sort or another played a central role in the life of that spirit. Beside the conventional denominations—Anglican, Roman Catholic, Quaker, and a Free Church that welcomed Baptists, Congregationalists, Methodists, and Presbyterians—Theosophists, Christian Scientists, and Spiritualists attracted smaller yet dedicated bands. The most prominent of these more esoteric sects was the Alpha Union, a group devoted to the realization of universal health and harmony. It was headed by a Scottish Congregationalist, J. Bruce Wallace, whose writings in the 1880s on Laurence Gronlund's *Cooperative Commonwealth* and Edward Bellamy's *Looking Backward* had helped introduce those two utopians to Howard. The Alpha Union was housed in a remarkable fantasia of a building, the Cloisters, built by the London heiress Annie J. Lawrence. It was, in the words of an early advertisement, to be "a place of 'plain living' where 'high thinking' shall be done, and in which the living spirit of man shall work out new and beautiful forms and schemes of expression."[58] The building contained a large semicircular cloister, whose central space was covered by canvas, serving as conference hall by day and dormitory by night, hammocks for sleeping arranged in such a way that they could be raised out of sight during the day. A startling tower with a conical roof made the building a landmark, as, in another way, did the pronouncements of its patroness. At the building's dedication she invoked "the unity, eternal reality, through all diverse, temporary and fragmentary seemings, the perfect inviolable whole, wherein sin and pain and death are not, and all contradictions are reconciled, all discords resolved."[59]

The Alpha Union conducted an annual Summer School of Religion, Psychology, and Sociology, which attracted students from home and abroad. Speakers lectured on a range of topics; the agenda for 1910 included talks entitled "Is It Possible to Obtain First Hand Evidence of the Next Life?" "Health Germs," and, from Bruce Wallace, "Exodus from Industrial Bondage."[60] C. B. Purdom's tongue-in-cheek account of his attendance at one of the first schools suggests that students received, if nothing else, a baptism in the heady language of universal brotherhood. "We were bathed in energizing currents of the Intellect. We were brought so near to the one Creative Intelligence that some of us could think no longer."[61]

The Alpha Union's effusions made Letchworth's citizens an easy target for caricature, if not scorn. John Buchan took a poke in his novel *Mr. Standfast.* Chapter 2, entitled "The Village Named Morality," described the community of Biggleswick, where houses were "badly built and oddly furnished: the bed was too short, the windows did not fit, the doors did not stay shut." Men were "rather weedy looking"; women "rather badly dressed and inclining to untidy hair." Of the town's religions: "I had already counted twenty-seven varieties . . . , including three Buddhists, a Celestial Hierarch, five Latter-Day Saints, and about ten varieties of Mystic whose names I could never remember." Buchan's conclusion: "A lot of ignorance, a large slice of variety, and a pinch or two of wrong-headed honesty—these are the ingredients of the pie. Not much real harm in it."[62]

Although treatment of that sort no doubt upset the company, confirming the directors' belief that cranks would bring ruination upon their scheme, it left the middle-class idealists of Letchworth unscathed. They knew that they evoked a

degree of ridicule. Indeed, they enjoyed ridiculing themselves, as their panto-
mimes proved. Yet they took their life at Letchworth with great seriousness and
found in it immense satisfaction. In the inaugural issue of *The City*, one of two
Letchworth monthlies published in the city's infancy, its editor, Harry Bryan
Binns, contributed a poem that reflected the vision these men and women
carried in their heads.

> I see a City being wrought
> Upon the rock of Living Thought.
> It was a bloodless dream until
> It quickened in a good man's will,
> Became a hope, became a vow,
> For me, for many, until now
> Upon the rock of Living Thought
> I see a City being wrought.[63]

They believed themselves a fortunate few. One of the early settlers wondered
after fifty years whether there might ever again be collected together "such a
brilliant circle of artists, medieval craftsmen, writers and musicians—innate
bohemians all—who had time and leisure to meet, to talk, to create beautiful
things, to make music for the sheer joy and love of it."[64] As Letchworth's
population grew, it became more difficult and more imperative than ever to
impart the spirit to newcomers. In 1909 the Residents' Union formed subcom-
mittees to plan lectures and distribute leaflets "which might help in making
[Garden City] ideals more widely known and appreciated among our residents."[65]

The men and women who had been Letchworth's first settlers had no difficulty seeing themselves as pioneers, and in the American sense of that term.
Never before in England had a city arisen from the land as Letchworth had.
That it was built across ancient fields could not convince these settlers that they
were not realizing their dream on virgin soil. They were assisted in this perception by unfriendly critics who could not understand the point of erecting a city
de novo—out in the "howling wilderness," as a hostile observer remarked at the
outset. Writing ten years after the groundbreaking, one of the pioneers declared
that the garden city ideal was "simply to demonstrate that by forethought it is
possible on 'prairie' land, to create a new town" possessing the best features of
town and country living.[66] Purdom wrote that the first residents "did truly look
upon the land with an eye of faith, and it was no wonder that, coming to build
their houses under such novel conditions, they should expect to see arise not

merely a new city but a new civilization." They would, in the words of one of their band, be their "own pious founders."[67]

They gloried in the fact that they had no past, even though so much at Letchworth derived from notions about a past in many ways superior to the present. "This is the City of the future," as Robert Gernon boasted. "And in a degree not elsewhere to be paralleled we are building and working altogether for the future. The past is not upon us to hinder us in our work. In a curious way we have almost escaped from the past and from the ancient traditions and are building afresh on new soil."[68] Believing in that, the pioneers often felt themselves and their vision betrayed by the commercial and financial reality that required constant concession. Yet Letchworth, in its early years, remained for many the vision of an attainable Englishness as well as an emergent city. It was a middle-class vision shaped and articulated by men and women who had chosen to live in a place where no one had ever lived before and had decided to partake of an experiment that no one had heretofore had the courage to conduct.

It was as well, however, a vision rooted in an ultimately conservative desire to transcend class through the imposition of a common culture derived not so much from future promise as from an invented past. In the summer of 1914 members of the Letchworth Arts Club engaged themselves in that quintessentially high-minded, middle-class pursuit, the production of a masque. Pageants, as well as May Day celebrations, were a characteristically important element in the "spirit of the place." This one, entitled "The Garden of the Leech," derived its theme from the ancient etymology of the word Letchworth, "the leech's garden"—though others insisted that it should be understood as "the farm by the rivulet." "The town's name," the printed foreword nonetheless declared, "considered as signifying the Leech's Holding, or Garden of Healing Herbs, gave the masque its point of departure. Garden City is in effect a place of healing, an experiment-ground for solutions to social ills and sores, and one where constructive thought may generate and bear fruit."[69] So it seemed to the masquers. And so it could still seem, despite disappointment and compromise, to the men and women whose dream it remained.

Chapter 7 Suburban High-
Mindedness at Hampstead

Devoted though he was to Letchworth and its spirit, in 1906 Raymond Unwin moved with his family to Hampstead, where he assumed the post of consulting architect and surveyor to the Hampstead Garden Suburb Trust. He remained in partnership with Barry Parker and continued to design for Letchworth. But his efforts now focused on this new project—the garden suburb.

To true believers in the ideals of the garden city, Unwin's move seemed a sad, surprising defection. As Howard found it necessary to insist, in a letter to *The Builder* in 1910, there was a vast but frequently ignored difference between a garden city and a garden suburb. The former was a "self-contained town—industrial, agricultural, residential." It must, Howard declared, be understood as "prepar[ing] the way for a national movement" and as a social institution of vital importance to the well-being of the country, "stemming the tide of the population now leaving the countryside and sweeping into our over-crowded cities." Garden suburbs, however, did no more than provide "that the normal growth of existing cities shall be on healthy lines." Though useful, even in the case of hideously overcrowded London, they nonetheless tended "to drive the country yet further afield" and failed to "deal with the root evil—rural depopulation."[1]

In 1911, Ralph Neville expressed a forthright impatience with garden suburbs that the invariably courteous Howard had no doubt felt but had foreborn from expressing. Addressing the council of the Garden City and Town Planning Association he declared that the "main idea" of the garden city movement "had got swamped by a multitude of smaller ideas," and that "it was important to bring back to the public mind" the fact that garden suburbs, whatever their immediate advantages, were "not really the chief object of the Garden City Association."[2] The term "garden suburbs" was further cheapened, in the minds of purists, when unscrupulous developers began to use it to describe any hastily planned subdivision along a city's edge. As *The Times* lamented, "Garden Suburbs are not made by purchasing a few fields, cutting them up into 'eligible sites,' and allowing the buyers to erect upon them any sort of house that may please their errant fancy. That way chaos lies; and the final result will be indistinguishable from the existing suburban conditions which are a reproach to Greater London."[3]

When the term "garden suburb" thus bespoke both the betrayal of a conception and the commercialization of an ideal, how difficult it was for those who had labored to bring Letchworth into being to accept Unwin's decision to devote himself to Hampstead. "I could not conceive how a man who believed in the garden city as he did could forsake it for a cause so inferior as that of a garden suburb," C. B. Purdom wrote to Barry Parker's widow many years after the move. He speculated, as did others, that the departure was a result of Unwin's inability to work with the hardheaded W. H. Gaunt. Yet Mabel Parker, in a letter at the same time to F. J. Osborn, declared that although neither Unwin nor Parker "could possibly have felt any sympathy with the outlook G. brought," she had never understood that there had been a "complete falling out." She observed as well that the founder of Hampstead Garden Suburb, Henrietta Barnett, had insisted that Unwin move there if he was to take charge of the enterprise. Osborn opined that although, as we have seen, "temperamentally [Gaunt] would not be in tune with Unwin, especially in aesthetic matters," their differences were not so great to have caused Unwin "to abdicate the scheme." Indeed, Unwin continued to design for Letchworth from his Hampstead office, as Parker designed for Hampstead from Letchworth. Osborn concluded, undoubtedly correctly, "that both partners realized the wider scope that they would have for advancing good planning methods by taking part in Mrs. Barnett's project as well as in Letchworth, and that it was not necessary for both to reside in Letchworth."[4]

In spite of the purists' disparagement of garden suburbs, proponents of the Hampstead scheme argued that experimentation at the city's edges, where most uncontrolled urban growth was then occurring, was as necessary to the revitalization of the nation as were the planning and building of such garden cities as Letchworth. In *Nothing Gained by Overcrowding!* published in 1912, Unwin made a case for the garden suburb and enlisted Howard himself as an ally. He cited Howard's assertion that once a city had reached a population of thirty thousand, it "might need to provide for the development all around it of subsidiary towns at a short distance, intimately connected with it. The fact that many . . . towns have already exceeded the limit in size which is deemed desirable by the advocates of the Garden City is, no doubt, unfortunate, but it can hardly be urged as a good reason for making no protest from the Garden City point of view against these towns being allowed to grow up in a homogeneous manner, swallowing up and obliterating the country all round, like the spreading of flood water over a shallow valley." Unwin defended efforts, such as the one in Hampstead, to secure "definite belts of open space" around existing cities, and then to develop them "by means of detached suburbs grouped around some centre and separated from the existing towns by at least sufficient open ground to provide for fresh air, recreation and contact with growing nature." In a lecture that same year he again coopted Howard as an ally, arguing for "Mr. Howard's Garden City idea applied to town development" and urging the laying out of what he called "individual suburbs," each with its own municipal buildings, churches, schools, and recreational facilities.[5]

Beyond the understandable desire to tackle a different and clearly important urban planning problem, there lay the fact that Hampstead offered Unwin an opportunity to experiment with ideas that he had begun to absorb from the work of Camillo Sitte—for example, Sitte's insistence on the importance of urban irregularity, tightness, and *place.* We have seen that Unwin himself acknowledged by 1907 that the spaces at Letchworth were too often disproportionately large.[6] A garden suburb up against London's constantly encroaching sprawl would encourage a general plan whose urban compactness might naturally reflect the concepts that Sitte had championed and that Unwin was finding increasingly congenial.

Without question, Unwin understood that whatever final plan he conceived for Hampstead Garden Suburb, it was bound to attract considerable attention, and hence focus thinking on important town planning issues. When F. J. Osborn wrote years later of the "wider scope" for the advancement of good planning methods that participation in the Hampstead project would afford

Parker and Unwin, he no doubt had in mind the fact that its highly visible creator was the redoubtable and imperious Henrietta Octavia Barnett, a woman well versed in the ways of attracting attention to the causes and schemes that she espoused. Although prepared to efface herself and her labors in the semi-autobiographical biography she wrote of her husband, the founder of Toynbee Hall, Henrietta Barnett was nonetheless a power in her own right.[7] Her work, alongside that of Samuel Barnett and the couple's equally reform-minded upper-middle-class allies, was continuing proof of the urban historian Walter Creese's observation that "no matter how cumulative and broad the forces of urban resolution might appear to be toward the end of the nineteenth century, they were still being initiated by well-placed and highly articulate personalities in Britain."[8]

Although she once described herself as nothing more than a "general servant" at Toynbee Hall, she could as easily be described as its co-founder. The Arts and Crafts architect C. R. Ashbee, an early resident at the Hall, recorded Barnett's predominating influence in his journal. "Mrs. Barnett is . . . the Prior and the Prioress of this place—the worthy head. A fine, noble, bright-eyed, vigorous woman she appears; and one that will have her own way and not be sparing of her opinion."[9] A protégé of the equally formidable social reformer Octavia Hill, Henrietta Barnett had written and spoken extensively and with characteristic certainty for over a quarter of a century on problems associated with poverty, and of ways to solve them by means of those programs and prescriptions to which she and Samuel had attached their label of "practicable socialism."

The Barnetts owned a house on the edge of Hampstead Heath, where they retreated on weekends from the debilitating atmosphere and taxing pressures of their labors in East London, and where they brought East End neighbors to enjoy the respite with them. When, in 1903, it became clear that the Charing Cross, Euston, and Hampstead railway (the present Northern Line) would extend services to Golders Green, Henrietta Barnett foresaw the consequences as further suburban overcrowding and jerry-building, and determined to mount a successful campaign to extend the heath. Around that extension she then proposed to build a suburb responding to human needs that, despite the efforts that she and others had pioneered, had remained unfulfilled in London slums.

Hampstead Garden Suburb was to address urban problems that Barnett believed could be more naturally solved in a garden suburb than in a garden city. She did not hesitate to tangle with Ebenezer Howard on that hotly disputed subject. In a 1910 speech to members of the German Town Planning

Association, according to a report in the *Hampstead and Highgate Express,* "she contrasted Hampstead with Letchworth, which was a noble attempt to create a city. But it was an artificial city, while at Hampstead they could see an effort to treat a suburb—the natural growth of an existing city—so that it could be made beautiful and desirable to live in." Howard of course replied with the by now standard argument that it was suburbs that were unnatural, and that only with "carefully thought-out plans for building new towns" could the "art of town planning . . . be in the fullest and most real sense carried out."[10] One has the sense that had Henrietta Barnett been the first to conceive of the garden city she would have championed it with her accustomed vigor. Since it was the suburb that had become her crusade, however, once the heathland had been purchased, that cause became the "natural" one.

With the purchase of the heath extension, the community would be guaranteed eighty acres of green space, providing residents the rare opportunity to breathe fresh, healthy air in perpetuity. Around that space the suburb would be designed to address four specific goals, spelled out in a letter of intention first published in 1905 and reiterated in articles by Henrietta Barnett and in annual prospectuses. First: "We desire to do something to meet the housing problem, by putting within the reach of working people the opportunity of taking a cottage with a garden within a 2d. fare of Central London, and at a moderate rent." Second: "Our aim is that the new suburb may be laid out as a whole on an orderly plan." By providing residents with a carefully designed environment, open spaces "within reach of every child and old person," "good views or glimpses of distant country," varied street configurations, and an attractive central district, the suburb's promoters hoped "to take away some of the anxiety now caused by town extension." Third: "We aim at preserving natural beauty," this goal a corollary of the preceding one. "Our object is so to lay out the ground that every tree may be kept, hedgerows duly considered, and the foreground of the distant view be preserved, if not as open fields, yet as a garden district, the buildings kept in harmony with the surroundings."[11]

The fourth object was the most original, and certainly the most expressive of the Barnetts' own lifelong concerns. "We desire to promote a better understanding between the members of the classes who form our nation." The intention was not, therefore, merely to provide housing for workers. "We propose that some of the beautiful sites round the Heath should be let to wealthy persons who can afford to pay a large sum for their land and to have extensive gardens." In this way, those paying rents of 7/6 per week and those paying as much as £400 per year "would share in the church, the chapel, the public library, and the open spaces, not by forced, artificial methods, but as inhabitants of the garden suburb."12

Whenever she wrote about her vision and the project that was its embodiment, Barnett championed the cause of reconstituted community. Once again, the image of the hierarchical village was evoked: when the rich sought comfortable neighborhoods and, in the process, deserted the poor, she declared in a 1905 *Contemporary Review* article, those localities they left behind were "deprived of the contagion of refinement which contact brings, and the richer people lose the inspiration which knowledge of strenuous lives and patient endurance provokes." The English system of government, she continued, "is based on the belief that there is in every district a leisured and cultivated class able to give time and thought to municipal and other public duties, and when such a class is absent the whole suffers both financially and ethically." This was the message the Barnetts had broadcast at the time they founded Toynbee Hall. Now, twenty-five years on, Henrietta Barnett was prepared to acknowledge that the Hall had been no better than an "artificial protest against the massing in one locality of the poor." The suburb, which would bring together men and women from different classes as genuine neighbors, would encourage the kind of social intercourse that its founders fondly believed had existed before the advent of industrialization and the uncontrolled growth of cities. "The old-fashioned village"; "the big house and the cottage"; "the cottage and the manor-house of the English village": over and over a pre-industrial ideal was celebrated. And with it, the expectation that class antagonisms gradually would vanish. Class division bred suspicion, Henrietta Barnett wrote, "and the sod of suspicion cannot produce the strong tree, in whose branches its people rest in happy security."13

Like so many who worked to invent an Englishness as a way of making England a better land and a stronger nation, Barnett never doubted the paramount importance of environment. She had paid close attention to George Cadbury's insistence on gardens as a means of both physical and moral regeneration, quoting him approvingly in one of the several articles she wrote on the Hampstead scheme: "The benefit, physically, morally, and even spiritually is so great that it would have been worth cultivating the gardens even if there had been no profit from the labour expended."14 The harvest of a workingman's garden was thus measured not only in vegetables for the table but in the improved character of the gardener and his family. Barnett could wax as lyrical as Cadbury about the soul-gratifying consequences of domestic horticulture: "father working, mother watching, children helping." Values would improve, along with digestion: "Pennies will not be needed for 'sweeties' as the 'goose gogs' are enjoyed; the pickles will give place to the lettuces; the hastily obtained indigestible 'relish' to 'the vegetables we growed.'" Father, especially, would experience a gratifying alteration for the better. "Speaking for my sex," Mrs. Barnett once declared, "one of our delights in the possession of a garden is to know that our men are healthily and happily employed and out of mischief. I myself always feel perfectly happy when my Canon [her husband] is occupied taking plantains out of the lawn."[15] The words echo high-minded paternalist—in this case, maternalist—certitude as to what is good and what is not, and an equally high-minded determination to impose that certitude on those unfortunate enough to be without the knowledge themselves.

This was unquestionably a conservative agenda. Yet it is a measure of the congruence of conservative and radical goals within the garden city movement that a committed socialist such as Unwin would have found the proposal appealing. He too understood the need to create new, liberating environments for workers and their families. He too looked to the past for models on which to construct the communities of the present. And, along with the Barnetts and so many others of similar temperament and point of view, he subscribed to the belief that "disinterested" reformers recognized what was best for England's sadly deprived citizenry.

Henrietta Barnett knew from the commencement of her efforts at Hampstead that the two objectives of her campaign—the heath extension and the garden suburb—must be understood as part of one overall scheme. Eton College owned the land in question: the 80 acres to be added to Hampstead Heath and the additional 243 acres that were to form the nucleus of the suburb. To raise money for the first parcel, Barnett organized the Hampstead Heath Extension Council in June 1902, with herself as honorary secretary. The council sought the purchase price—ultimately £36,000—from both private donors and public bodies. A small army of volunteers folded circulars and stamped and addressed envelopes. In the course of three mailings, Henrietta Barnett personally signed thirteen thousand letters, including some sent, as the council's final report put it, as "personal reminders to negligent persons of their public duties"—almost certainly the tart language of the honorary secretary. Among the largest contributors were Andrew Carnegie and Harold Harmsworth (Alfred's brother), each of whom subscribed £1,000.[16]

The Extension Council's report also expressed gratitude to those who had "faced not always courteous municipal bodies" in the course of the campaign.

39. Henrietta Barnett, c. 1910. "The only person . . . who could recite the Ten Commandments as if she had just made them up."

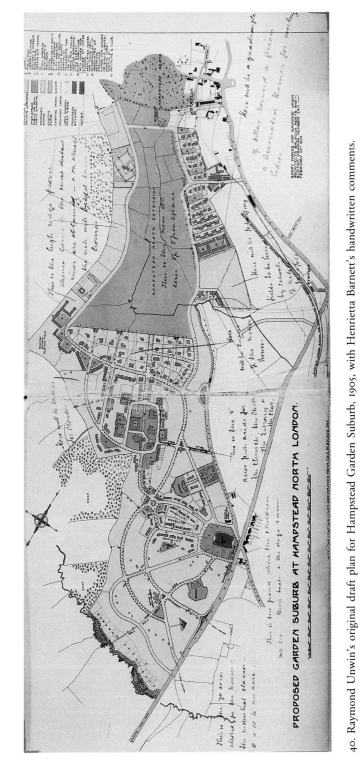

40. Raymond Unwin's original draft plan for Hampstead Garden Suburb, 1905, with Henrietta Barnett's handwritten comments.

41. Illustration from M. H. Baillie Scott and Raymond Unwin's Hampstead Garden Suburb promotional brochure, *Town Planning and Modern Architecture.* The charm of the countryside.

42 and 43. Unwin's admiration for enclosed medieval towns was reflected in the photograph of Rothenburg, from his *Town Planning in Practice*, and in his proposal for the wall between Hampstead Garden Suburb and the heath.

44. The wall as built, suggesting that the planners and promoters of the Suburb were concerned with keeping the heath and its frequenters at bay.

·PROPOSED SHOPS· HAMPSTEAD GARDEN SUBURB· PARRY PARKER AND RAYMOND UNWIN ARCHITECTS

45. The Finchley Road shops and offices, Hampstead Garden Suburb. Designed by Unwin's associate A. J. Penty. Again, the appeal of the medieval.

46. Unwin's prototype, perhaps, for the central square at Hampstead Garden Suburb. From *Town Planning in Practice.*

47 St. Jude's, Hampstead Garden Suburb, designed by Edwin Lutyens.

48. The Free Church, Hampstead Garden Suburb, also by Lutyens. The two churches illustrate the degree to which Henrietta Barnett was willing to allow grandeur to triumph over cosiness.

9. The Institute, Hampstead Garden Suburb. By Edwin Lutyens. A temple to high-mindedness.

50. An illustration from Baillie Scott and Unwin's *Modern Architecture and Town Planning*. Note the attention to detail: the walls, the sunken garden. The houses have been drawn as if at the edge of the countryside. They are, in fact, at the center of the Suburb.

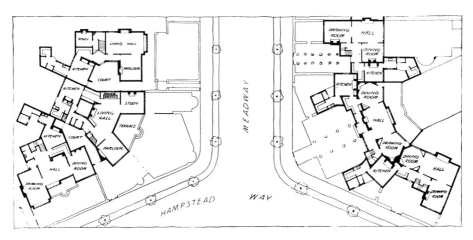

51 and 52. Suburban "cottages" for the upper middle class. From Baillie Scott and Unwin's *Modern Architecture and Town Planning.*

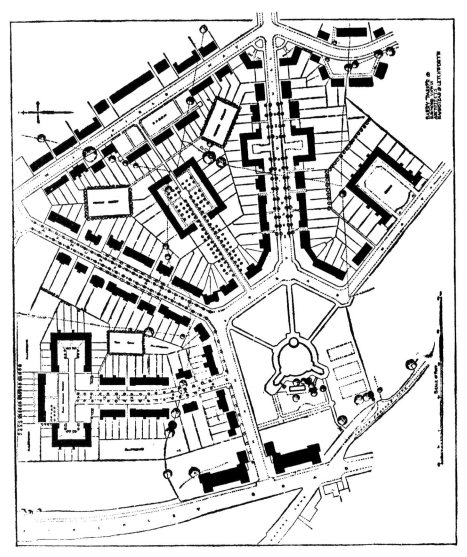

53. Unwin's plan for the working-class village at Hampstead Garden Suburb. The pond (right center) was never built. Note the tennis courts, which were.

54 and 55. Workers' cottages at Hampstead Garden Suburb. Asmuns Place and Hampstead Way.

56. The artisan at home. Illustration from Baillie Scott and Unwin's *Town Planning and Modern Architecture*.

57. The clubhouse, Willifield Green. Parker and Unwin, architects. Like the Finchley Road shops, the building displays Unwin's admiration for the picturesque.

58. Waterlow Court, Hampstead Garden Suburb. M. H. Baillie Scott, architect. The vintage suburb at its best.

Henrietta Barnett labored long, and in the end with considerable success, to make nearby borough councils and the London County Council understand their obligation to support her campaign to preserve open land to the ultimate benefit of all of London. In the case of the Hampstead Borough Council, the local authority most likely to profit from both the extension and, even more, the suburb, she made it clear that construction of the latter would not begin until the former was secured. Knowing that Hampstead suffered a shortage of workers' housing, she used the suburb as a not so subtle bribe to persuade the councillors to invest in the heath. The suburb's historian has expressed the strategy succinctly: "No working class housing to relieve Hampstead's problems unless Hampstead played its part in getting the 80 acres."[17] The ploy succeeded. When the vote was taken, one of the councillors who supported the scheme declared "that the chance of getting working class dwellings in that neighborhood was far greater if these eighty acres were acquired than if they let things alone, for in the latter event the builders would only put up such houses as would suit their pockets."[18] The borough voted £5,000 toward the purchase of the heathland; their example was followed by the Borough Councils of Islington (£2,500) and St. Pancras (£1,000), by the Middlesex County Council (£2,000) and, after considerable pressure from Barnett and her allies, by the London County Council (£8,000).

Indeed, none of this support came without intense campaigning. Barnett assembled a powerful group of lobbyists to assist her in her battles with local officialdom—the nucleus of what would become the board of the Hampstead Garden Trust. A "syndicate of eight," she called them: "a veritable showman's happy family: two earls, two lawyers, two free churchmen, a bishop and a woman."[19] In addition to herself, the group included Lord Crewe, at various times leader of the House of Lords, lord president of the Privy Council, and secretary of state for India; Lord Grey, soon to be governor general of Canada; Sir John Gorst, a highly visible member of Parliament and former solicitor general; and Robert Hunter, one of the founders of the National Trust. Her bishop was Arthur Winnington-Ingram, not just any bishop, but bishop of London. Her two free churchmen, Walter Hazell and Herbert Marnham, both enjoyed highly respectable reputations as church laymen and Hampstead residents. The willingness of these men to lend their prestige and, more significantly, their time to the effort is testimony to Barnett's formidable and, one cannot help but conclude, all but irresistible determination. When the land was conveyed from Eton to the London County Council in March 1907, Samuel Barnett wrote to his brother with obvious pride in the authoritative role that

Henrietta had played in the transfer of land that had once belonged to Henry VIII. "Henricus Octavius gave it to Eton, and Eton sold it to Henrietta Octavia. It is a great triumph. The way is now clear for Garden Suburb."[20]

By that time, indeed, the syndicate had been reconstituted as a smaller board of directors of the Hampstead Garden Trust, Ltd., which with mortgages and the issuance of shares was able on May 1, 1907, to purchase the land—again from Eton—on which the original suburb was built, for £107,500. The new board was further testimony to the extent of Henrietta Barnett's connections to the world of the highly influential. Its chairman was Alfred Lyttelton, who had served as colonial secretary in Arthur Balfour's Conservative government and was a neighbor of the Barnetts in Westminster, whence they had moved following Samuel's appointment as canon of the abbey in 1906. Other directors included Robert Hunter, Herbert Marnham, and Henrietta herself, of the original eight, along with Frank Debenham, a member of the drapery firm of Debenham and Peabody and of the London County Council, and Henry Vivian, the leading advocate of the co-partnership housing movement.

The board's task had been, if anything, more difficult to achieve than that of the Heath Extension Council. As was true with Letchworth, investors were not easily persuaded to put money into a scheme that seemed to most no more than philanthropic. A letter writer to the *Hampstead and Highgate Express* claimed to have shown the proposal to a developer, who had called it unrealistic. The scheme was "worthy of being the offspring of a disciple of St. Francis; only an ecclesiastic could or would have denied it." It was, in fact, "mere moonshine; no millionaire would lend his money for such a purpose."[21] Businessmen, Samuel Barnett lamented in a letter to his brother, were not accustomed to an investment of this sort. "Their ideal is the giver of money who receives thanks and an approving conscience."[22] One such potential investor, when approached by the board, replied that he "had given considerable time to the matter, but feared that no building scheme would pay unless houses were more crowded, for people did not want gardens."[23] Meanwhile, Hampstead residents grew alarmed at the prospect of just such crowding, and at the thought of those who might soon become their neighbors. One worried householder wrote *The Times* to express his angry concern. "It is really a delightful programme. Get your wealthy persons to subscribe to retain as much as possible of Hampstead as a heath recreation or pleasurable heath and garden ground. Then convert a part of it into a building estate (the very thing you subscribed to prevent); . . . then bring up all the poor from various parts of London, with their howling, undisciplined and ignorant products [children?] . . . to live in 'kindly neighborliness.'"[24]

Of course, the suburb was not to be built on the heath extension, as Henrietta Barnett and others were quick to point out. But the fear expressed in the letter helps explain why she felt compelled to lecture in the ensuing months to meetings of the Hampstead Women's Institute and at the Hampstead public library to small but, from the trust's perspective, extremely important audiences. A year later she was still at work, mailing out five thousand prospectuses, addressing a dinner meeting in London, held to honor Ralph Neville and his work on behalf of garden cities, at which—at least according to her admiring husband—"she made the speech of the evening as she lightly touched the great meaning of the movement which is enlarging people's imagination."[25] Without question, her clear sense of that "great meaning" enabled her to speak of it with convincing determination, just as it turned that determination into the certainty that London *would* have the suburb community she believed it so desperately needed.

Henrietta Barnett claimed to have known from the moment she read *The Art of Building a Home* that Unwin was the planner she wanted for her project. "I read on and on, not ever noticing who wrote what, until putting down. I said, 'That's the man for my beautiful green golden scheme.'" This despite the fact that the trust had first offered the post to the distinguished and highly visible architect Richard Norman Shaw.[26] Yet Barnett was clearly impressed by Unwin's much-publicized work at Letchworth. She found his concept of neighborly quadrangles particularly appealing. In a brochure prepared to attract investors, the trust reprinted illustrations from Parker and Unwin's book, along with captions indicative of the sort of life to be led at Hampstead: "A corner of a proposed quadrangle forming a tennis court around which will live young men, clerks, etc.—who can thus get wholesome exercise before the rapid two-penny tube takes them into London to their work."[27]

The caption, almost certainly written by Henrietta Barnett, suggests the degree to which she was prepared to impose a style of life on the men, women, and children who were to live in her suburb. On a map sketched for her by Unwin she wrote—in much the same certain style as the caption—of who was to do what, and where: "This is the pond where the children will sail their boats and swim"; "This is the high ridge from whence some of the more distant views are obtained—and on which the rich will build their houses."[28] Henrietta Barnett's vision was not simply a concept, it was replete with a degree of detail that must have made Unwin's task even more daunting than the one he and Parker had undertaken at Letchworth.

Unwin was appointed consulting architect in May 1906, with a mandate to lay out the estate, negotiate for the lease of building sites, approve house plans, and oversee workmanship and the use of materials. Until that time, the most notable development approximating a garden suburb in or near London was Bedford Park, at Chiswick, which dated from 1875. The street layout there, by and large a conventional block system, probably disqualifies it as a garden suburb, at least as the concept was to develop under Unwin's inspiration and supervision at Hampstead. Yet the width of the streets and incorporation into the planning of mature trees planted by the estate's previous owner, the curator of the nearby Royal Horticultural Society gardens, resulted in what Walter Creese has described as a "revolutionary consciousness of space brought alive by light filtering through the trees." Creese notes that the absence of stiffness, a consequence of the sensitive placement of houses so as to produce pleasing vistas between buildings as well as up and down the streets, gave the suburb the look of a much older community. It possessed, as one contemporary journal expressed it, the "snug warm look of having been inhabited for at least a century." To which Creese adds: "The English dual requirement, the seeking of new images through the restoration of old values, was cogently expressed."[29]

That requirement was, of course, one to which Unwin was particularly sensitive. He had almost certainly visited Bedford Park; its roster of architects included Shaw, and the adventurous Arts and Crafts designer C. F. A. Voysey. And he undoubtedly came away impressed by the manner in which both the overall layout and the arrangement of individual buildings—houses, shops, an inn, a clubhouse, and an art school—came together into a pleasing communal whole. Unwin's charge, however, required him to produce something more than a variant on Bedford Park. He was to relate the suburb to the heath and in some manner as well to the dreary suburban sprawl of adjacent Finchley Road; and he must design for a community composed—unlike middle-class Bedford Park—of men and women from both the working and middle classes, bringing them into a kind of proximity that would promote social harmony and a degree of intermingling without in any marked degree challenging fundamental class relationships.

Unwin was aided in his task by a 1906 Act of Parliament, which he assisted in drafting, that specifically exempted Hampstead Garden Suburb from the bye-law restrictions that had blighted suburban development with their well-meant but poorly considered insistence on uniformity. The Hampstead act's main provisions were that there should be no less than fifty feet between houses on opposite sides of any road, that houses would be limited to eight per acre, and—most important for Unwin's purposes—that minor "accommodation roads," cul-de-sacs serving the sort of quadrangles and *places* that Unwin considered so important to his schemes, would be exempt from the byelaws governing roadway widths and could be laid out in whatever way seemed most appropriate to the directors and their chief planner. Not surprisingly, the trust proved itself a formidable lobbyist as the bill was debated. The Hendon Urban District Council petitioned in opposition to the provision allowing variances on the accommodation roads. In response, the directors instructed Henry Vivian, who was to introduce the bill in Parliament, to "seek an informal talk with Mr. John Burns [president of the Local Government Board] to show how [the present] byelaws would injure the Garden City movement." Should it be deemed appropriate or necessary, a larger deputation was prepared to call on Burns as well.[30]

Assisted by the flexibility that Parliament granted him, Unwin proceeded to tackle his two major planning problems. In the case of the first, the relation between the suburb itself and the landscape surrounding it, Unwin's solution was interestingly ambiguous. In a stylish and profusely illustrated promotional brochure he wrote with the architect M. H. Baillie Scott, he declared his intention to "bring together the best that the English village and the English city have to give."[31] Leafing through the booklet's pages, one encounters in pictures and captions the authors' repeated and deliberate evocation of the rural qualities Unwin was determined to preserve as a bulwark against the bustling crowds disgorged daily at the Golders Green underground station. The caption beneath a photograph of Wyldes Farm celebrated its origins as part of Henry VIII's original grant to Eton; it was there, indeed, on a far edge of the suburb, that Unwin himself lived from 1907 until his death in 1940. In 1909, the American Arts and Crafts journal *The Craftsman* wrote approvingly of the way in which "the whole place reminds one of an English village on a large scale and in perfect repair, and anyone who has ever seen an English village knows that nothing else in the world fulfills quite so completely all that one has dreamed of as an ideally beautiful and restful place to live."[32] Unwin's original scheme, dated 1905—the one bearing Henrietta Barnett's confident annotations—does recall rural patterns. The layout of curving, tree-lined streets, the "village" center, with shops, churches, and library, reflect the informal, settled cosiness that Unwin prized and that he understood to be the essence of rural community. Special effort was made to replace walls, particularly back walls enclosing outbuildings and laundry yards, with hedges, or, whenever possible, with open greenswards and commons that would contribute to the sense of rural openness.

Yet from certain vantage points, and in those enclosed or semi-enclosed courts and quadrangles that Unwin fancied, the suburb expressed a frank, self-conscious urbanity that Letchworth never achieved. Along the border between the heath extension and the suburb, Unwin proposed a wall reminiscent of one he had seen and photographed at Rothenburg. The effect, when executed according to the design of his draftsman, Charles Wade, was to evoke not so much an English village as a small central European medieval town. This image was reinforced by the landmark tower of St. Jude's Church, which rose from the suburb's central square. Even more frankly urban was a set of office buildings, shops, and flats designed by another of Unwin's assistants, Arthur Penty, along the Finchley Road. These buildings represented another kind of wall, and bespoke the town-country ambivalence that continued to characterize Unwin's work as a planner. Their impressive heft reflects Unwin's admiration for the kind of townscape that Sitte preached and that Unwin increasingly respected, just as their all but quaint medieval style evoked the particular urbanity that Unwin found most acceptable. At the same time, the buildings' ground-floor shops fronted on Finchley Road, not into the suburb. Thus Unwin, though he acknowledged the necessity for urban commerce, did not appear to welcome it within the suburb itself. Instead, he employed large commercial buildings to isolate his placid community from the world at its gates. As commerce turns its back on the suburb, the suburb sets its face toward the green and pleasant landscape that to this day gives Hampstead Garden Suburb its distinctive charm.

Unwin's layout of the streets and dwellings within the suburb's insulated precincts achieves that amalgam of English city and English village of which Unwin and Baillie Scott had boasted in their promotional pamphlet. Houses were clustered in quadrangles and closes in such a manner that "each individual house gains in dignity and architectural effect by the grouping."[33] Unwin was simultaneously employing the same concept at Letchworth. Yet at Hampstead there was a tightness about his and others' designs that resulted in a more genuinely urban environment. Barry Parker, in an article for *The Craftsman*, described the process by which the whole became more than the sum of its parts. "One by one the special features of each house were dropped by each client as due consideration was given to the desirable quietness and composure of the external appearance of houses which were so close together as to be almost in the nature of a terrace."[34]

Parker and Unwin were re-creating the urbanity of Oxford and Cambridge, or of cathedral towns. To have moved beyond those old-fashioned forms and designed an even more compact cityscape would have belied the suburb's purpose and would have been antithetical to Unwin's own anti-urban instincts. Only in the laying out of blocks of two-story working-class flats along Addison Way did Unwin succumb wholeheartedly to Sitte's aesthetic. There he capitalized on the street's irregular junction with Hogarth Hill to create that feeling of semi-enclosed *place* about which he was writing so approvingly, moving his buildings close enough to the street's edge so as to create an almost citylike illusion.

As he planned the suburb, Unwin remained conscious of the injunction that Henrietta Barnett had declared the "fundamental principle" that was to govern the suburb's design, and that echoed his own communitarian convictions: "That the part should not spoil the whole, nor that individual rights be assumed to carry the power of working communal or individual wrongs."[35] Yet neither Henrietta Barnett nor Unwin apparently supposed that the principle would in any way interfere with the drafting or implementation of a scheme that separated workers and their families from the houses of their middle-class neighbors. Though class antagonisms were to be banished from the suburb, class distinctions would remain. "In the Garden Suburb Estate," Barnett wrote, "it will be an essential condition of building that the dwellings of all classes be made attractive with their own distinctive attractions, as are the cottages and manor house of the English village; the larger gardens of the rich helping to keep the air pure, and the sky view more liberal; the cottage gardens adding that cosy, generous element which ever follows the spade when affectionately and cunningly wielded as a man's recreation."[36]

As originally planned, one-third of the houses built in the suburb would be available for the "industrial classes." Expensive building sites around the heath extension were to be sold at prices high enough to permit the financing of an estate at rates that would enable families from the inner city to afford cottage accommodation. Of the original 240 acres, seventy were set aside for workers' dwellings, from thirty to seventy for "clerks" and persons who could afford to pay from £30 to £60 per year in rent; and forty-five for houses with rents of more than £100 per year.[37] By 1912, however, only 166 of more than 1,000 houses and flats erected were rented for less than 10 shillings a week, though the Hampstead Garden Trust provided accommodations to its own workers for from 3/3 to 5/9 a week.[38]

In a lengthy review of Unwin's *Town Planning in Theory and Practice* that appeared in a 1910 issue of *The Craftsman,* the journal's editor praised Unwin's determination to bring classes together within the communities he designed.

"In planning new towns Mr. Unwin turns to the example of the English village, where all classes of houses are mingled along the village street or around the green, from the laborer's small cottage to the large house of the wealthy farmer, doctor or local manufacturer, and even at times the mansion of the lord of the manor."[39] While unquestionably true that Unwin derived inspiration from the English village, *The Craftsman*'s American editor was putting a democratic gloss on its configuration that even Unwin, much as he liked to imagine the village as a genuine community, would have found hard to swallow. In any event, whatever his—or Henrietta Barnett's—hopes for lively and mutually beneficial social intercourse between classes in the suburb, they were dampened by the economic reality that the rich, before purchasing an expensive leasehold, needed reassurance that the poor were to be kept at arm's length. In their promotional brochure, written a year before the *Craftsman* review, Unwin and Baillie Scott went out of their way to convince their readers—potential purchasers of what Henrietta Barnett, in her written comments on Unwin's first plan, had called the "richer houses"—that Hampstead Garden Suburb was, in fact, not one community but two. "At one end of the estate where Hampstead golf course forms a boundary, only houses of a larger type with good gardens are under erection. At the northern end, in pleasant contrast, the cottages are being built, public greens and open spaces are being laid out, and the charm of an old English village is being successfully recreated."

As further evidence that Hampstead was no pie-in-the-sky community, the authors included the following homily on suburb industrial relations. "The British workman . . . seems to have had an exciting lesson or two up at Hampstead. Considerably more than 2000 of him have been sacked in nine months in the gracious work of inculcating the lesson that for a fair day's pay it is well that he should do a good day's work of his hands and his head." Unwin and Baillie Scott remark as well that the woodwork for buildings on the estate was being finished in joinery shops in Leicestershire, "at country prices," rather than in East London, whose workers were in theory to be among the beneficiaries of communities such as Hampstead.[40]

How to reconcile these observations with Unwin's enthusiastic embrace of social democracy, as exemplified in the egalitarian educational scheme he had promulgated at Letchworth only four years before, let alone with the undiluted socialism of his youth? Certainly the maternalistic "spirit of the place" that Henrietta Barnett infused into the life of her suburb was a far cry from Letchworth's semi-utopian pioneerism. But as with Letchworth, so with Hampstead: without the financial support of upper-middle-class investors, the experiment would fail. As the *Architects' and Builders' Journal* observed in 1912, "Whatever may be taught as to the principle, the fact remains that people who live in houses of a certain class and standard do not want to have their dwellings contiguous to or mingled with others of a lower class or standard; and the immediate result of making the attempt would almost certainly be to lower the rental value of the better class of houses." More to the point, perhaps: "In practice it will be found that neither class desires the amalgamation."[41] Barnett had never proposed building houses for rich and poor in close proximity. Yet she continued to profess her belief that the "amalgamation" would nonetheless prove beneficial to both classes, and to insist that the suburb, despite its layout, would encourage the much-needed reunion she sought to promote. In an article written for the first issue of the suburb's monthly magazine that same year, she once more declared that "it is only by the frequent interchange of thoughts and acts which neighbourhood fosters, that the invisible barriers can be broken down, that circumstances are seen to be of no consequence compared to community of interest, similar tastes and mutual respect for character."[42]

One obvious place where members of the otherwise divided community might have encountered each other in the manner imagined by Henrietta Barnett was in its central square. In his preliminary plan, Unwin had proposed a "cosy" Sitte-esque arrangement to include parallel rows of shops leading into a green, on which were to be located church, chapel, public hall, library, picture gallery, and museum. A key element in this plan was the shops, the one feature that would bring residents, rich or poor, high- or low-minded, into daily touch with each other. And yet when the central square was built, the shops had disappeared from the plan, and hence from the suburb altogether.

This significant change was a consequence of the appointment of Edwin Lutyens as consulting architect to the trust. Lutyens was engaged in May 1906, during the same meeting that Unwin was officially hired, though Unwin had already been working on preliminary plans. The choice of Lutyens was almost certainly the work of Alfred Lyttelton, whose country house he had remodeled. It illustrates, as does the initial offer of the consultantship to Richard Norman Shaw, the trust's determination to secure the services of an architect of "fashion," to encourage and reassure investors. Lutyens was a rising star already championing an elegant neo-Georgian style at odds with the Arts and Crafts aesthetic. In a letter to his wife at the time of his appointment, he wrote of passing through Chipping Campden, the "headquarters of that most—to me— distasteful [C. R.] Ashbee, now artist and furniture freakist."[43]

Lutyens was as light-heartedly arrogant as he was supremely talented, with an ego to match that of Henrietta Barnett. Her own "old-fashioned" tastes accorded more with Unwin's; as a consequence, she often found herself battling Lutyens's determination to turn the suburb, and particularly the central square, into something far grander and more monumental than either she or Unwin had envisioned. Lutyens, though eager to avoid friction, nonetheless had little patience with her aesthetic limitations. "A nice woman, but proud of being a philistine—has no idea much beyond a window box full of geraniums, calceolarias and lobelias, over which you can see a goose on a green."[44] Though Lutyens liked to laugh at Henrietta Barnett, and was on more than one occasion vexed by what he considered her obtuseness, he generally reserved his ire for lesser fry—administrators of the various building societies that financed construction of much of the suburb's housing: people like Henry Vivian, the champion of co-partnership, who were, in Lutyens's opinion, too often small-minded and short-sighted.

The relationship between Lutyens and Unwin appears to have been amicable enough, although one of Unwin's assistants, A. J. Penty, claimed in his diary that "Lutyens hoped to kick him [Unwin] off the suburb."[45] No other evidence for this sort of animosity exists. To a town planning conference in 1910, Unwin remarked with equanimity that "when the Trust were in a position to commission Mr. Lutyens to design the whole of the buildings in and around [the] central square as one consistent group, a more formal layout of the area was adopted than that originally planned, to suit Mr. Lutyens's finer Renaissance scheme of treatment."[46]

In another talk at the same meetings, however, he spoke of his own conviction that suburban centers should be designed so as "to gather . . . residents of many different classes, and to present that development of the vast areas covered by houses of one class without any relation . . . to local life."[47] Initially, it is clear that both Unwin and Henrietta Barnett assumed that any such design would include shops; they were present in Unwin's preliminary scheme of 1905, and in another rough sketch that Henrietta sent in a letter to one of the directors, Herbert Marnham, in the winter of 1908. Yet in a prospectus issued by one of the suburb housing societies a year later, a rendering of Lutyens's most recent proposal shows not only that have the shops disappeared, but also that rows of four-story flats have transformed the square into a formal, elegant urban space. Henrietta appears to have taken violent objection to this scheme. Lutyens described her in a letter to his wife as "awfully upset . . . on the ground of the other houses near being over-shadowed." He added that "Unwin warns me that it will make things difficult between me and Mrs. B. in the future. She evidently won't forget it."[48]

In the end the two compromised. The buildings were lowered; the shops disappeared. And with their disappearance the suburb was deprived not only of important domestic conveniences but also of a gathering place as natural as it was necessary, where residents from both sides of the community might have come together in some degree of social comfort. Unwin tried to promote a marketplace in 1912, after the suburb acquired a further 112-acre parcel to the east of the original tract: "an open-air market, where those who grow in their gardens more vegetables than they need for themselves can exchange with those who grow more flowers and fruit."[49] But the idea, attractive on both aesthetic and social grounds, was never realized. Indeed, inspired perhaps by the formality of Lutyens's square, Unwin imposed an axial plan on the extension, three avenues radiating eastward in a manner that recalls his plan for Letchworth, turning their backs on the more villagelike townscape that has come to be known as the "vintage" suburb.

Under Lutyens's hand the central square emerged not as a social gathering place but as a powerful expression of the suburb's high-minded intentions. It had always been the plan to build two large churches, Anglican and Free, on the highest point of the suburb's original 240 acres. In an undated letter to Herbert Marnham, her free church ally, Henrietta Barnett declared that the two churches "would be an outward and visible sign of your and my faith that worship is the highest act of human life and that the individuality given us by Our Creator must find its expression in varied methods of worship."[50] In Lutyens's hands, that commission resulted in two remarkably striking buildings, expressive of both the power of faith and their designer's determination to leave his bold architectural impression on the community and its inhabitants. Construction of an imposing institute on the square's eastern side, between the two churches, completed a triad that declared the determination of the suburb's founders to impose a striving after that "best self" attainable by means of a life of spiritual and intellectual enrichment.

The square was—and remains—imposing. But it is not particularly welcoming. One enters it as if stepping into a semi-sacred space. And in fact not many appear to enter it at all: few noisy children; no bustling crowds. And no sense that this is a community's common center. What common life there was in the suburb's early days focused around a clubhouse for workers, built in the midst of their separate "village" on Willifield Green (and destroyed by a parachute land mine in 1940), complete with bowling green, ninepin pitch, and allotment gardens. With the self-assurance in which she cloaked all her endeavors, Barnett wrote that her "long and large experience of workmen's clubs in East London had told me what was mainly wanted for a place of rest and recreation for those whose labour had rendered hands horny and bodies weary."[51] Whatever may have been wanted, construction of the clubhouse at Willifield could have done nothing to encourage the mingling of classes that Barnett continued to declare her intention and that was supposed to give the suburb its distinctive social advantage.

Although both Unwin and Lutyens had been appointed consulting architects to the trust, it was Unwin who carried out the daily assignments associated with laying out roads and walkways and approving plans for all buildings to be constructed on the site. Prospective residents could choose a design from among a number available for consideration at the trust office, or they could submit plans of their own to Unwin's office.[52] The trust remained the suburb's sole landowner, thereby retaining any unearned increment in land values, and in so doing pledging allegiance to garden city ideals. It leased plots to individual builders but at the start had no intention of building houses itself. Most of the dwellings, for both middle- and working-class residents, were financed through co-partnership societies similar to those at Letchworth and elsewhere in England.[53]

Some of the most adventurous building schemes, however—a striking group of houses by Baillie Scott at the juncture of Meadway and Hampstead Way, the "great wall" by the heath—were undertaken by the Garden Suburb Development Company, which was not a co-partnership but a conventional limited liability company that worked in close collaboration with the trust.[54] The three most active co-partnership societies, First, Second, and Third Hampstead Tenants Ltd., leased "cottages" for 6s to 9s per week and, for larger houses, up to £130 per year. Every tenant was required to take up £50 worth of stock, or the equivalent of two years' rent, should that be larger, with the option of paying that amount in one lump sum or weekly installments, at the end of each year receiving interest on the investment. These policies, where imposed on working-class co-partners, all but guaranteed respectable residents of the sort that Henrietta Barnett believed most susceptible to her improving schemes, the sort of which she had found far too few during her years in East London. By 1912, 1,060 houses and flats had been built in the suburb, 796 by co-partnership societies.[55]

The Unwin–Baillie Scott brochure promised designs conforming to Arts and Crafts principles. If the authors were prepared to dilute the pure milk of

Barnett's gospel to reassure middle-class purchasers about the likelihood of social intercourse with the industrious classes, they remained uncompromising in their pronouncements on the matter of style, insisting that Hampstead was to be one suburb whose houses and gardens were in no way characteristically "suburban." "Those museums of absurdities which constitute the modern Englishman's home," Baillie Scott wrote, "must be seen in all their deplorableness by their occupants, and all the unspeakable products of the modern tradesman's art must be sacrificed." He added that an invasion of London's suburbs by an "alien power" would not by any means represent an unmitigated disaster. "It would be something to know that 'Acacia Villa' and 'The Laurels' were no more to shelter their unhallowed household gods." Inside: "Instead of an accumulation of transitory rubbish, we shall have a few good things."[56] Here, certainly, an expression in explicitly architectural terms of Barnett's high-minded cultural credo, and further evidence of why she found Unwin an appealing partner.

In spite of these high-minded fulminations, the houses built for middle- and upper-middle-class residents, while almost universally designed with considerable thought and meticulous attention to detail, represented a range of styles and tastes. Baillie Scott adhered most closely to the Arts and Crafts rubric. His impressive houses at the juncture of Hampstead Way and Meadway, composed together as a gateway into the central portion of the estate, contain variations on the open yet cosy plan—large living halls, bay windows, and inglenooks— that were the hallmark of the movement. Though of impressive size, they were constructed with what the brochure described as "simple and substantial materials." A pair of elegant Georgian houses in a grassy square adjacent to the Heath, designed by Michael Bunney, were planned far more conventionally: vestibule and small central hall, morning room, drawing room, and dining room. Some of the most attractive middle-class housing was designed by Geoffry Lucas around a close in Hampstead Way (the grouping now referred to as Lucas Square). Unwin and Baillie Scott chose to depict it in *Town Planning and Modern Architecture* as an illustration of Unwin's oft-reiterated insistence on the importance of "scientific planning" as a way of "improv[ing] the general appearance of an estate. Although attractive in themselves, it is obvious how much each individual house gains in dignity and architectural effect by grouping." Yet the plans show a quite conventionally arranged interior space: again, a central hall, drawing room, dining room, and offices.[57]

One has the sense that despite the brave words of Unwin and Baillie Scott, developers feared that unless they provided the amenities expected in what were seen by most potential clients as "city" houses, those clients would not come to live at Hampstead. As the *Architects' and Builders' Journal* observed in 1912, it was probably a mistake to introduce elements associated with the countryside into houses for the rich this close to town. "Town dwellers are not cottagers. Their lives may be needlessly complex, their luxuries far too many; but you cannot, indeed, have at one and the same time the simplicity of the rustic and the culture of the other class."[58] As a consequence, Unwin and Baillie Scott were compelled to extol the green and white marble vestibule floor and a series of plaster friezes adorning a large house near the heath extension. Parker and Unwin continued to design what they referred to as cottages, even though these were clearly sizable houses for middle-class clients, containing, in one case, two sitting rooms, a kitchen, four bedrooms, a bath, and a dressing room.[59] Yet it is difficult to avoid the sense that what may have continued to appeal to the Letchworth pioneer as appropriate to that more adventurous environment might well have struck the potential middle-class Hampstead Garden Suburbanite as at best quaint and at worst sadly out-of-date.

For working-class tenants, Parker and Unwin and other architects designed houses similar to those at Letchworth, though generally more effectively because they were more tightly placed. Almost all consisted of living room or parlor, kitchen, scullery, and bath on the ground floor, two or three bedrooms and WC on the first. Where feasible, two-bedroom and three-bedroom houses were planned next to or close to each other. In the case of cottages in Wordsworth Walk, a working-class close, for example, the smaller dwellings rented for 7/8 per week, the larger for 13/6, the likely result being a "mixed" neighborhood, the families of skilled and semi-skilled workers living side by side.[60] Here, if nowhere else, the trust was prepared to encourage a degree of social heterogeneity; whether tenants welcomed the experiment is not apparent.

No one attempted to convince the working class of the virtues of one large living room. Yet Unwin remained eager to encourage the ideal that such a room invoked. An illustration in the brochure of one of the cottages that he and Parker designed in Temple Fortune Lane shows an old man sitting in his inglenook, a book on his lap. Despite a mantel-shelf full of what Baillie Scott would no doubt have labeled "transitory rubbish," the photograph exudes the kind of benign high-mindedness that responded both to Unwin's vision of intelligent democracy and Henrietta Barnett's notions of proper cultural deference.

There nowhere appears in the minutes of the trust, nor in various local journals, the sort of disappointed, angry discussion that continued to occur at

Letchworth concerning the quality of working-class housing. One comes across occasional complaints about the room sizes in cottages renting at the low end of the scale. "There is no doubt," the 1907 Report of Hampstead Tenants, Ltd., itself acknowledged, "that the rooms in the cottages at 6/6 are very small." But, the Report added, "the gardens are comparatively large."[61] Corners were not cut at Hampstead in the way they had to be in Letchworth. In all likelihood, the reason for the difference lies in the fact that the trust was willing to subsidize ground rents on land used to build workers' housing—at least until after World War I, a luxury that First Garden City, Ltd., could not afford.[62]

Critics of Hampstead and Letchworth agreed that neither community provided sufficient housing for unskilled workers and their families. At a meeting of the trust in October 1910, Unwin was asked to pursue the matter with the co-partnership societies.[63] A year later an anonymous article in the suburb's monthly newspaper, the *Town Crier*, pointed out the embarrassing fact that none of the cleaning women engaged by residents could afford to live in the high-priced community where they worked. "So far as we know there is not to be found within the Suburb any dwelling place with a rent low enough to be within the reach of a woman supporting herself by casual work. . . . By a curious paradox, these pleasant homes and cheerful places in which we live are intimately dependent upon the existence of other homes in squalid and crowded quarters, where our workers, like all the similar body of casual workers in suburbs which do not claim to be 'ideal,' have and always have had to herd." The writer acknowledged that there was little the trust or the building societies could do by themselves to solve the problem, declaring only that "until this problem of the housing of at least so much casual labour as we can ourselves maintain in fairly regular employ is faced, the slums and the Garden Suburb will remain as far asunder as the poles."[64]

If the suburb was able to house few if any poor people, it did succeed in providing attractive accommodation for various other groups marginalized by the standard geographical and social grid that unimaginative developers and rigid byelaws imposed on suburbs. From the beginning, Henrietta Barnett had insisted that there be special housing for the elderly, for convalescents, and for single women.[65] And working with Unwin, she managed to achieve her purpose. The Orchard, a quadrangle of forty-eight flats—a "four-square Elizabethan building," Hampstead Tenants, Ltd., called it—for old people, opened in October 1909. Each small apartment contained a living room with bed recess, scullery and WC. Bathrooms and a wash house were provided on the ground floor.[66] Rents ranged from 3/6 to 4/6 per week. The Orchard was

Elizabethan in more than architectural style. It was run, in one respect, like a traditional alms house. Those willing to subscribe to a fund for its construction and maintenance had the right to nominate tenants—one tenant for each £50 donation. Residents soon complained that they felt exploited, with tours by interested visitors impinging on their privacy and encouraging the idea that they were charity cases. Visitors left "with the notion that the Orchards is a philanthropic settlement, the inmates of which are to consider themselves perpetually on view." The *Town Crier* observed that the building was "neither a peep show or a poorhouse." It was time "this little comedy" ended, the Orchard being occupied by residents who paid a fair rent and deserved their privacy.[67]

Far more controversial was Homesfield, a group of six homes designed by Unwin and erected around a close. Because Henrietta Barnett's experience in East London had taught her much about the debilitating effect of environment on character, she was determined to use Hampstead as a kind of experimental station to prove that even in cases deemed close to hopeless, a change of scene would produce a change in behavior. In the first two of the houses, built with money contributed by George Cadbury and the Barnetts, lived boys and girls who would otherwise have been sent with their parents to the workhouse. Supervised by housemothers, Barnett wrote, the children "learned much under [their] guidance and example, joined to the indefinite but potent influences of beauty, the song of birds, the dance of squirrels, and the mystery of growing things." In the third and fourth houses, administered by the Salvation Army, lived children from even more "sad and degraded" backgrounds. A fifth house was run as a rest home "for tired young female servants" and out-of-work maids. It's matron, according to Barnett, did "invaluable work in character building and ideal creating." The sixth house was an "Eventide Home" for sixteen women, who were provided not only with a garden to work in but an "alone room" to which "anyone can retire whose nerves or temper feels frayed."[68]

The entire scheme, obviously close to Barnett's heart and therefore supported by her fellow directors, was not welcomed by those who lived in the working-class area of the suburb where it was located. Neighbors complained of noise and objected that the project had been railroaded past co-partnership shareholders without proper notification or discussion. "Is there any reason why tenants who have taken up shares to enable them to live in this desirable spot and have spent money on their houses and gardens should suddenly have buildings of this description dumped down in their midst?"[69] An early manifestation of that now-familiar lament "Not in my back yard!"

There were no complaints, however, about the best-known "associated living" scheme at Hampstead, a quadrangle designed by Baillie Scott in 1909, containing small flats for unmarried middle-class working women and named for Sydney Waterlow, the founder of the long-established Improved Industrial Dwellings Company that underwrote the building. Henrietta Barnett wrote that she was determined to provide decent accommodation for hard-working, independent women who too often "lodged in rooms over-filled with furniture and attended by disagreeable land ladies."[70] The scheme succeeded in a way that the Letchworth equivalent, Homesgarth, did not, almost certainly because of its appeal to suburban Londoners and because there was in the minds of the suburb's governors none of the timid, half-heartedness that inhibited the realization of Ebenezer Howard's plans. Henrietta Barnett was Hampstead's inspirator, as was Howard Letchworth's. But Barnett not only inspired, she ruled, and in a manner that Howard must occasionally have envied.

Waterlow Court contained forty-nine flats, most of them provided with a large, beamed living room, bedroom, bath, and scullery. There were as well nine two-bedroom and five three-bedroom flats. A dining hall and common room were on the ground floor; kitchen, housekeeper's flat, and three servant's bedrooms occupied the first and second floors in the same block. One-bedroom flats rented for from one pound fourteen shillings to £2 per month. Maid service cost 3s per week. The success of Waterlow Court encouraged the building of Meadway Court in 1913, another and more expensive "associated living" scheme with rents of up to £125 per year.[71]

Waterlow Court is one of the finest architectural achievements in the suburb. The *British Architect*, often skeptical about Arts and Crafts practitioners and their efforts at both Letchworth and Hampstead, had no doubts. "Whilst a good many folk have been talking about ideality, one architect at least has come somewhere pretty near its achievement."[72] Baillie Scott, in working a contemporary variation on the ancient university quadrangle, devised a form completely appropriate for the building's use, and certainly expressive of the suburb's very "best self."

Walter Creese has written of how Unwin's use of courtyards and quadrangles encouraged within the suburb "a mood of inwardness, of serene self-content-ment."[73] That mood was fostered as well by Henrietta Barnett's insistence that the suburb become an all-but-enchanted community, apart from the world outside, a secret garden where high-mindedness was cultivated with as much loving care as allotment flowers, fruits, and vegetables. She took every public opportunity to bespeak her sense of this specialness. At the ground-breaking for

St. Jude's Church, in 1907: "This is our hope, that the outside of the new St. Jude's will aid those who see it to seek higher things, and in seeking perhaps it will be given to them to comprehend something of what is meant by 'The Beauty of Holiness.'" At a reception for residents in 1910 to discuss plans for the building of the institute: "With an eye of faith she saw hundreds of students banded in friendship, keen and ever keener to learn, with minds so full and lives so enriched by nobler interests that there would be no room for the meaner imaginings." At a Saturday evening "conversazione" that same year, introducing a talk by Unwin on "Beauty in Foreign Towns": "On Sunday would come to those who were so happy to be religious the aid of spiritual food; but on Saturday nights one was glad for the aids to the higher air which intellectual interests gave."[74]

Elsewhere, Saturday nights meant the public house and the music hall, of which there were of course neither within the suburb. There, instead, were organizations "seeking to develop the true spirit of comradeship, and to secure 'the utmost for the highest.'"[75] If Barnett occasionally mystified her readers with such airy phrases, she left them in no doubt that they were privileged to share with her the spirit of this place that was essentially her personal creation. In an article titled "Outside Criticisms of the Suburb," written in 1913 for the trust's monthly journal, *The Record,* she responded to outsiders who sneered that residents were being dragooned into attending cultural programs of various sorts.

> Truly the idea of a common intellectual life and common social activities in which all may share if they choose and none are compelled to share . . . seems to be a thing so novel that outsiders are fain to regard it as a crafty agency for making prigs of us all. We who live in the Suburb know better. We live and let live. Yet probably the majority of people in the Suburb can appreciate and admire the action of a public-spirited landlord who is not satisfied with doing the minimum of what his tenants demand, but anticipates more than their material needs and provides for them without waiting for public pressures.[76]

In those words one hears that "serene self-contentment" that, if it was the suburb's hallmark, was certainly its founder's as well.

Cultural life centered on the institute, designed by Lutyens and opened for use in 1911, classes having previously been held elsewhere. At a meeting that December, Barnett boasted that 750 men and women had attended a total of 1,027 classes, and at fees of 3 to 5 shillings. She spoke of how the institute might "create an atmosphere" and declared that the "atmosphere which should exist in our Institute should be, first, serious purpose; secondly, conscientious care of detail; and thirdly, entertainment and interest."[77]

The Record included each month an account and listing of institute classes and activities rivaling in length and comprehensiveness the similar reports that one finds in the Letchworth *Citizen*. In August 1912, thirty-one suburb organizations were listed as having made use of the building during the previous fifteen months, including the Horticultural Association, the Oddfellows' Society, the Conservative and Liberal Associations and the British Socialist Party, the Ethical Society, the Theosophical Society, the Orchestral Society, and the British Union for the Abolition of Vivisection. As important to the cultural life of the community were the classes organized by the Institute Classes Sub-Committee, of which Henrietta Barnett was chair. These were listed under various categories: languages, arts and crafts, commercial, nature study, physiology and nursing first aid, and Swedish drill. In addition, a series of debates and conferences was advertised, among them: Raymond Unwin on "School Clinics"; "The Beggar at Our Door," a discussion chaired by suburb director Frank Debenham; "Are Strikes Avoidable?" with garden city advocate Aneurin Williams as one of the speakers; and "Some Aspects of Imperial Preference," with Henry Vivian, champion of co-partnership, among the debaters. The Novel Literary Club, "Mrs. S. A. Barnett, president"; the Child Study Society; and the Shakespeare Society were among the flourishing organizations that made the institute their home.[78]

Not everyone was content with the intellectual fare that the institute provided. A persistent suburb critic who wrote a series of letters—"The Letters of Julius"—to the *Town Crier*, attacked the programs as demeaning to the intelligence of suburb residents. "You must remember that you are not dealing with people whose consciousness of the higher things of life is just awakening: it is no part of your task to arose their dormant faculties, and slumbering souls. . . . You have presumed that you are called upon to work out their intellectual and social salvation; you ought to be well content to leave them the opportunity of working it out for themselves."[79] "Julius" was reminding those who managed the institute's affairs that the line between promotion and paternalism was a fine one.

Fees for use of the institute's facilities were modest enough for most middle-class families, though probably out of range for all but the most affluent and steadily employed artisans. Day membership for the reading room was 10/6 per year, for example. Those unable to afford the full tuition for classes paid a registration fee and whatever else they could afford. The *Daily Telegraph* praised this scheme as an "interesting attempt to show that a community composed of all classes of society can . . . enjoy classes, lectures, societies and other direct and indirect means of enriching life by thought and knowledge."[80] And yet when, in 1914, the suburb leased Turner's Wood, a seventy-acre common adjacent to the estate, *Garden Cities and Town Planning* reported that "it is proposed to allow residents to use this on payment of two guineas a year each, which will entitle them to a key. The wood is to be surrounded by an unclimbable fence."[81] Here, clearly, was one place where the "community of all classes" was to be segregated into its two major components.

Events at the clubhouse on Willifield Green, in the heart of the working-class sector of the suburb, appear to have centered around athletic activities, choral groups, and dancing classes. A bowling green and ninepin pitch, men's and ladies' gymnasiums, a library and reading room, and a billiard room were available to members. Most amenities here as well required the payment of fees, some not insubstantial: for the ladies' gym, 17/6d for the period from October to March.[82] Classes for men and women met weekly. Although the club was advertised as having been designed to accommodate the interests of working-class families, it remained the property of Hampstead Tenants, Ltd., the co-partnership company that built it and continued to control its use. In 1911 the elected house committee was astonished to learn that the company had fired an assistant steward. As reported by the *Town Crier,* the ensuing flap proved the unwillingness of those in charge to tolerate members' interference with their management. "Certain members—quite properly, as it seems to us—resenting the procedure adopted, endeavoured to intercede [on behalf of the dismissed steward] with the Finance Committee and were told, of course in the best official style, to mind their own business. A small storm arose in consequence, and a good many things were done both by the Finance Committee and by the recalcitrant members to which neither side will wish us to allude."[83] The *Daily Mail,* delighted to wash the suburb's dirty linen publicly, reported confrontations with Henry Vivian, president of the company, on the front porch of the clubhouse, and a demand that the offending protesters identify themselves so that they could be expelled. Meanwhile, those sympathizing with the dismissed steward organized a boycott of the club's billiard room, which, the *Daily Mail* reported, was working a financial hardship on the institution.[84]

Such embarrassments damaged the image of the suburb as a place where social harmony reigned. Beyond obvious and probably inevitable clashes, such as the clubhouse fracas, there was a kind of occasional condescension, even on the part of the democratically inclined *Town Crier,* that cannot have assisted in bringing classes together with any degree of genuine social comfort. Under the heading "actually overheard in the Suburb," for example:

> Imagine two fathers, the same number of mothers, and about four times that number of children, filing past the "Baillie Scott" houses on Saturday evening last summer, probably out from, say, Finchley, to see the sights, and trailing home in the inconsequential manner so well known to amateur travellers. . . .
> "Look, muvver—'Meadway!'"
> "Yus. Look Ted—'Midway!' I wonder what it means."
> "Why, midway between the 'eath and somewhere else, o' course."
> General satisfaction—and especial admiration on the part of Ted's wife at the wonderful elucidation of the mystery.[85]

A mildly amusing anecdote, presumably, in the opinion of the magazine's editor and his middle-class readers. But not the sort of tidbit to encourage working-class readers to believe that they were fully accepted members of the suburb, any more than they were fully responsible members of a clubhouse that had been designed for them but belonged to someone else.

Education in Hampstead Garden Suburb was education by class. Nothing suggests that Unwin attempted to persuade the directors to institute the sort of democratic system he had championed at Letchworth. In the Garden City he was a participating citizen of the community. In the Garden Suburb he appears to have been no more than a well-paid and favorably regarded employee. Construction of a state-supported elementary school was delayed for several years as a result of continuing squabbles between the suburb trustees and the Hendon Education Committee. The trust wanted the school built within the suburb, yet it was unwilling to allow the Education Authority use of the building after school hours. The trustees demanded a two-story building, which would take up less room. The committee insisted on—and eventually got—a one-story design. Matters came to a head at a meeting on Willifield Green, boycotted by the trustees, at which Hendon committee members argued that delay was a consequence of suburb intransigence. *The Town Crier* agreed. "The School question is not a matter of estate management, and in dealing with it the residents cannot have an undivided loyalty. . . . We are citizens first, residents on a particular estate afterwards, nor can we admit that we have surrendered any of our rights and duties as citizens by the fact of such residence, still less that we have delegated them to any one else. The Directors of the Trust cannot stand between us and the local authority, nor can they expect our unquestioning support in disputes with it."[86]

The elementary school, finally completed in January 1913, was located near

Willifield Green, in the heart of the suburb's working-class community. Until it was finished, some elementary school students were accommodated at the institute, rented from the trust by the Hendon Authority. Meanwhile, middle-class secondary school children were housed as well in the institute while suitable facilities were built, by private subscription, for them. Notices were distributed, reassuring parents that the two student bodies would remain thoroughly isolated from each other. "There will be running, in different parts of the Institute, entered by different doors, the Elementary State-supported Schools for infants and . . . the Kindergarten branch of the Secondary School with fees from 2 1/2 guineas upward."[87] Yet Henrietta Barnett continued to write as if those "different doors" did not exist. Only eight months earlier she had once again declared it to be the suburb's goal to break down "invariable barriers" and promote "community of interest."[88]

Three years before, Samuel Barnett wrote to his brother that his wife "had come into a Kingdom."[89] The kingdom was of her own creation, where her position as undisputed ruler afforded her the luxury of an empress's clothes. Things were so if she said they were so. There were some who challenged her understanding of her own considerable accomplishments, or who suggested that "invariable barriers" could not be broken down without democratic participation in the processes of suburb government. These she dismissed as, at best, men and women without a true understanding of the suburb's mission, or, at worst, pesky troublemakers. Suburb governance was, in fact, a tangled affair. The trust, the various co-partnership societies, the Hampstead Borough Council, the Hendon Urban District Council, and the Hendon Education Committee possessed particular and often conflicting authorities and jurisdictions. It was with the trust, however, that residents most frequently found themselves at odds.

Dissatisfaction with the way the trust managed the suburb's public and semi-public facilities and amenities, plus increasing frustration over the delays in school construction, led to the formation of the Residents' Association in 1911, an outgrowth of the Ratepayers' Association, whose function had been to watch over the affairs and policies of the local taxing authorities, the Hampstead and Hendon councils. And the trust, not surprisingly, did not look fondly on this instrument for the expression of community opinion. At a meeting the previous year, Alfred Lyttelton, president of the board, had expressed the trustees' belief "that as the present community represented only about one-third of the ultimate population of the Suburb, it was not advisable to proceed further at present with the formation of a Residents' Association."[90] Undeterred, the petitioners persevered, and with the trust's consent, if not its active approval, the association came to life, proclaiming its determination to work with the trust for the benefit of the suburb community. At an early meeting, one of its supporters declared that whereas in the past "the Trust had energized for them," now it was their hope that "the Trust would work with them."[91]

One of the association's first actions was to publish the *Town Crier,* edited by suburb resident Charles Crump, who soon adopted a generally critical stance toward the trust and its policies and methods. The trust retaliated with *The Record,* advertising itself as the "official organ of the Board," whose aim it would be to "keep to the front the ideals which gave form and substance to the Hampstead Garden Suburb," and to "inform the world of what life means on the Suburb." The *Town Crier* gave *The Record* a stiffly polite welcome. "It is a good thing to have . . . an organ for expressing the official point of view. The franker and plainer that expression is the more the Suburb will have reason to welcome our new contemporary."[92]

With clenched editorial teeth and frozen smiles the two journals then proceeded to do sedate battle over the question of suburb governance. In its November 1911 issue, the *Town Crier* challenged the trust with words taken from a recent article by Samuel Barnett: "Will the world of the future any more than the world of the past be saved by good despots? Is there not something in human nature which demands a choice in its own government?"[93] The previous June, in a leader entitled "The Two Schools," the paper had asked citizens of the suburb to concede the fact that they faced a governmental dilemma. On the one side stood the "large majority of the residents" who subscribed to the ideal of a "self-sufficing, self-governed community, developing on self-chosen lines." Standing against this ideal were the directors, who saw the suburb developing under their "paternal guidance," believing that "any permanent good can only come from their greater experience and that their power of commanding and utilizing expert knowledge justifies any determination they may make to govern without taking counsel of the residents." The writer (in all likelihood the paper's editor, Charles Crump), while proclaiming himself "by inheritance, by temperament, by education . . . a convinced adherent of the first ideal," acknowledged that the trust was a "paternal government" and that "nothing but a radical alteration" in its constitution could make it otherwise. Given that implacable fact, all he could hope for was that the "war" between the two ideals might be fought "with mutual respect, in spite of the well known law that in all collisions, even of opinion, more heat than light is commonly generated."[94]

The editor was a realist, if nothing else. While Henrietta Barnett remained the trust's honorary manager and its most powerful director, suburb government would be exercised in accordance with a paternalist ideal. In her 1913 *Record* article, "Outside Criticisms of the Suburb," she had stoutly declared that she would rather affairs were in the hands of "an oligarchy . . . responsible directly for the financial stability and prosperity of the whole undertaking, than in those of an unlimited democracy of the tenants who would have a direct interest in sacrificing the future to the present."[95] Although she was writing in this instance of the management of co-partnership housing societies, her sentiments applied as well to the governance of the suburb itself. She and her fellow directors must be allowed to put the best interests of the community ahead of the selfish temporary demands of special pleaders. That injunction lay at the heart of the gospel of high-minded social reform: trust us to know what is right, and to act on your behalf, in your best interests. At the opening of a flower show on Bank Holiday, 1909, Barnett spoke of the need to cultivate the "flower of trust." "Let us all trust each other, our motives, our intentions, our aims. . . . Let our . . . gardens grow the flower of trust; and that flower will not grow near the weed of suspicion."[96]

Those unwilling to trust Henrietta Barnett experienced the force of her indomitable determination. Brigid Grafton Green, for many years the suburb's archivist and a collector of Barnett anecdotes, reports the comments of a neighbor: "She was the only person I've ever known who could recite the Ten Commandments as if she had just made them up"; and of her secretary, who recalled her saying once, "you know, I agree with Jesus . . . "[97] Not surprising, then, that when she received a petition from 323 residents in 1911, complaining about delays in the opening of the elementary school, she replied frostily that the course pursued by the trust was "recognized by most of the inhabitants of the Estate as public-spirited and . . . worthy of local support." Those who elected to complain to what she referred to as "my Board" must remember that the directors "did not feel bound" to communicate with residents "through an Association." "If there are some who misunderstand and complain, it is, I would suggest, both easier and wiser for those who hear such complaints to seek information before joining in protests or fostering, if not creating grievances."[98] In this spirit was community to be nurtured.

And yet it would be wrong to leave the matter there. Henrietta Barnett's authoritarianism made her, at times, extraordinarily difficult to deal with, and, as Edwin Lutyens understood, an easy enough target for gentle ridicule. And yet perhaps her supreme self-confidence encouraged an equal degree of self-assuredness in the architects who worked for her at Hampstead. It may have been her singleness of mind that inspired "her" architects to design as boldly as they often did, with the result that the Hampstead work of Unwin, Lutyens, Baillie Scott, and others combines into a collection of buildings and townscapes far more distinguished than the sum of its parts, an astonishingly delightful and impressive urban achievement.

Chapter 8 Epilogue

In 1914, Raymond Unwin left his post as consulting architect for Hampstead Garden Suburb (and a year later dissolved his partnership with Barry Parker) to accept appointment as chief town planning inspector to the Local Government Board, and then, four years later, as chief housing architect to the Ministry of Health. His departure signaled the end of the first chapter in the history of the English garden city movement. True, it had done little to address the problems of class conflict. Nor had it proved conclusively, as Howard hoped it would, that urban reconstitution could take place without significant state assistance. Yet it had set examples that, if followed, might assist in the prevention of further congestion in Britain's existing cities, by providing alternatives that were both physically beneficial and aesthetically pleasing. Above all, it had generated a set of principles and ideals that gained acceptance not only in Britain but throughout much of the western world. The years before 1914 witnessed not only the developments analyzed in this book but also the spread of the garden city gospel in Europe and America—indeed, throughout much of the world. Howard's book was translated into French, German, and Russian before 1914. By that time Garden City Associations had been established in eleven countries, and an International Garden Cities Association founded.[1]

The historian Anthony Sutcliffe credits the spread of garden city ideals to a band of dedicated propagandists and intermediaries; he names the Englishman T. C. Horsfall, the Frenchman Georges Benoit-Lévy, the German Hermann Muthesius, and the American George Howe as the most prominent among those who ensured that town planning principles in general and those of garden city and garden suburb enthusiasts in particular received a wide and favorable hearing. Sutcliffe argues as well that the excitement generated throughout Europe and the United States by planning schemes was the result of a "surge in creative internationalism," reflected in a large increase in the number of international organizations and in the growth of interest in Esperanto immediately before World War I.[2]

While that may well be true, it is important to remember that as far as Britain was concerned, the movement, in the minds of its supporters, remained closely identified with a particularly English vision. John Burns, working-class president of the Local Government Board in the Liberal government of 1906, and the man most responsible for the Town Planning Act of 1909, spoke of that vision at an international conference on town planning the following year. "I conceive the city of the future as Ruskin, Morris, Wren and Professor [Patrick] Geddes wished a city to be—that is, an enlarged hamlet of attractive healthy homes. . . . It is not an accident that the beautiful manor house, the restful vicarage, the stately homes of England, the beautiful public schools and colleges have turned out the Ruskins, the Kingsleys, the Morrises, the Nelsons, the Newtons, and the Darwins."[3] No matter that neither Christopher Wren nor Patrick Geddes, one of Europe's leading planning theorists in 1910, would have or did subscribe to Burns's sense of what a city ought to be. Burns was dealing not with history but with myth, articulating an Englishness that, in the institutions and heroes it honored, bespoke those hierarchical relationships that garden city so often seemed to invoke.

Unwin's departure from Hampstead to the Local Government Board signaled the emergence of the state as an increasingly influential and powerful participant in the process of planning towns and building houses. We noted at the beginning of this study the way in which a liberalist, interventionist Englishness was part of an accepted consciousness among reformers. Wartime necessity brought that consciousness to full flower. Unwin's initial task was to design state-financed housing estates for munitions makers. That work led, in turn, to his central role in the drafting of the Tudor Walters Committee Report,

which urged state support for the construction of working-class housing, regu-
lated by town-planning schemes that conformed to Unwin's clearly formulated
principles of urban layout. The result was the Housing Act of 1919, pledging
government programs for the construction of 500,000 houses—"homes fit
for heroes"—within three years. That this ambitious goal was never met, for
reasons having largely to do with postwar Britain's faltering economy, did not
diminish a growing acceptance of the necessity for state intervention to accomplish a task now understood as far too massive to be undertaken by private
initiative.

Chapter two of the English garden city movement was thus the history of
interwar planning by governmental bureaucracies at both the local and national levels. Some favored construction of what had come to be called satellite
towns, close by existing cities and to a degree dependent on them, yet separated
from them by greenbelts. C. B. Purdom, Letchworth's chronicler and champion before 1914, became a leading spokesman for the satellite concept, having
outlined it in a pamphlet he published in 1917—"The Garden City After the
War." As successive governments continued to build extensive housing estates
at the edge of existing cities, however, others—Unwin among them—recog-
nizing the threat of massive suburban sprawl, argued that the immediate need
was not for new satellite towns but rather for well-designed garden suburbs.

These projects, whether towns or suburbs, were planned and brought into
being by an expanding bureaucracy of housing experts. Unwin's metamorpho-
sis into a reform-minded civil servant is evidence of a change that, as one recent
historian has argued, made of town planning less a cause than a discipline.[4]
Though Unwin's later work as a civil servant no doubt remained grounded in
his early convictions, that of younger professionals depended increasingly on a
thorough knowledge of detailed codes, regulations, and techniques: the planner as expert, rather than the planner as reformer.

In direct opposition to these postwar trends stood the garden city's leading
pioneer, Ebenezer Howard. While his disciples were arguing the inevitability of
state intervention, he was preparing to launch a second, privately financed
garden city at Welwyn, halfway between London and Letchworth. Howard had
pressed the case for another garden city while Letchworth was still in its infancy.
He first raised the issue in 1901. Both Ralph Neville and Aneurin Williams
opposed him at the time, arguing that a second attempt would not succeed
without substantial government assistance.

When, in 1919, Howard managed to secure fifteen hundred acres as a first
step toward the establishment of Welwyn Garden City, others associated with

the cause were not pleased. They believed, correctly, as it transpired, that sufficient financial backing would be even more difficult to obtain than it had been for Letchworth. Both C. B. Purdom and F. J. Osborn did their best to persuade Howard to understand Welwyn not as an offshoot of Letchworth but as a London satellite, the first of twenty or so such communities to be built specifically to relieve metropolitan overcrowding. Those heady dreams soon evaporated with the onset of economic depression and the abandonment by the Lloyd George government in 1921 of the ambitious housing schemes inspired by Tudor Walters.

Welwyn survived because of its directors' willingness to sacrifice unearned increment, as the Letchworth directors had, to immediate financial necessity. Attractively laid out according to designs by the Canadian Beaux-Arts architect Louis de Soissons, it incorporated elements of Unwin's earlier Letchworth scheme, most notably in middle-class residential districts, which featured cul-de-sacs and closes. Yet Welwyn never claimed itself as a bold social experiment the way that Letchworth had. It was, as much or more than its progenitor, a city divided by class: working class to the east of the mainline railway, middle class to the west. Although Welwyn did attract industry, its proximity to London meant that many who lived there did so as commuters. As one historian of town planning has observed, "Welwyn Garden City was regarded as a quiet community of no particular cachet, where Londoners of modest means and interested in gardening might move."[5] People had traveled to Letchworth in its early days to see the future. People traveled to Welwyn to eat their evening meal and sleep amid the tepid joys of a well-planned and aesthetically pleasing satellite suburbia.

The future lay with towns such as Wythenshawe, a community designed by Barry Parker on the outskirts of Manchester between 1927 and 1941. Commissioned by the city of Manchester, it incorporated, in mature form, the design principles that Parker and Unwin had together developed and articulated before World War I. And it was able to depend for its success, in a way that neither Letchworth nor Welwyn had, on the taxing and borrowing power of a large and financially stable municipal authority. It might thus appropriately serve as the centerpiece of the second chapter in the history of the garden city movement in Britain, midway between Letchworth and Hampstead and such New Towns of the post–World War II era as Stevenages, Harlow, and Cumbernauld, which represent the garden city's third phase.

The increasingly central role of the state during the interwar and postwar years signals the degree to which that second strand of Englishness discussed at the outset of this study—the interventionism of liberal consensus—moved from background to foreground in the history of the garden city movement. At the same time, however, those values enshrined in the Englishness of the garden city ethos in its early years—admiration for the past, for country ways, for social harmony—found general expression in the politics and culture of the 1920s and '30s. The middle class increasingly craved a countryside that was, at the same time, becoming more accessible. Peter Mandler writes of an "urge to identify with the countryside, to represent urbanity and modernity by analogy with the rural past." This on the part of men and women unable to construct an identity—a "home"—of their own, who felt compelled to borrow an identity from a social order whose extinction might have been expected in the previous century.[6] Alex Potts, in Raphael Samuel's collection of essays on patriotism, analyzes the same impulse, the need to discover the countryside, which became "an obsession among a not-so-privileged middle class who on many counts felt marginal and who wished to possess a true inner identity more valuable than its external social persona."[7] To the extent that the garden city movement popularized "country" aesthetics, it enabled those who sought identity in the past to find it. Unwin's lanes and cul-de-sacs, his cottages and closes became the exemplar for hundreds of "garden-type" suburbs and developments catering to this need to partake of "country," in territory that was by no stretch of the imagination any longer countryside.

Stanley Baldwin well understood the potent magic of the image and remodeled the Conservative party to reflect it. While never turning his back on modernization—as Mandler observes, Baldwin presided over a road-building and electrification program that "shredded the countryside"—he nonetheless cloaked change in a "gentle, modest, domesticated, cottage-loving image that fitted neatly with established trends within the middle class."[8] Baldwin could extol the virtues of gardening with the assurance of a George Cadbury: "Nothing can be more touching than to see how the working man and woman after generations in the town will have their tiny bit of garden if they can, will go to gardens if the can, to look at something they have never seen as children, but which their ancestors knew and loved."[9] Baldwin hoped to seduce his fellow countrymen and women with the notion that all Britons shared a set of homely values. Despite powerful evidence to the contrary—depression, a general strike—he projected an image of social harmony and inclusiveness closely akin to the message broadcast by garden city supporters. Around a community of common culture, as defined by its propagators, a cohesive citizenry would strive for what Alex Potts has called an "ideal modernity," free of class divisions and rooted in age-old, pre-industrial values.[10]

This newly defined modernity had about it qualities more feminine than masculine. Alison Light has written of how "the 1920s and '30s saw a move away from the formerly heroic and officially masculine public rhetorics . . . to an Englishness at once less imperial and more inward-looking, more domestic and private—and, in terms of pre-war standards, more 'feminine.'" Light notes the way that the "little man"—"the suburban husband pottering in his herbaceous borders"—became the new exemplar of civilian virtue.[11] And one is reminded of Henrietta Barnett's definition of happiness: watching as her husband dug plantains from the lawn.[12] This England is inward-looking; it is charming; it is cosy; it is "little" England, as opposed to "Great" Britain. It is that landscape of the south, rolling and soft and welcoming. It is, quite clearly, the landscape of the garden city, as envisioned and then to a significant degree realized by Barry Parker, Raymond Unwin, and others in the years before World War I.[13]

Celebration of the past and of the hierarchical order of pre-industrial villages; fear of class conflict and of the cities that were its breeding ground; certainty that a common culture was to be defined by arbiters who better than the rest understood the meaning of "best": these attitudes are embedded in the history of interwar Britain, as they are in that of the early garden city movement. To understand this is to understand why a generation went to war in 1939, as Alun Howkins reminds us, singing

There'll always be an England
While there's a country lane.
As long as there's a cottage small
Beside a field of grain.[14]

It was this Englishness that men and women turned to when frightened either by the coming of a world war, or—as in the case of those who lived before 1914—by the realities of class division and the threat of class conflict, or by the apparent inevitability of democracy. Englishness replaced grim realities with the cosy village, where all lived healthy lives, cultivated their gardens, and accepted their place within a hierarchy governed by an elite that understood its obligations to those whom it both ruled and served. That this myth was powerful enough to engulf as many as it did suggests how weakly rooted were more democratic alternatives to it. It demonstrates as well how much of what does happen in the world is driven by fear of what may happen.

Notes

INTRODUCTION: THE MATTER OF ENGLISHNESS

1. C. F. G. Masterman, "Realities at Home," and P. W. Wilson, "The Distribution of Industry," in C. F. G. Masterman, ed., *The Heart of the Empire* (New York, 1973), 7–8, 234.

2. Robert Colls and Philip Dodd, eds., *Englishness: Politics and Culture, 1880–1920* (London, 1988).

3. Philip Dodd, "Englishness and the National Culture," in Colls and Dodd, *Englishness*, 1.

4. Raphael Samuel, *Theatres of Memory* (London, 1994), 6.

5. Linda Colley, "Looking for Ourselves," *Times Literary Supplement*, 2 May 1997, 9.

6. John Taylor, *A Dream of England: Landscape, Philosophy, and the Tourist's Imagination* (Manchester, 1994), 21.

7. Colley, "Looking for Ourselves," 8.

8. Barry Parker and Raymond Unwin, *The Art of Building a Home* (London, 1901), 107–108.

9. Ibid., 92.

10. Ibid., 95, 100.

11. Alex Potts, "'Constable Country' Between the Wars," in Raphael Samuel, ed., *Patriotism: The Making and Unmaking of British National Identity* (London, 1989), 3: 173.

12. James Vernon, "Englishness: The Narration of a Nation," *Journal of British Studies,* April 1995, 246.

13. Samuel A. Barnett, "A Scheme for the Unemployed," *Nineteenth Century,* November 1888, 754.

14. Walter L. Creese, *The Search for Environment. The Garden City: Before and After* (New Haven, 1966), 5.

15. Alun Howkins, "The Discovery of Rural England," in Colls and Dodd, *Englishness,* 36.

16. James Bryce, quoted in Dennis Smith, "Englishness and the Liberal Inheritance After 1886," Colls and Dodd, *Englishness,* 254–255.

17. Robert Colls, "Englishness and the Political Culture," in Colls and Dodd, *Englishness,* 36.

18. Matthew Arnold, *Culture and Anarchy* (New York, 1895), 85.

19. *Report of the Interdepartmental Committee on Physical Deterioration,* Parliamentary Papers, 1904, vol. 22, Cd. 2175; vol. 1: 15.

20. Taylor, *A Dream of England,* 22.

21. P. Lyttelton Gell, *The Municipal Responsibilities of the "Well-to-Do"* (n.p., n.d.), Toynbee Hall Papers. Quoted in Standish Meacham, *Toynbee Hall and Social Reform, 1890–1914* (New Haven, 1987), 39–40.

22. Brian Doyle, "The Invention of English," in Colls and Dodd, *Englishness,* 90.

23. Dodd, "Englishness and the National Culture," 2.

24. Colley, "Looking for Ourselves," 8.

CHAPTER 2. BOURNVILLE AND PORT SUNLIGHT: THE EXEMPLARS

1. See Gillian Darley, *Villages of Vision* (London, 1975); Nicholas Taylor, *The Village in the City* (London, 1973).

2. Richard Dennis, *English Industrial Cities in the Nineteenth Century* (Cambridge, England, 1984), 176–177. For Europe and America, see Bridgett Meakin, *Model Factories and Villages* (London, 1905), 351ff.

3. E. Ackroyd, "On Improved Dwellings for the Working Classes," in John Burnett, *A Social History of Housing* (London, 1986), 150.

4. Walter L. Creese, *The Search for Environment. The Garden City: Before and After* (New Haven, 1966), 15, 39.

5. Colin Bell and Rose Bell, *City Fathers* (London, 1972), 261–262.

6. For the concept of this fourth class, see Harold Perkin, *The Origins of Modern English Society* (London, 1969), and *The Rise of Professional Society* (London, 1989).

7. A. G. Gardiner, *Life of George Cadbury* (London, 1923), 99.

8. Ibid., 122. Testimony before a committee of the Upper House of Convocation on moral principles and social problems, 1906.

9. Ibid., 121.

10. *The Garden City Conference at Bournville: Report of Proceedings* (London, 1901), 32, 43.

11. Gardiner, *Life of George Cadbury,* 121.

12. Angus Watson, *My Life* (London, 1927), 140.

13. *Liverpool Daily Post,* 6 August 1913, in Port Sunlight Archives, 29.

14. *Progress,* January 1900, 147.

15. *Liverpool Daily Post,* 6 August 1913.

16. Ibid.; *Progress,* May 1903, 179; October 1906, 301.

17. William Lever, "Land for Houses," speech delivered to the Birkenhead Liberal Club, October 1898, in William Lever, *The Six Hour Day and Other Industrial Questions* (London, 1918), 163–164.

18. William Lever, *Co-Partnership and Efficiency* (Port Sunlight, 1912), 6, and *Education and the Common Life* (Bolton, 1912), 13.

19. Lever, *Education and the Common Life,* 9, 10–11.

20. Edward Cadbury, *Experiments in Industrial Organization* (London, 1912), 1.

21. Ibid., xvii.

22. Ibid., 69.

23. Ibid., 254–255.

24. Ibid., 233–234.

25. *A Descriptive Account of Cocoa and of Its Manufacture by Cadbury Brothers* (Bournville, 1882), 11–12.

26. Patrick Joyce, *Work, Society and Politics* (Brighton, 1980).

27. Cadbury, *Experiments in Industrial Organization,* 6.

28. Accounts of Alice Bond and William Davenport in "Personal Reminiscences, Bridge St. and Bournville," 1929, Cadbury Archive, Bournville.

29. Account of Cephas Edwards in "Personal Reminiscences."

30. Cadbury, *Experiments in Industrial Organization,* 254.

31. Gardiner, *Life of George Cadbury,* 103.

32. *Bournville Works Magazine,* July 1911, 199; December 1911, 359, 366; July 1912, 195, 202; October 1912, 293.

33. Gardiner, *Life of George Cadbury,* 121.

34. Ibid., 69.

35. George Cadbury, Jr., *Town Planning with Special Reference to the Birmingham Schemes* (London, 1915), 26; Burnett, *Social History of Housing,* 166; J. A. Dale, "Bournville," *Economic Review* 15 (January 1907): 14.

36. W. A. Harvey, *The Model Village and Its Cottages: Bournville* (London, 1906), 12; Bournville Village Trust, *The Bournville Village Trust* (1901), n.p.; (1909), 8.

37. Bournville Village Trust, Deed of Foundation, Cadbury Archive, Bournville.

38. *Architectural Review* 19 (1906): 192.

39. J. S. Nettlefold, *Practical Housing* (Leftwich, 1908), 54.

40. *The Bournville Village Trust* (1901), n.p.; (1909), 8.

41. Harvey, *Model Village and Its Cottages,* 18.

42. Ibid., 58–59.

43. Ibid., 53, 60.

44. *Architectural Review* 19 (1906): 192.

45. Harvey, *Model Village and Its Cottages,* 23–24; Wilhelm Miller, *What England Can Teach Us About Gardening* (New York, 1911), 137–138.

46. William Thompson, *Housing Up to Date* (Leicester, 1907), 3–4; Gardiner, *Life of George Cadbury,* 155; speech by George Cadbury, reported in *The British Architect,* 27 September 1901, 220.

47. Harvey, *Model Village and Its Cottages,* 14.

48. Dale, "Bournville," 21.

49. Ibid., 24.

50. Bournville Village Trust, *Bournville Village Trust, 1900–1955* (Bournville, 1955), 84.

51. *Bournville Village Trust* (1909), 18.

52. *Birmingham Daily Mail,* 25 February 1902, 2.

53. "Notes and Comments," *Architect and Contract Reporter,* 7 July 1911.

54. Bournville Village Trust, *Annual Report,* 1914, 5.

55. Dale, "Bournville," 20.

56. Bell and Bell, *City Fathers,* 276.

57. "Residents' Handbook and Rules," Bournville Village Trust archives.

58. Gardiner, *Life of George Cadbury,* 259.

59. Elizabeth Cadbury, undated speech, Birmingham Public Library MSS. 466/152/91.

60. Elizabeth Cadbury, Presidential Address, 1907, Birmingham Public Library MSS. 466/152/11.

61. Gardiner, *Life of George Cadbury,* 316.

62. Charles Wilson, *The History of Unilever: A Study in Economic Growth and Social Change* (London, 1954), 1: 37, 41.

63. Ibid., 45–46.

64. William Lever, address, *Birkenhead News,* 24 November 1900.

65. W. L. George, *Labour and Housing at Port Sunlight* (London, 1909), 23, 42–43, 46–50; Wilson, *History of Unilever,* 1: 147.

66. *Progress,* February 1905, 43, 36.

67. Ibid., 42.

68. W. H. Lever, *Co-Partnership* (Port Sunlight, 1912), 4; Second Viscount Leverhulme, *Viscount Leverhulme by His Son* (London, 1927), 25.

69. Wilson, *History of Unilever,* 1: 153, 157. The quotation is from *The Encyclopedia Britannica,* 14th ed., in its article on Lever.

70. W. H. Lever, *Co-Partnership and Efficiency* (Port Sunlight, 1912), 5, 13–14.

71. *Progress,* August 1913, 104.

72. Ibid., 105.

73. Lever, "Combines," in *Six Hour Day,* 271.

74. Lever, *Co-Partnership,* 20.

75. *Progress,* February 1912, 39.

76. Wilson, *History of Unilever,* 1: 144; George, *Labour and Housing at Port Sunlight,* 100.

77. Quoted in M. Georges Benoit-Lévy, "Port Sunlight," in *Garden City.* Translated and printed as a supplement in *Progress,* October 1904.

78. W. L. George, *Engines of Social Progress* (London, 1907), 126.

79. W. H. Lever, speech at ground-breaking ceremony, in E. H. Edwards, *Messrs. Levers' New Soap Works* (Liverpool, 1888), 28–29.

80. W. H. Lever, *The Buildings Erected at Port Sunlight and Thornton Hough* (Port Sunlight, 1902), 27.

81. Ibid., 17.

82. Ibid., 9.

83. Walter Tomlinson, *The Pictorial Record of the Royal Jubilee Exhibition, Manchester, 1887* (Manchester, 1888), quoted in Creese, *Search for Environment*, 128.

84. Creese, *Search for Environment*, 128.

85. Port Sunlight Archives, PSHA 10.

86. Interview with J. Lomas-Simpson, in Michael Shippobottom, "Viscount Lever: A Study of an Architectural Patron and His Work" (Master's thesis, University of Manchester, 1977), 70.

87. Lever, *Buildings Erected at Port Sunlight*, 11.

88. Creese, *Search for Environment*, 131.

89. George, *Labour and Housing at Port Sunlight*, 69.

90. Ibid., 71.

91. Lever, *Buildings Erected at Port Sunlight*, 15.

92. *Progress*, October 1901, 363.

93. W. H. Lever, *Art, Beauty, and the City* (Port Sunlight, 1915), 6; Lever, *Six Hour Day*, 156, 158.

94. *Progress*, May 1900, 342; October 1900, 536–539; November 1902, 114.

95. *Progress*, October 1903, 373–374; George, *Labour and Housing at Port Sunlight*, 118.

96. Lever Brothers, *The Village of Port Sunlight* (Port Sunlight, n.d.), 5. George, *Labour and Housing at Port Sunlight*, 83.

97. *Progress*, October 1900, 550–551.

98. *Progress*, August 1903, 303.

99. George, *Labour and Housing at Port Sunlight*, 184; Benoit-Lévy, "Port Sunlight."

100. Watson, *My Life*, 137; George, *Labour and Housing at Port Sunlight*, 177–178.

101. For statistics, see Lever Brothers, *Visit of the International Housing Conference to Port Sunlight, August 9, 1907* (Port Sunlight, 1907), 3–9.

102. *Progress*, May 1901, 184.

103. *Progress*, September 1901; October 1906, 327.

104. *Progress*, February 1901, 51, 56.

105. *Progress*, March 1900, 231.

106. *Progress*, August 1902, 293–294; October 1903, 383–384.

107. *Progress*, March 1905, 94.

108. Thomas H. Mawson, *Civic Art* (London, 1911), 209.

CHAPTER 3. EBENEZER HOWARD AND THE GARDEN CITY ASSOCIATION

1. For a discussion of these trends, see Anthony Sutcliffe, *Towards the Planned City: Germany, Britain, the United States, and France* (New York, 1981), esp. 29, 32–33, 103, 132, 139.

2. T. C. Horsfall, *The Improvement of the Dwellings and Surroundings of the People: The Example of Germany* (Manchester, 1906), 16.

3. T. C. Horsfall, "Housing of the Labouring Classes," unpublished lecture, 1900. Quoted in Sutcliffe, *Towards the Planned City*, 70.

4. J. S. Nettlefold, *Practical Housing* (Letchworth, 1908), 8.

5. See S. Martin Gaskell, "The Suburb Salubrious," in Anthony Sutcliffe, ed., *British Town Planning: The Formative Years* (Leicester, 1981), 16–61.

6. William Ashworth, *The Genesis of Modern British Town Planning* (London, 1959), 84.

7. *Royal Commission on the Housing of the Working Classes, Report, 1884–5.* Quoted in John Nelson Tarn, *Five Per Cent Philanthropy* (Cambridge, 1973), 114.

8. Hansard Third Series, CCC (1885), 652. Quoted in Anthony Wohl, *The Eternal Slum* (Montreal, 1977), 247.

9. William Thompson, *The Housing Handbook* (London, 1903), 25. A publication of the National Housing Reform Council.

10. John Burnett, *A Social History of Housing, 1815–1985* (London, 1986), 184–185.

11. James Cornes, *Modern Housing in Town and Country* (London, 1905), xvi.

12. *Sheffield Daily Independent,* 28 September 1904, 4.

13. Dan H. Lawrence, ed., *Bernard Shaw, Collected Letters 1898–1910* (London, 1965), 188.

14. Stanley Buder, *Visionaries and Planners: The Garden City Movement and the Modern Community* (New York, 1990), 9.

15. Ebenezer Howard, interview in *The Spectator,* 5 June 1926, in Robert Beevers, *The Garden City Utopia: A Critical Biography of Ebenezer Howard* (New York, 1988), 7.

16. Ibid., 14; Buder, *Visionaries and Planners,* 15–17, 39.

17. Avner Offer, *Property and Politics, 1870–1914: Landownership, Law, Ideology, and Urban Development in England* (Cambridge, 1981), 187, 194–195.

18. Ibid., 197.

19. James Silk Buckingham, *National Evils and Practical Remedies* (London, 1849), chap. 4.

20. Howard Papers, in Hertfordshire County Council Record Office, D/EHo F1, F3 (hereafter cited as Howard Papers).

21. Edward Gibbon Wakefield, *A View of the Act of Colonization* (London, 1849).

22. Alfred Marshall, "The Housing of the London Poor," *Contemporary Review* 45 (1884): 224.

23. Thomas Spence, *The Rights of Man* (London, 1793), 3, 11–12.

24. Edward Bellamy, *Looking Backward* (London, 1888), 44.

25. Ebenezer Howard, "Lecture to the Fabian Society," 11 January 1901, Howard Papers, D/EHo F9.

26. Ebenezer Howard, *Garden Cities of To-morrow,* ed. F. J. Osborn (London, 1946), 48.

27. Ibid., 46, 48.

28. Ibid., 51–55.

29. Ibid., 98, 56–57.

30. Ibid., 106.

31. Ibid., 146.

32. Robert Fishman, *Urban Utopias in the Twentieth Century: Ebenezer Howard, Frank Lloyd Wright, and Le Corbusier* (New York, 1977), 4.

33. Beevers, *Garden City Utopia,* 5, 42–43.

34. Howard, *Garden Cities of To-morrow,* frontispiece.

35. Ebenezer Howard, "Commonsense Socialism," 1892, Howard Papers, D/EHo F10.

36. Howard, *Garden Cities of To-morrow,* 104, 108.

37. Ebenezer Howard, "Responsibility of the Masses for the Condition of the Classes," 1900, Howard Papers, D/EHo F1.

38. *Fabian News,* December 1898, 39.

39. *Builder,* 9 August 1902, 129.

40. C. B. Purdom, *The Building of Satellite Towns* (London, 1925), 55.

41. Northcliffe to Howard, 24 February 1912, Howard Papers, D/EHo F25.

42. Howard scrapbook, Welwyn Garden City Central Library. Quoted in Beevers, *Garden City Utopia,* 72.

43. Garden City Association, *The Garden City Conference at Bournville: Report of Proceedings* (London, 1901), 1.

44. Ralph Neville, "Cooperation and Garden Cities," in Garden City Association, *Garden City Conference,* 25.

45. Beevers, *Garden City Utopia,* 79–80.

46. "Memorandum of Association of the Garden City Pioneer Company," printed as an appendix to Howard, *Garden Cities of To-morrow* (London, 1902), 180.

47. *Evening Standard,* 17 April 1905, 3.

48. *The Times,* 24 March 1906, in press cutting book, 1905, First Garden City Heritage Museum (hereafter FGCHM), 180.

49. For a list and description of many of these projects, see Patrick Albercrombie, "A Comparative Review of Examples of Modern Town Planning and 'Garden City' Schemes in England," *Town Planning Review* (1910): 111–116. See also Gordon Cherry, *The Evolution of British Town Planning* (Leighton Buzzard, 1974), 39.

50. C. B. Purdom, *The Garden City* (London, 1913), 202–203.

51. Ebenezer Howard, "Preface," in G. Montague Harris, *The Garden City Movement* (London, 1906), 13.

52. Fred Knee to Thomas Adams, 19 September 1902. FGCHM file, "Collection of Source Material."

53. Beevers, *Garden City Utopia,* 74–77; Shaw's letter is in the British Library, Add. MS, 50513, ff. 247–267.

54. Neville, "Cooperation and Garden Cities," 21.

55. Ralph Neville to Ebenezer Howard, 23 June 1903, and 13 November 1903, Howard Papers, D/EHo F25.

56. Co-Partnership Tenants, Ltd., *The Pioneer Co-Partnership Suburb* (London 1912), 6–7.

57. Henry Vivian, "The Garden City Tenants' Scheme," in First Garden City, Ltd., *Where Shall I Live?* (London, 1906), 55.

58. *Daily Herald,* 31 July 1912, in press cutting book, 1912–1913, FGCHM, 132.

59. See Beevers, *Garden City Utopia,* 90.

60. Garden City Association, *Garden City Conference,* 9–10.

61. Ralph Neville, "The Basis of British Efficiency," *The Garden City* (November 1904), 1–2.

62. *Garden Cities and Town Planning* (August 1913), 195.

63. Ralph Neville, *Garden Cities* (Manchester, 1904), 16.

64. Reprinted in *Garden Cities and Town Planning,* November 1909, 268.

65. Ebenezer Howard, "Garden Cities: Manufactures and Labour," in Garden City Association, *Garden City Conference,* 56.

66. Garden City Association, *Housing in Town and Country* (Report of the 1906 Conference) (London, 1906), 16.

67. Hugh E. Seebohm, "The First Garden City Company," *Independent Review,* May 1904, 528–529.

68. Barry Parker, "Copartnership Building of Houses," *The Craftsman,* May 1912, 194.

69. Beevers, *Garden City Utopia,* 80.

CHAPTER 4. BARRY PARKER AND RAYMOND UNWIN: PRINCIPLES AND PRACTICE

1. W. R. Lethaby, "The Builder's Art and the Craftsman," in R. Norman Shaw, *Architecture: A Profession or an Art* (London, 1892), 152–153.

2. M. H. Baillie Scott, *Houses and Gardens* (London, 1906), 97.

3. C. R. Ashbee, *A Book of Cottages and Little Houses: For Landlords, Architects, Builders, and Others* (London, 1906), 92–93.

4. C. F. A. Voysey, "The English Home," *British Architect,* 27 January 1911, 60.

5. M. H. Baillie Scott, "The Ideal Suburban Home," *Studio* 4 (1894): 128.

6. Freda White, "Raymond Unwin," in "Personal Papers," 8 September 1961, Unwin Papers, Manchester University Archives, (hereafter UP).

7. Michael Day, "Sir Raymond Unwin and R. Barry Parker: A Study and Evaluation of Their Contribution to Site-Planning Theory and Practice" (Master's thesis, Manchester University, 1973), 10.

8. Raymond Unwin, Journal, 26 July 1887, UP.

9. Ibid., 8 June 1887.

10. Ibid., 21 August 1887.

11. Ibid., 18 July 1887; 5 June 1887; 31 May 1887.

12. Raymond Unwin, "The Architect's Contribution," *RIBA Journal,* November 1931, 9.

13. Ibid., 10.

14. Raymond Unwin, Journal, 4 July 1887, UP.

15. Edith M. O. Ellis [Mrs. Havelock Ellis], *Three Modern Seers* (London, 1910), 41–42; James Hinton, *The Law-Breaker and the Coming of the Law* (London, 1884), 15.

16. Raymond Unwin, "Edward Carpenter and 'Towards Democracy,'" in Gilbert Beith, ed., *Edward Carpenter: In Appreciation* (London, 1931), 235.

17. Edward Carpenter, *Towards Democracy* (London, 1885), 48.

18. Raymond Unwin, "The Dawn of a Happier Day," January 1886, UP, UN/15/2, n.p.

19. Raymond Unwin, "Down a Coal Pit," MS for article published in *Commonweal,* 7 July 1890. UP, "Publications and Articles," n.p.

20. Raymond Unwin, Journal, 6 May 1887.

21. Unwin, "Edward Carpenter and 'Towards Democracy,'" 239.

22. Edward Carpenter, "Transitions to Freedom," *Forecasts of the Coming Century* (Manchester, 1897), 186.

23. Unwin, "Dawn of a Happier Day," n.p.

24. Raymond Unwin, "Scrambling," MS for an article published in *Commonweal* in 1886, UP, "Publications and Articles," n.p.

25. Quoted in Peter Davey, *Architecture of the Arts and Crafts Movement* (New York, 1980), 171.

26. Day, "Sir Raymond Unwin and R. Barry Parker," 11–14.

27. Barry Parker, "Raymond Unwin," *RIBA Journal,* 15 July 1940, 209.

28. Barry Parker, "Speeches on the Occasion of the Presentation of the Royal Gold Medal [of the Royal Institute of British Architects] to Sir Raymond Unwin," UP, "Publications and Articles," n.p.

29. Lethaby, "Builder's Art and the Craftsman," 161.

30. Barry Parker, "Building for Professional People," *The Craftsman*, October 1910, 47.

31. Preface, *Catalogue of Works Exhibited by Members of the Northern Art Workers' Guild* (Manchester, 1903), n.p.

32. See Frank Jackson, *Sir Raymond Unwin: Architect, Planner and Visionary* (London, 1985), 24–26, 37; Dean Hawkes, *Barry Parker and Raymond Unwin, Architects* (London, 1980), 9.

33. Barry Parker and Raymond Unwin, *The Art of Building a Home* (London, 1901), iii; Barry Parker, Introduction, "Modern Country Homes in England," *The Craftsman*, April 1910, 3.

34. Parker and Unwin, *Art of Building a Home*, ii.

35. Barry Parker, *Our Homes* (Buxton, 1895), 3.

36. Barry Parker, "Some Principles Underlying Domestic Architecture," *Journal of the Society of Architects*, September 1895, 181.

37. Parker and Unwin, *Art of Building a Home*, 16.

38. Ibid., 21.

39. Parker, Introduction, "Modern Country Homes in England," 4.

40. Jackson, *Sir Raymond Unwin*, 39.

41. Barry Parker, "Democracy's Influence in Architecture," *The Craftsman*, July 1912, 433.

42. Ibid.

43. Parker and Unwin, *Art of Building a Home*, 9.

44. Ibid., 33.

45. Raymond Unwin, "Gladdening versus Shortening the Hours of Labour," 21 February 1897, UP, 15/4.

46. Raymond Unwin, Journal, 23 June 1887, UP.

47. See p. 3.

48. Parker and Unwin, *Art of Building a Home*, 92.

49. Ibid., 86.

50. Raymond Unwin, *Cottage Plans and Common Sense* (London, 1902), 3.

51. Barry Parker, "Buildings Suggested by the Site," *The Craftsman*, May 1911, 179.

52. Barry Parker, "Relation of House to Garden," *The Craftsman*, September 1911, 606.

53. Unwin, "Gladdening versus Shortening the Hours of Labour."

54. G. B. Brown, "The Joseph Rowntree Village Trust," *The Garden City*, September 1906, 169.

55. Ibid., 197.

56. Parker and Unwin, *Art of Building a Home*, 3–4.

57. Unwin, *Cottage Plans and Common Sense*, 11.

58. Lawrence Weaver, *The Country Life Book of Cottages* (London 1913), 23.

59. Raymond Unwin, ed., *A Nation's New Houses* (London [1919]), 6.

60. Parker and Unwin, *Art of Building a Home*, 5.

61. Daily Mirror, *The Perfect Home and How to Furnish It* (London, 1913), 180–181.

62. Barry Parker and Raymond Unwin, "The Interior Decoration of Our Homes," *Letchworth Magazine*, December 1906, 141.

63. Barry Parker, "Some Principles of Domestic Architecture," *British Architecture* (1895): 242 (a speech read before the Society of Architects).

64. Barry Parker, "Planning Groups of Cottages," *The Craftsman*, March 1912, 655.

65. Parker and Unwin, *Art of Building a Home*, 64.

66. Katharine Bruce Glasier, "Labour's Northern Voice," August 1940, UP, 13/2.

67. See Jackson, *Sir Raymond Unwin*, chap. 4, esp. 109–110.

68. Raymond Unwin, talk to the Cambridge Social Discussion Society, *Cambridge Independent Press*, 16 February 1906, 3; Unwin, "The Planning of the Residential Districts of Towns" (address to the Seventh International Congress of Architects), *RIBA Journal*, July 1906, appendix, lvi.

69. Raymond Unwin, "'Wholesale' Planning," in E. G. Culpin, ed., *Practical Application of Town Planning Powers* (Report of the National Town Planning Conference arranged by the Garden City and Town Planning Association, December 1909) (London, 1910), 38.

70. Raymond Unwin, *Town Planning in Practice* (London, 1909), 138.

71. Unwin, *Cottage Plans and Common Sense*, 4.

72. Raymond Unwin, "The City Development Plan," in Royal Institute of British Architects, *Transactions: Town Planning Conference, London, 10–15 October 1910* (London, 1911), 254.

73. Raymond Unwin, "Town Planning at Hampstead," *Garden Cities and Town Planning*, May 1911, 84.

74. Raymond Unwin, "Karlsruhe," *Architectural Review*, January 1911, 58.

75. Le Corbusier, *L'Urbanisme* (Paris, 1959), in François Loyer, *Architecture of the Industrial Age* (Geneva, 1983), 266.

76. See Jackson, *Sir Raymond Unwin*, 103; George R. Collins and Christine C. Collins, *Camillo Sitte: The Birth of Modern City Planning* (London, 1965).

77. New Earswick Trustees, *One Man's Vision: The Story of the Joseph Rowntree Village Trust* (London, 1954), xiii.

78. Unwin, *Town Planning in Practice*, 79.

79. Unwin, *Cottage Plans and Common Sense*, 4–5.

80. Barry Parker, "The Court in Domestic Architecture," *The Craftsman*, January 1912, 409.

81. Parker and Unwin, *Art of Building a Home*, 104–105.

82. Ibid., 101–102; *Cambridge Independent Press*, 16 February 1906, 3.

83. Parker and Unwin, *Art of Building a Home*, 106.

84. Unwin, "Gladdening versus Shortening the Hours of Labour."

85. See, for example, Raymond Unwin, "The Planning of Towns and Suburbs," *RIBA Journal*, March 1910, 365.

CHAPTER 5. LETCHWORTH: BEST LAID PLANS

1. *Daily News*, 10 October 1903, in press cutting book, 1903–4, FGCHM, 85; C. B. Purdom, "At the Inception of Letchworth," *Town and Country Planning*, September 1953, 427.

2. Typescript, pp. 1–2, in press cutting book, 1903–4, FGCHM, 42.

3. C. B. Purdom, *The Garden City* (London, 1913), 34–35; *Garden City*, July 1906, 127.

4. W. A. Cadbury to Ebenezer Howard, 16 July 1903, FGCHM file, "Negotiations for site

of Garden City"; Ebenezer Howard to Alfred Harmsworth, 30 June 1903, FGCHM file, "Collection of Source materials." See Stanley Buder, *Visionaries and Planners: The Garden City Movement and the Modern Community* (New York, 1990), 59.

5. *Builder,* 23 January 1904, 75.

6. *Daily Graphic,* 5 September 1903, in press cutting book, 1903–4, FGCHM, 32.

7. C. B. Purdom, *The Letchworth Achievement* (London, 1963), 9.

8. Aneurin Williams, "Land Tenure in Garden City," in Purdom, *Garden City,* 216 (appendix A).

9. Ibid., 218, 219.

10. Ibid., 216, 217.

11. Ebenezer Howard, "Our First Garden City," *St. George's Magazine,* July 1904, 182.

12. Thomas Adams, "Garden Cities and Small Holdings," *Garden City,* January 1907, 249; "Correspondence," May 1907, 330.

13. *North Hertfordshire Mail,* 9 August 1906, in press cutting book, 1905–9, FGCHM, 13.

14. C. B. Purdom, *The Building of Satellite Towns* (London, 1925), 68, 81.

15. Ibid., 164.

16. Form letter from Thomas Adams, December 1906, FGCHM file, "Correspondence, 1902–1906"; Michael Simpson, *Thomas Adams and the Modern Planning Movement* (London and New York, 1985), 21–22.

17. *Builder,* 23 May 1913, 585.

18. [First Garden City, Ltd.], *London and the Manufacturer: Letchworth vs. London* (Letchworth, 1907), n.p.

19. *Manchester Evening News,* 14 June 1908, in press cutting book, 1908–10, FGCHM, 4; Purdom, *Building of Satellite Towns,* 107; Purdom, *Garden City,* 43.

20. Ebenezer Howard, "Garden Cities: Manufacturers and Labour," in Garden City Association, *The Garden City Conference at Bournville: Report of Proceedings* (London, 1901), 54.

21. Purdom, *Garden City,* 145.

22. First Garden City Company, Ltd., *Report of the Annual General Meeting, 1913* (Letchworth, 1913), 9–10.

23. Interview, *Letchworth Citizen,* 5 March 1943, n.p.

24. Raymond Unwin, "The Planning of Garden City," in Purdom, *Garden City,* 222–223.

25. Raymond Unwin to Thomas Adams, 11 July 1904, FGCHM file, "Negotiations for the Site of Garden City."

26. *Cambridge Independent Press,* 16 February 1906, 3; Raymond Unwin, "The Planning of Garden City," in Purdom, *Garden City,* 229.

27. First Garden City, Ltd., *Guide to Garden City* (London, 1906), 30.

28. F. H. Purchas, "The First Garden City," *Estate Magazine,* April 1910, 150.

29. Raymond Unwin to Ebenezer Howard, 27 July 1903, FGCHM file, "Negotiations for Site of Garden City."

30. *RIBA Journal,* December 1909, 68.

31. Raymond Unwin, "The Beauty of Towns," delivered in February 1907, reprinted in *Town and Country Planning,* October 1954, 528.

32. "Suggestions," undated, UP, UN 12/24, i, iii.

33. Thomas Adams to Raymond Unwin, 24 August 1904; Raymond Unwin to Thomas Adams, 23 August 1904, FGCHM file, "Negotiations for the Site of Garden City."

34. Purdom, *Garden City,* 66.

35. E. G. Culpin in *Garden City and Town Planning Review,* April 1914, 82.

36. *Letchworth Citizen,* 22 March 1912, 4.

37. W. H. Gaunt, "A Few Notes upon a Recent Essay on Architecture," *The City,* September 1910, 109.

38. H. C. Lander, "Architecture in Letchworth," *The City,* October 1909, 227.

39. Raymond Unwin, "The City Development Plan," in RIBA Town Planning Conference, *Members' Handbook* (London, 1911), 248; Raymond Unwin, *Town Planning in Practice* (London, 1909), 294.

40. Unwin, "The Planning of Garden City," 225.

41. Purdom, *Garden City,* 73.

42. Ibid., 84.

43. Raymond Unwin, "Cottage Building in Garden City," *Garden City,* June 1906, 110.

44. Purdom, *Garden City,* 157, 268–269 (appendix E).

45. Ibid., 265.

46. Howard Society Archives, Letchworth, "Notes on Howard Cottage Society, Ltd.," n.p.

47. *Letchworth Citizen,* 22 March 1912, 4.

48. *North Hertfordshire Mail,* 6 September 1906, in press cutting book, 1906–13, FGCHM, 10.

49. *Garden City,* April 1906, 55.

50. *Letchworth Citizen,* 18 October 1912, 3; 25 October 1912, 3; 17 January 1913, 3.

51. Purdom, *Garden City,* 160–161.

52. J. H. Elder-Duncan, *Country Cottages and Week-End Homes* (London, 1906), 17–18.

53. Purdom, *Garden City,* 50; *The Architect and Contract Reporter,* 12 January 1906, 37.

54. Purdom, *Garden City,* 50–51.

55. Barry Parker and Raymond Unwin, "The Cheap Cottage: What Is Really Needed," *Garden City,* July 1905, 55.

56. *Building News,* 19 July 1907, 64.

57. *Garden City,* October 1906, n.p.

58. *Garden City,* September 1907, 431.

59. *The City,* February 1909, 35.

60. H. G. Wells, "Joint Households," *Daily Mail,* 25 May 1905. See also Lynn F. Pearson, *The Architectural and Social History of Cooperative Living* (London, 1988), 64–66, 90.

61. Ibid., 56–63.

62. Ebenezer Howard, *Garden Cities of To-morrow,* ed. F. J. Osborn (London, 1946), 54.

63. Howard papers, D/EHo F3.

64. H. Clapham Lander, "The Advantages of Co-operative Dwellings," in Garden City Association, *The Garden City Conference at Bournville,* 64–65.

65. Ibid., 61.

66. Purdom, *Garden City,* 98–99.

67. Ebenezer Howard, "Letchworth Co-operative Houses," *Garden City,* October 1907, 436–438.

68. Prospectus, Letchworth Co-operative Homes, Ltd., FGCHM file, "Homesgarth."

69. *Westminster Gazette,* 24 November 1910, in press cutting book, 1910–11, FGCHM, 83.

70. First Garden City, Ltd., Directors Minute Book, 24 November 1910, 54; 2 July 1908, 234; Files, Letchworth Garden City Corporation.

71. Prospectus, Letchworth Co-operative Houses, Ltd., 3 June 1911, FGCHM file, "Homesgarth."

72. Ebenezer Howard, "A New Outlet for Woman's Energy," *Garden Cities and Town Planning Magazine,* June 1913, 152.

73. *Letchworth Citizen,* 5 September 1913, 3; 24 October 1913, 2.

74. See, for example, an undated and unattributed newspaper article by Howard entitled "Co-operative Housekeeping. Applying the Principle to a Working Class Scheme," in FGCHM file, "Homesgarth."

75. *Architects and Builders Journal,* 29 November 1911, in press cutting book, 1910–11, FGCHM, 193.

76. *Letchworth Citizen,* 5 January 1912, 4.

CHAPTER 6. LETCHWORTH: "THE SPIRIT OF THE PLACE"

1. First Garden City, Ltd., *The Garden City Movement: Report of the Speeches Delivered at the Meeting Held on the Letchworth Estate, Friday, October 9, 1903* (Hitchin, [1903]), 10.

2. *North Hertforshire Mail,* 23 August 1906, in press cutting book, 1906–13, FGCHM, 5.

3. Residents' Council Minute Book, report of the annual meeting, 3 January 1906, FGCHM file, "Garden City Association, 1902–7."

4. *North Hertfordshire Mail,* 31 January 1907, in press cutting book, 1906–7, FGCHM, 138.

5. Harved Craske to Aneurin Williams, 13 November 1907, FGCHM file, "Directors."

6. First Garden City, Ltd., *Report of the Annual General Meeting* (Letchworth, 1908), 8, 11.

7. *Letchworth Citizen,* 15 February 1908, 3.

8. *Letchworth Citizen,* 13 December 1912, 5.

9. *Letchworth Citizen,* 3 February 1913, 3; A. W. Brunt, *The Pageant of Letchworth, 1903–1914* (Letchworth, 1942), 8, 11–12.

10. *Letchworth Citizen,* 22 February, 1908, 1.

11. *Standard,* 9 October 1907, in press cutting book, 1906–13, FGCHM, 38.

12. Raymond Unwin, "Social Experiments," *Commonweal,* 5 March 1887, UP.

13. J. J. Kidd, "Socialist Society," *Letchworth Magazine,* September 1906, 37.

14. *Letchworth Citizen,* 21 March 1908, 4.

15. *Letchworth Citizen,* 15 September 1911, 3; C. B. Purdom, *The Building of Satellite Towns* (London, 1925), 64.

16. G. P. Nowers, "The Call of the Future," *The City,* February 1909, 28; *Letchworth Citizen,* 22 April 1911, 5.

17. W. H. Gaunt, "Letchworth as an Industrial Centre," in First Garden City, Ltd., *"Where Shall I Live?" Guide to Letchworth and Catalogue of the Urban Housing and Rural Homesteads Exhibition* (London, 1907), n.p.

18. *Letchworth Citizen,* 15 March 1912, 2.

19. *Letchworth Citizen,* 29 March 1912, 3.

20. *Daily Herald,* 19 April 1912, in press cutting book, 1911–12, FGCHM, 58; *Letchworth Citizen,* 19 April 1912, 3.

21. *Letchworth Citizen,* 25 April 1913, 3.

22. *Letchworth Citizen,* 13 May 1913, 5.

23. Harved Graske to George Bates, W. F. Kensett, and A. W. Brunt, 13 May 1913, FGCHM file, "Directors."

24. *Daily Citizen,* 14 May 1913, in press cutting book, 1913–17, FGCHM, 29.

25. Ebenezer Howard, untitled speech to trade unionists, n.d. ("about 1907"), Howard Papers, D/EHo.Fı.

26. Ethel Henderson, "The Ideals of Letchworth, the First Garden City," manuscript, n.p., FGCHM.

27. See p. 88.

28. Speech of the Reverend C. Stuart Smith, *Letchworth Citizen,* 14 March 1913, 3.

29. *North Hertfordshire Mail,* 17 January 1907, in press cutting book, 1906–7, FGCHM, 119.

30. Charles Lee, Diary, entry for 22 November 1908, FGCHM file, "Early Letchworth Memories."

31. *Letchworth Citizen,* 24 May 1912, 2.

32. Quoted in C. B. Purdom, *The Garden City* (London, 1913), 151.

33. Ibid., 110.

34. Ebenezer Howard, "The Land Question at Letchworth," *The City,* August 1909, 182.

35. *Letchworth Citizen,* 11 January 1908, 3; *The City,* August 1909, 175.

36. *The Times,* 2 January 1905; *Hertfordshire Reporter,* 24 February 1905, in press cutting book, 1904–5, FGCHM, 7, 33.

37. *Clarion,* 6 November 1903, in press cutting book, 1904–5, FGCHM, 11.

38. Robert Gernon, "Wanted a Music Hall," *Bedfordshire Express,* 5 October 1907, in press cutting book, 1907–8, FGCHM, 136.

39. *Garden City,* 5 June 1906, 120.

40. Ebenezer Howard, *Garden Cities of To-morrow,* ed. F. J. Osborn (London, 1946), 102.

41. Ralph Neville, "Co-operation and Garden Cities," in Garden City Association, *The Garden City Conference at Bournville: Report of Proceedings* (London, 1901), 11.

42. Quoted in W. G. Furnston, *The Skittles Inn* (Letchworth, 1914), 10–11.

43. *North Hertforshire Mail,* 29 August 1907, in press cutting book, 1906–13, FGCHM, 57.

44. *Letchworth Citizen,* 27 October 1911, 3.

45. Raymond Unwin, "Education at Garden City," reprinted from the *Journal of Education* in *Bedfordshire Express,* 30 December 1905, in press cutting book, 1905, FGCHM, 103.

46. *Hertfordshire Reporter,* 1 July 1905, in press cutting book, 1904–5, FGCHM, 96.

47. *Garden City,* February 1906, 22; *Garden City and Town Planning,* February 1909, 172–173; Purdom, *Garden City,* 172–173.

48. Purdom, *Garden City,* 173–174; W. H. G. Armytage, *Heavens Below: Utopian Experiments in England, 1560–1960* (Toronto, 1961), 375.

49. FGCHM file, "Adult School," n.d.; *Letchworth Citizen,* 24 January 1913, 3.

50. Mary E. Nicholson, "Social Life at Letchworth," in First Garden City, Ltd., *"Where Shall I Live?"* 30.

51. C. H. Hynett to F. J. Osborn, 14 July 1953, FGCHM file, "Early Letchworth Memories."
52. First Garden City, Ltd., *Guide* (London, 1906), 89; First Garden City, Ltd., *"Where Shall I Live?"* 91–100; *Letchworth Garden City Directory* (Letchworth, 1910), 28–32.
53. Purdom, *Garden City,* 54.
54. Letchworth Dramatic Society, Annual Report, 1907–8, 4; "The Letchworth Theatre: A Souvenir of the Hundredth Performance," 10 December 1913, in Letchworth Dramatic Society album, FGCHM.
55. F. J. Osborn, "Letchworth's First Fifty Years," *Town and Country Planning,* September 1953, 406.
56. *Vegetarian Messenger,* December 1907, in press cutting book 1907–8, FGCHM, 184.
57. Charles Lee, "From a Letchworth Diary," *Town and Country Planning,* September 1953, 435–437.
58. *Garden City,* December 1907, 471; Stanley Buder, *Visionaries and Planners: The Garden City Movement and the Modern Community* (New York, 1990), 39.
59. V. W. Miles, *The Cloisters, Letchworth* (Letchworth, 1967), 17.
60. *Bedfordshire Express,* 13 August 1910, in press cutting book, 1910, FGCHM, 240.
61. *Letchworth Magazine,* September 1906, 65.
62. John Buchan, *Mr. Standfast* (London, 1961), 47, 49.
63. *The City,* January 1909, 1.
64. Truda Fitzwater-Wray to F. J. Osborn, n.d., FGCHM file, "Early Letchworth Memories."
65. Residents Union, Minutes of meeting of 18 August 1909, FGCHM file, "Garden City Association."
66. *St. James Gazette,* 4 March 1906, in press cutting book, 1904-5, FGCHM, 56; *Letchworth Citizen,* 14 February 1913, 3.
67. Purdom, *Garden City,* 51; *The City,* February 1909, 28.
68. Robert Gernon, letter to the *Hertfordshire Express,* 8 January 1908, in press cutting book, 1908–13, FGCHM, 44.
69. Foreword, "The Garden of the Leach: A Masque of Letchworth," FGCHM file, "Event Programmes, Scripts."

CHAPTER 7. SUBURBAN HIGH-MINDEDNESS AT HAMPSTEAD

1. *The Builder,* 11 June 1910, 665.
2. *Garden Cities and Town Planning,* November–December 1911, 228.
3. *The Times,* 11 October 1910, in press cutting book 1910–11, FGCHM, 7.
4. Mabel Parker to Fredric J. Osborn, 16 September 1963; Fredric J. Osborn to Mabel Parker, 27 September 1963; Mabel Parker to C. B. Purdom, November 1963; C. B. Purdom to Mabel Parker, 8 November 1963. FGCHM file, "Pamphlets and Articles by Barry Parker and Raymond Unwin."
5. Raymond Unwin, *Nothing Gained by Overcrowding!* (London, 1912), 1–2; "The Town Extension Plan," *Old Towns and New Needs* (Warburton Lectures of 1912) (Manchester, 1912), 47–48.
6. See p. 106.

7. See Seth Koven, "Henrietta Barnett (1851–1963): The (Auto)biography of a Late Victorian Marriage," in Susan Pedersen and Peter Mandler, eds., *After the Victorians: Private Conscience and Public Duty in Modern Britain* (London, 1994), 31–53.

8. Walter L. Creese, *The Search for Environment. The Garden City: Before and After* (New Haven, 1966), 220.

9. Hampstead Garden Suburb Trust, Ltd., *Cottages with Gardens for Londoners* (London, 1907), 18; C. R. Ashbee, Journal, 28 June 1886. Quoted in Koven, "Henrietta Barnett," 41.

10. *Hampstead and Highgate Express*, 3 September 1910, in press cutting book, 1910, FGCHM, 271.

11. Henrietta Barnett, "Science and City Suburbs," in *Science in Public Affairs*, ed. J. E. Hand (London, 1906), 55–57.

12. Ibid. See also Hampstead Garden Suburb, "Prospectus," 21 July 1908, FGCHM files, "Bournville to Hampstead."

13. Henrietta O. Barnett, "A Garden Suburb at Hampstead," *Contemporary Review*, February 1905, 234–235, 239–240.

14. Henrietta O. Barnett, "The Garden Suburb at Hampstead," in Henrietta O. Barnett and Samuel A. Barnett, *Towards Social Reform* (London, 1909), 336.

15. Barnett, "Science and City Suburbs," 65–66; [Brigid Grafton Green], *Suburb Heritage* (London, 1975), 4.

16. Hampstead Heath Extension Council, *Report* (London, 1908), 13, 15.

17. Brigid Grafton Green, *Hampstead Garden Suburb, 1907–1977: A History* (London, 1977), 6.

18. *Hampstead and Highgate Express*, 6 February 1904, in press cutting book, 1904–5, FGCHM, 37.

19. Henrietta O. Barnett, *The Story of the Growth of Hampstead Garden Suburb* (London, 1928), 6.

20. Samuel A. Barnett to Frank G. Barnett, 16 March 1907, Barnett Papers, London County Council, F/BAR/325.

21. *Hampstead and Highgate Express*, 9 January 1909, in press cutting book 1, Hampstead Garden Suburb Archives (hereafter HGSA), 16.

22. Samuel A. Barnett to Frank G. Barnett, 7 April 1906, Barnett Papers, F/BAR/361.

23. Garden Suburb Trust Minute Book, 23 February 1905 (letter from Sir Richard Farrant), HGSA.

24. *The Times*, 28 December 1904, in press cutting book 1, HGSA, 46.

25. Garden Suburb Trust Minute Book, 23 February 1905, HGSA; Samuel A. Barnett to Frank G. Barnett, 17 March 1906, Barnett Papers, F/BAR/359.

26. Barnett, *Story of the Growth*, 7; Garden Suburb Trust Minute Book, 27 November 1905, HGSA.

27. Hampstead Garden Trust, *The Proposed Garden Suburb at Hampstead* (London, n.d.), 10.

28. The original map is in HGSA.

29. Creese, *Search for Environment*, 89. The quotation is from *The Pioneer*, 17 July 1880.

30. Garden Suburb Trust Minute Book, 6 March 1906, HGSA.

31. Raymond Unwin and M. H. Baillie Scott, *Town Planning and Modern Architecture at Hampstead Garden Suburb* (London, 1909), 2.

32. "Rapid Growth of the Garden City Movement, Which Promises to Reorganize Social Conditions all over the World," *The Craftsman,* December 1909, 307.

33. Unwin and Baillie Scott, *Town Planning and Modern Architecture,* 29.

34. Barry Parker, "Symmetry in Building: The Result of Sincerity," *The Craftsman,* June 1911, 186.

35. Barnett, "A Garden Suburb at Hampstead," 233.

36. Ibid., 232.

37. Ibid., 233; Barnett, "Science and City Suburbs," 71.

38. Alan A. Jackson, *Semi-Detached London* (London, 1973), 79.

39. "Town Planning in Theory and Practice: The Work of Raymond Unwin," *The Craftsman,* January 1910, 400.

40. Unwin and Baillie Scott, *Town Planning and Modern Architecture,* 27, 43.

41. *Architects' and Builders' Journal,* 4 April 1912, in press cutting book, 1912, FGCHM, 61.

42. [Henrietta O. Barnett], "Hampstead Garden Suburb Trust," *The Record,* August 1912, 4.

43. To Emily Lutyens, 6 May 1906, Lutyens Papers, Royal Institute of British Architects, LuE/8/2/7(i).

44. Christopher Hussey, *The Life of Sir Edwin Lutyens* (London, 1950), 190 (To Herbert Baker).

45. A. J. Penty, diary transcripts, entry for 2 March 1914. "Suburb Architects" file, HGSA.

46. *Royal Institute Of British Architects Town Planning Conference, 1910* (London, 1911), 74.

47. Ibid., 250.

48. To Emily Lutyens, 7 April 1904, Lutyens papers, LuE/10/3/8(i–ii).

49. Raymond Unwin, "The Hampstead Garden Extension," *The Record,* August 1912, 8.

50. "Central Square" file, HGSA.

51. Barnett, *Story of the Growth,* 15.

52. Unwin and Baillie Scott, *Town Planning and Modern Architecture,* 34.

53. See pp. 64–65.

54. Grafton Green, *Hampstead Garden Suburb,* 9.

55. *Garden Cities and Town Planning,* May 1912, 94.

56. Unwin and Baillie Scott, *Town Planning and Modern Architecture,* 13, 17.

57. Ibid., 29, 31.

58. *Architects' and Builders' Journal,* 25 September 1912, in press cutting book 4, HGSA, 135.

59. Unwin and Baillie Scott, *Town Planning and Modern Architecture,* 74, 43.

60. *Architects' and Builders' Journal,* 1 November 1911, in press cutting book 4, HGSA, 20.

61. *Hampstead Record,* 5 October 1907, in press cutting book 2, HGSA, 28.

62. Grafton Green, *Hampstead Garden Suburb,* 10.

63. Garden Suburb Trust Minute Book, 21 October 1910, HGSA.

64. "The Suburb and the Slums," *Town Crier,* December 1911, 109.

65. Barnett, "Garden Suburb at Hampstead," 236.

66. Hampstead Tenants Societies, *Co-Partnership in Housing* (London, n.d. [pre-1914]), 23–24.

67. Barnett, *Story of the Growth,* 14; *Town Crier,* September 1911, 68.

68. Barnett, *Story of the Growth,* 21–24.

69. *Town Crier,* May 1912, 28.

70. Barnett, *Story of the Growth,* 20.

71. *Garden Cities and Town Planning,* November 1909, 246; *The Record* [the "official" suburb journal], October 1913, 43.

72. *British Architect,* 9 July 1909, 22.

73. Creese, *The Search for Environment,* 239.

74. Barnett, *Story of the Growth,* 28; *Finchley and Hendon Times,* 28 October 1910, in press cutting book 3, HGSA, 10; *Hampstead and Highgate Express,* 26 February 1910, in press cutting book, 1910, FGCHM, 36.

75. [Henrietta O. Barnett], "Life in a Garden Suburb," *The Record,* November 1913, 45.

76. "Resident" [Henrietta O. Barnett], "Outside Criticisms of the Suburb," *The Record,* June 1913, 173.

77. *Hendon and Finchley Times,* 22 December 1911, in press cutting book 4, HGSA, 47.

78. *The Record,* August 1912, 16–19; October 1912, 47.

79. *Town Crier,* May 1914, 19.

80. *The Record,* September 1913, 21; *Daily Telegraph,* 12 September 1910, in press cutting book, 1910, FGCHM, 285.

81. *Garden City and Town Planning,* May 1914, 103.

82. *The Record,* October 1912, 47.

83. *Town Crier,* November 1911, 93.

84. *Daily Mail,* 17 October 1911, in press cutting book, 1911–12, FGCHM, 123.

85. *Town Crier,* April 1911, 12.

86. *Town Crier,* January 1912, 123.

87. *Town Crier,* December 1911, 106.

88. *The Record,* August 1912, 4.

89. Samuel A. Barnett to Francis G. Barnett, 4 June 1909, Barnett Papers, F/BAR/393.

90. Garden Suburb Trust Minute Book, 3 March 1910, HGSA.

91. *Hampstead and Highgate Express,* 20 January 1911, in press cutting book 3, HGSA, 28.

92. Garden Suburb Trust Minute Book, 13 February 1912, HGSA; *The Record,* August 1912, 22; *Town Crier,* September 1912, 88.

93. *Town Crier,* November 1911, 91.

94. *Town Crier,* June 1911, 31.

95. "Outside Criticisms of the Suburb," *The Record,* June 1913, 173–174.

96. *Hampstead and Highgate Express,* Bank Holiday edition, 1909 [n.d.], in press cutting book 2, HGSA, 73.

97. Grafton Green, *Hampstead Garden Suburb,* 8.

98. Henrietta O. Barnett to (?), 17 November 1911, "Henrietta O. Barnett and Samuel A. Barnett letters" file, HGSA.

CHAPTER 8. EPILOGUE

1. Stanley Buder, *Visionaries and Planners: The Garden City Movement and the Modern Community* (New York, 1990), 134, 140. See also Steven V. Ward, "The Garden City Introduced," and Dennis Hardy, "The Garden City Campaign: An Overview," in Stephen V. Ward, ed., *The Garden City, Past, Present, and Future* (London, 1992).

2. Anthony Sutcliffe, *Towards the Planned City* (New York, 1981), 176.

3. [Royal Institute of British Architects], *Town Planning Conference, London, 10–15 October, 1910: Transactions* (London, 1911), 64. Quoted in Sutcliffe, *Towards the Planned City,* 170.

4. Buder, *Visionaries and Planners,* 108.

5. Ibid., 127.

6. Peter Mandler, *The Fall and Rise of the Stately Home* (New Haven, 1997), 225, 229.

7. Alex Potts, "'Constable Country' Between the Wars," in Raphael Samuel, ed., *Patriotism* (London, 1989), 3: 164.

8. Mandler, *Fall and Rise of the Stately Home,* 241.

9. Stanley Baldwin, *On England* (London, 1926), 8. From a speech to the Royal Society of St. George, May 6, 1924.

10. Potts, "'Constable Country' Between the Wars," 163.

11. Alison Light, *Forever England: Femininity, Literature, and Conservatism Between the Wars* (London, 1991), 8.

12. See p. 152.

13. See Raphael Samuel, "Preface," in Samuel, ed., *Patriotism,* 1: xii.

14. Alun Howkins, "The Discovery of Rural England," in Robert Colls and Philip Dodd, eds., *Englishness: Politics and Culture, 1880–1920* (London, 1988), 84.

Index